Nawa F 2

Reader's Choice

6TH EDITION

D1567244

MICHIGAN

Sandra Silberstein

Barbara K. Dobson

Mark A. Clarke

ISBN 978-0-472-03858-9 (print)
ISBN 978-0-472-12907-2 (e-book)

2026 2025 2024 2023   4 3 2 1

Contents

Introduction for Students

Welcome to the sixth edition of *Reader's Choice*. This book has been written to meet the needs of teachers and students in a rapidly changing globalized world. The purpose of this introduction is to acquaint you with the book and with our approach to teaching reading in English to speakers of other languages.

We believe that reading is an active process in which effective readers bring their understanding of the world to bear on text. Whether reading a book or an article, an infographic or a chart, or surfing the web—regardless of the content or form of the material—successful readers rely on an attitude of independence and the coordination of a number of skills and strategies. Efficient readers approach material with goals in mind, and they adjust their behavior accordingly. They develop expectations, and they read to confirm, reject, or adjust those expectations. Most of this is done without conscious attention to the process. The material in *Reader's Choice* gives you practice in this kind of independent, efficient, and critical reading.

We believe *Reader's Choice* is most effective when it is used in situations where curiosity and active participation are encouraged. It is a tool that will help you and your teachers develop a partnership for learning. You will see that we speak directly to students in the directions and exercises. To the extent possible, we have tried to permit you to get to know us and our approach to teaching and learning—and to living. We encourage you to take a playful approach to the readings and exercises in this book and to interact with the book and each other in ways that permit you, as individuals, to develop your own attitude and approach to learning. You will find interesting and provocative readings on topics that matter. We hope you enjoy using the book as much as we have enjoyed writing it.

When you look at the Contents page you will notice that there are three kinds of units in *Reader's Choice*. The odd-numbered units (1 through 7) contain language skills work. These exercises give you intensive practice in using word-, sentence-, and discourse-level reading strategies. The even-numbered units (2 through 8) contain reading selections that give you the opportunity to use the skills you have learned to interact with and evaluate the ideas of texts. Finally, Unit 9 consists of a longer, more complex reading selection.

Basic language and reading skills are introduced in early units and reinforced throughout the book. The large number of exercises provides opportunities for repeated practice. Do not be discouraged if you do not finish each exercise, if you have trouble answering specific questions, or if you do not understand everything in a particular reading. The purpose of the tasks in *Reader's Choice* is to help improve your problem-solving skills. For this reason, the process of attempting to answer a question is often as important as the answer itself.

Reader's Choice contains exercises that provide practice in both language and reading skills. In this **Introduction**, we will first provide a description of language skills exercises followed by a description of the reading skills work contained in the book.

Language Skills Exercises

Word Study Exercises

Upon encountering unfamiliar vocabulary in a passage, there are several strategies available to readers. First, you can continue reading, realizing that often a single word will not prevent understanding the general meaning of a selection. If further reading does not solve the problem, you can use one or more of three basic skills to arrive at an understanding of the unfamiliar word. You can use context clues to see if surrounding words and grammatical structures provide information about the unknown word. You can use word analysis to see if understanding the parts of the word leads to an understanding of the word. Or, you can use a dictionary to find an appropriate definition. *Reader's Choice* contains numerous exercises that provide practice in these three skills.

Word Study: Context Clues

Guessing the meaning of an unfamiliar word from **Context Clues** involves using the following kinds of information:

   a. knowledge of the topic about which you are reading
   b. knowledge of the meanings of the other words in the sentence (or paragraph) in which the word occurs
   c. knowledge of the grammatical structure of the sentences in which the word occurs

When these exercises appear in skills units, their purpose is to provide practice in guessing the meanings of unfamiliar words using context clues. Students should not necessarily try to learn the meanings of the vocabulary items in these exercises. The **Vocabulary from Context** exercises that accompany reading selections have a different purpose. Generally the first exercise should be done before reading a selection and used as an introduction to the reading. The vocabulary items have been chosen for three reasons:

   a. because they are fairly common and therefore useful for students to learn
   b. because they are important for an understanding of the passage
   c. because their meanings are not easily available from the context in the selection

Word Study: Stems and Affixes

Another way to discover the meanings of unfamiliar vocabulary is to use word analysis, that is, to use knowledge of the meanings of the parts of a word. Many English words have been formed by combining parts of older English, Greek, and Latin words. For instance, the word *bicycle* is formed from the parts *bi,* meaning "two," and *cycle,* meaning "round" or "wheel." Often knowledge of the meanings of these word parts (along with context) can help the reader to guess the meaning of an unfamiliar word. Exercises in **Word Study: Stems and Affixes** provide practice in this skill at regular intervals throughout the book. You will find a bonus set of stems and affixes exercises in **Appendix A.** **Appendix B** lists all of the stems and affixes that appear in *Reader's Choice.*

Word Study: Dictionary Use

Sometimes the meaning of a single word is essential to an understanding of the total meaning of a selection. If context clues and word analysis do not provide enough information, it will be necessary to use a dictionary. The **Dictionary Study** exercises that accompany some of the reading selections require students to use the context of an unfamiliar vocabulary item to find an appropriate definition from the dictionary entries provided.

Sentence Study Exercises

Sometimes comprehension of an entire passage requires the understanding of a single sentence. **Sentence Study** exercises give students practice in analyzing the structure of sentences to determine the relationships of ideas within a sentence. You will be presented with a complicated sentence followed by tasks that require analyzing the sentence for its meaning. Often you will be required to use the available information to draw inferences about the author's message.

Paragraph Reading and Paragraph Analysis Exercises

These exercises give you practice at the paragraph level. Some of the paragraph exercises are designed to provide practice in discovering the general message. You will be asked to determine the main idea of a passage: that is, the idea that is the most important, around which the passage is organized. Other paragraph exercises are meant to provide practice in careful, detailed reading. You will be required not only to find the main idea of a passage but also to guess vocabulary from context, to answer questions about specific details in the paragraph, and to draw conclusions based on an understanding of the passage.

Discourse Focus

Effective reading requires the ability to select skills and strategies appropriate to a specific reading task. The reading process involves using information from the full text and knowledge of the world in order to interpret a passage. Readers use this information to make predictions about what they will find in a text and to decide how they will read. Sometimes we need to read quickly to obtain only a general idea of a text; at other times we read carefully, drawing inferences about the intent of the author. Discourse-level exercises introduce these various approaches to reading, which are then reinforced throughout the book. These reading skills are described in more detail in the discussion that follows.

Nonprose Reading

Throughout *Reader's Choice,* nonprose selections (charts and graphs, an infographic, a survey, and a subway map) provide practice reading material that is not primarily arranged in sentences and paragraphs. It is important to remember that the same problem-solving skills are used to read both prose and nonprose material.

Reading Skills Exercises

You will need to use all of your language skills in order to understand the reading selections in *Reader's Choice.* The book contains many types of selections on a wide variety of topics. These selections provide practice in using different reading strategies to comprehend texts. They also give practice in four basic reading skills: **skimming, scanning, reading for thorough comprehension,** and **critical reading.** An introduction to each of these is presented, with exercises, in Unit 1 and practiced throughout the even-numbered units.

Skimming

Skimming is quick reading for the general idea(s) of a passage. This kind of rapid reading is appropriate when trying to decide if careful reading would be desirable or when there is not time to read something carefully.

Scanning

Like skimming, **scanning** is also quick reading. However, in this case the search is more focused. To scan is to read quickly in order to locate specific information. When you read to find a particular date, name, or number, you are scanning.

Reading for Thorough Comprehension

Reading for thorough comprehension is careful reading in order to understand the full meaning of the passage. At this level of comprehension, the reader is able to summarize the author's ideas but has not yet made a critical evaluation of those ideas.

Critical Reading

Critical reading demands that readers make judgments about what they read. This kind of reading requires posing and answering questions such as, *Does my own experience support that of the author? Do I share the author's point of view? Am I convinced by the author's arguments and evidence?*

Of course, effective readers use combinations of these skills and strategies simultaneously. Systematic use of the exercises and readings in *Reader's Choice* will give you practice in the basic language and reading skills necessary to become a proficient reader. Additional suggestions for the use of *Reader's Choice* in a classroom setting are included in the *To the Teacher* section on the website: www.press.umich.edu/esl/.

Acknowledgments

As *Reader's Choice, 6th Edition* goes to press we are somewhat surprised to discover that we have been working together for almost 50 years—23 on either side of the turn of the century! Since we began our collaboration, the landscape of English language teaching has changed dramatically, as have the demands on teachers and students. We are grateful for the support of many individuals as we have adjusted to the shifting demands of the times–colleagues and fellow teachers who have commented on and critiqued materials as the complexity of issues required adjustments in approach and technique, and graduate students who endured multiple drafts with consistent attention and good humor.

And, of course, a heartfelt "Thank you!" for the continuing loyalty of *RC* teachers who have collaborated with us in creating classrooms that promote student agency and critical thinking.

We are pleased to have enjoyed the consistent support of the University of Michigan Press throughout the years. In particular, Kelly Sippell, steadfast editor from 1996 to 2021, consistently championed author autonomy and textual integrity. Kelly, we wish you the most carefree and adventuresome retirement possible; we wouldn't be where we are today without your extraordinary editorial skills, your professionalism, and your energy and enthusiasm. And we thank Charles Watkinson, Director, UM Press and Katie LaPlant, Associate Textbook Editor, for ushering *Reader's Choice* into the digital age. We are grateful for their creativity and commitment toward this new endeavor.

We have continued to enjoy the unwavering support of our spouses Doug, Tom, and Patricia, whose contributions to our efforts are often unacknowledged but never taken for granted.

Seattle, Ann Arbor, Denver, 2023

UNIT 1

> **BEFORE YOU BEGIN**
>
> 1. Do you read a menu the same way that you read a textbook?
>
> 2. If not, what are the differences?

Efficient readers read differently depending on what they are reading and their goals. There are four basic types of reading behaviors or skills: skimming, scanning, reading for thorough comprehension, and critical reading. Each is explained below, and exercises are provided to give you practice in each of these.

Skimming

Skimming is quick reading for general ideas. When you skim, you move your eyes quickly to acquire a basic understanding of the text. You do not read everything, and you do not read carefully. You read, quickly, such things as the title, subtitles, and topic sentences. You also look at pictures, charts, graphs, icons, etc., for clues to what the text is about.

> **GETTING ORIENTED**
>
> The infographic on pages 4–5 describes a place in the Pacific Ocean that you may have heard of. Skim "The Great Pacific Garbage Patch" to get a general idea of what information it presents and how it is presented.
>
> 1. Is this a place you want to travel to? Why or why not?
> 2. What is the overall topic of this infographic?
> 3. Look at the subheadings. What information is given in each section of the infographic; that is, what is the general topic of each section?
>
> Once you have a general idea of the information contained in a text and how it is organized, you can search for specific information.

The following questions give you practice in scanning. Use the information in "The Great Pacific Garbage Patch" to answer the following questions. True/False items are indicated by a T / F before a statement.

1. **T / F**   The Garbage Patch is a large area of polluted land.

2. **T / F**   Ocean currents affect the location of the Garbage Patch.

3. **T / F**   The city of Los Angeles is in danger of the Garbage Patch washing onto its beaches.

4. **T / F**   The Garbage Patch contains materials from both Asia and North America.

5. **T / F**   The Garbage Patch is made up largely of plastic.

6. **T / F**   Most of the material in the Garbage Patch comes from ships.

7. **T / F**   The infographic shows a new method of recycling plastic.

8. What is the difference between biodegradation and photodegradation?

   _____

   _____

9. **T / F**   It takes 450 years for a plastic bottle to break down into natural substances.

10. Why does the infographic show Spain and Portugal?

    _____

    _____

11. **T / F**   Garbage in the Pacific Ocean causes the North Pacific Gyre.

12. **T / F**   The Garbage Patch extends from the surface of the water to the ocean floor.

13. **T / F**   The Garbage Patch is a danger to ships.

14. **T / F**   Ships are working to clean up the Garbage Patch.

15. **T / F**   The Garbage Patch is getting smaller because people are recycling plastic more now than before.

16. Four of the following words from the infographic are similar in meaning. Circle the word that does not belong.

    debris   *garbage*   *gyre*   *litter*   *trash*

Reading for Thorough Comprehension

When you read for thorough comprehension, you try to understand the full meaning of a reading. You want to know the details as well as the general meaning of the selection. When you have thoroughly comprehended a text, you have done the following things.

1. You have understood the main ideas and the author's point of view.

2. You have understood the relationships of ideas in the text, including how they relate to the author's purpose.

3. You have understood most of the concepts in the passages, as well as the vocabulary. This may require you to guess the meanings of unfamiliar words from context or to look up words in the dictionary.

4. You have begun to note that some of the ideas and points of view that were not mentioned were, however, implied by the author. This is called drawing inferences. It is the beginning of critical reading, which will be the focus of the next activity.

The Great Pacific Garbage Patch

It is an area of marine debris, lying approximately 135° to 155° West and 35° to 42° North. Although it shifts every year and the exact position is hard to tell, it lies within the North Pacific Gyre and does not go anywhere, as it is confined by its currents.

The area

The Patch is around 2200 kilometers long and 800 kilometers wide

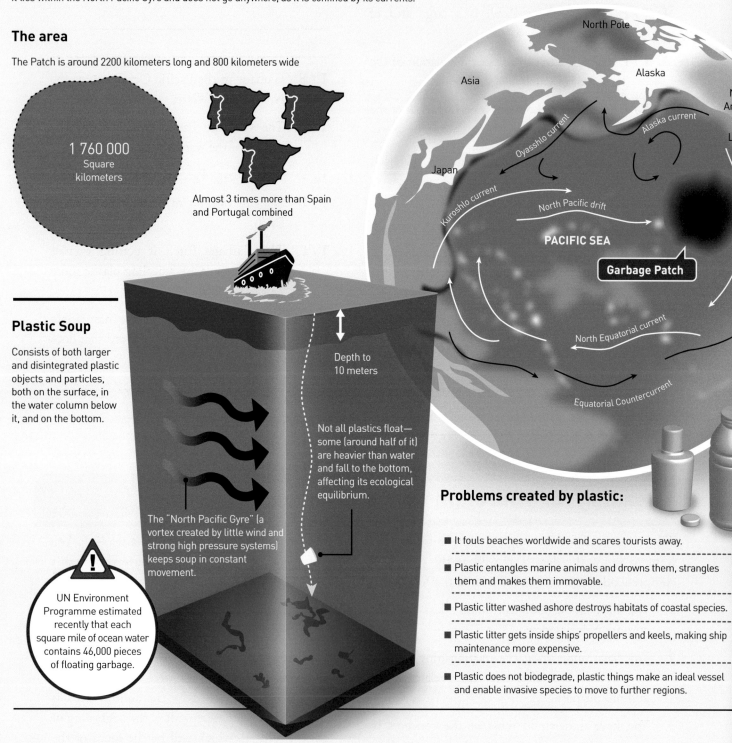

1 760 000
Square kilometers

Almost 3 times more than Spain and Portugal combined

Plastic Soup

Consists of both larger and disintegrated plastic objects and particles, both on the surface, in the water column below it, and on the bottom.

The "North Pacific Gyre" (a vortex created by little wind and strong high pressure systems) keeps soup in constant movement.

UN Environment Programme estimated recently that each square mile of ocean water contains 46,000 pieces of floating garbage.

Depth to 10 meters

Not all plastics float—some (around half of it) are heavier than water and fall to the bottom, affecting its ecological equilibrium.

North Pole

Asia

Alaska

N Am

Japan

Oyasshlo current

Alaska current

Lo

Kuroshlo current

North Pacific drift

PACIFIC SEA

Garbage Patch

North Equatorial current

Equatorial Countercurrent

Problems created by plastic:

■ It fouls beaches worldwide and scares tourists away.

■ Plastic entangles marine animals and drowns them, strangles them and makes them immovable.

■ Plastic litter washed ashore destroys habitats of coastal species.

■ Plastic litter gets inside ships' propellers and keels, making ship maintenance more expensive.

■ Plastic does not biodegrade, plastic things make an ideal vessel and enable invasive species to move to further regions.

How does it form?

Currents in the Pacific Ocean create a circular effect that pulls debris from North America, Asia, and the Hawaiian Islands. Then it pushes it into a floating pile of 100 million tons of trash.

Where does it all come from?

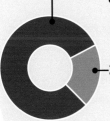

80%
Land, brought by sewer systems and rivers to the sea.

20%
Ships and ocean sources like nets or fishing gear, many containers fall into the sea after severe storms.

 Interesting facts

Less than 9% of plastic is recycled.
In the Central North Pacific Gyre, small pieces of plastic outweigh surface zooplankton many times over.

 Photodegradation

Plastic never biodegrades, it doesn't break down into natural substances. It goes through a photodegradation process, splits into ever smaller and smaller parts, which are still plastic.

How long does it take to photodegrade plastic:

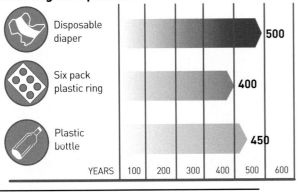

		YEARS	100	200	300	400	500	600
Disposable diaper							500	
Six pack plastic ring					400			
Plastic bottle						450		

Scanning is also quick reading, but when you scan, you are looking for something specific. Sometimes you are looking for a number or a word or the name of something. Sometimes you are looking for specific ideas. When you scan, you usually take the steps that follow.

1. Decide exactly what information you are looking for and what form it is likely to take. For example, if you wanted to know how much something cost, you would be looking for a number. If you wanted to know when something will start, you would be scanning for a date or a time. If you wanted to know who did something, you would be looking for a name. If you are looking for specific ideas, you would search for key words.

2. Next, decide where you need to look to find the information. You would turn to the sports section of a newspaper or website to discover who won a baseball game, and you would scan the "C" section of a directory for the phone number of Steven Cary.

3. Move your eyes quickly down the page or screen until you find what you want. Read to get the information.

4. When you find what you need, you usually stop reading.

This activity gives you practice in reading for thorough comprehension. To find out more about the Great Pacific Garbage Patch, you might do a web search. The US National Oceanic and Atmospheric Administration (NOAA) has published information about the Great Pacific Garbage Patch on the web. Some of it is reprinted below. Read the information from NOAA, and then do the activity that follows.

What are the "garbage patches"?

The "garbage patch," as referred to in the media, is an area of marine debris… in the North Pacific Ocean. The name "garbage patch" has led many to believe that this area is a large and continuous patch of easily visible marine debris items such as bottles and other litter… This is simply not true. While litter items can be found in this area, along with other debris such as… fishing nets, much of the debris mentioned in the media these days refers to small bits of floatable plastic debris. These plastic pieces are quite small and not immediately evident to the naked eye.

What's in a name? The name "garbage patch" is a misnomer. There is no island of trash forming in the middle of the ocean, nor a blanket of trash that can be easily seen. This is likely because much of the debris found here is small bits of floating plastic not readily visible.

How big are the "garbage patches"?

The reported size and mass of these "patches" have differed from media article to article…. There is

really no accurate estimate on the size or mass of the "garbage patch"….

What is the main debris type found in these patches?

Plastics. Likely because of the abundance of plastics and the fact that some common types of plastic float.

Can you see the "garbage patches" with satellite photos?

NO… Sightings of large concentrations of debris, especially of large debris items are not very common. A majority of the debris observed in the "garbage patch" is small plastic pieces. Small debris pieces are difficult to see due to their size, and many of these pieces may be suspended below the surface of the water, which would make them even harder to see, even with the human eye. For these reasons, the debris, or "patch" of debris is not visible with existing satellite technology.

Comparing information from two different sources can be helpful in learning about a new topic. Complete the table below to compare what the infographic and NOAA say about the Great Pacific Garbage Patch. Each row in the table asks a question. Answer each question first by filling in information from the infographic. Then answer it based on the information from NOAA. Your teacher may want to do the first row with you as an example.

	Infographic	NOAA
Where is the Garbage Patch?		
How big is the Garbage Patch?		
What is in the Garbage Patch?		
What does the Garbage Patch look like?		

Critical Reading

When we read critically, we draw conclusions and make judgments about the reading. We ask questions such as, "What inferences can be drawn from this? Do I agree with this point of view?" We often do this when we read, but in some cases it is more important than others, as, for example, when authors give opinions about important issues or when you are trying to make a decision.

Exercise 1

Use the infographic and the information from the NOAA website to answer the following critical reading questions.

1. Did your understanding of the Great Pacific Garbage Patch change after you read the information from NOAA?

    _____

2. What do you do when you find that information in one source differs from information in another source?

    _____

3. Do you think that the infographic is a good source of information about the Great Pacific Garbage Patch? Why or why not?

    _____

Exercise 2

One can also critically "read" a film. Ramin Bahrani's *Plastic Bag* provides a different perspective of the Great Pacific Garbage Patch. Go to the *Reader's Choice, 6th Edition: Companion Teaching Materials* website, and watch the film. It is a love story… sort of.

The film begins with the words, "They told me it's out there, the Pacific Vortex." If you're not certain of the meaning of the term *vortex*, look it up in an English or bilingual dictionary before you watch the film. Why do you think the film refers to the Great Pacific Garbage Patch as the Pacific Vortex?

After watching the film, answer the following questions.

1. What is the main idea or message of the film?

    _____

2. What do you think the following lines from the film mean?

    a. "Why were my moments of joy so brief?"

    _____

    b. "I wish you had created me so I could die."

    _____

3. Why do you think that the filmmaker made this a love story? Do you think that only the plastic bag is in love? Who besides the plastic bag may be in love?

    _____

4. Why do you think the filmmaker calls the woman the "maker?" In what way is she responsible for making the bag?

    _____

5. Do you think this is an effective film? Did you enjoy it? Did it make you think?

    _____

Nonprose Reading
Subway Map

New York City hosts more than 55 million visitors each year. The city has five boroughs*. One of them, Manhattan, has most of the sites that we think of when we think of New York: museums, universities, performance centers. One of the easiest ways to get around the city is by subway. Below is a partial map of Manhattan subways, from the south end of Central Park to the southern end of Manhattan Island. The exercises in this section will give you practice in nonprose reading.

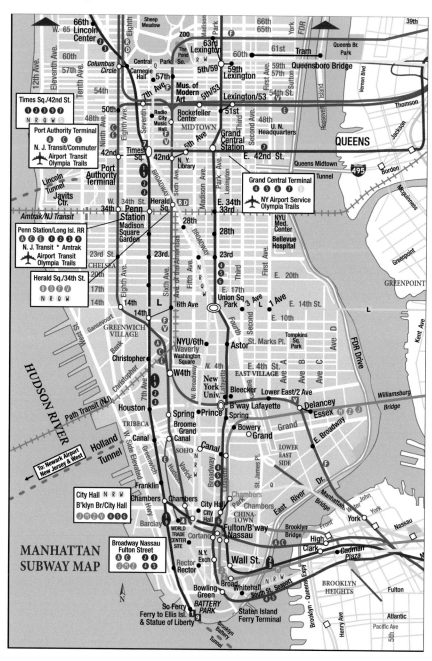

---

*Borough: part of a city with its own local government, division, administrative unit.

Scanning

Below are some common destinations for visitors to New York. Circle the following major locations on the subway map on page 8. Your teacher may want to read these aloud as you quickly scan to locate them.

Transportation Centers

1. Grand Central Station
2. Port Authority (Bus) Terminal
3. Penn Station
4. Ferry to the Statue of Liberty

Arts and Performance Centers

1. Lincoln Center for the Performing Arts
2. Madison Square Garden
3. Carnegie Hall
4. Museum of Modern Art
5. Radio City Music Hall

Famous Locations

1. Rockefeller Center
2. Wall Street
3. World Trade Center Site
4. China Town
5. United Nations
6. New York University
7. Central Park
8. Brooklyn Bridge

GETTING ORIENTED

Indicate if the statements below are true (T) or false (F). Your teacher may want to read these aloud as you quickly scan to find the answers.

1. **T / F**   The names of neighborhoods are shown in red.
2. **T / F**   The different subway lines are indicated by color.
3. **T / F**   All of the individual train routes within a subway line are indicated by numbers.
4. **T / F**   Avenues run east/west.

Comprehension

Answer the following questions. True/False questions are indicated by a T / F preceding a statement. Your teacher may want you to work on your own or in pairs.

1. You are arriving at Penn Station, and you will be staying near Columbus Circle. What subway will you take to get to your hotel? _____

2. You are staying near 8th Avenue and 58th Street, and you want to go to Carnegie Hall. Would you take the subway or walk? _____

3. You know that you will be visiting Rockefeller Center Monday and the site of the World Trade Center on Tuesday. You want to visit the Museum of Modern Art (MOMA) on one of those days. Which day would you visit the MOMA if you wanted to visit two sites that are near each other? _____

4. You are at Rockefeller Center, and you want to have dinner in Chinatown. How will you get there? Indicate which subway line(s) you would take and whether you will choose to walk at certain points.
   _____
   _____

5. You are at the site of the World Trade Center and want to visit Wall Street. How would you get there?
   _____
   _____

6. Your friends are going to drive you to the Newark Airport in New Jersey. They ask you to meet them at the subway station closest to the Holland Tunnel. At what station would you get off? If you are coming from Columbus Circle, will you need to change trains?
   _____

7. **T / F** You can visit Ellis Island and the Statue of Liberty on the same trip.

8. **T / F** You can take the Red 2/3 train directly from Columbus Circle to the South Ferry.

9. **T / F** The Yellow line stops at Chambers Street, near Chinatown.

Critical Reading

Your teacher may want you to work on the following questions in pairs or small groups.

1. Some of your friends will only have one day in New York City. They want to visit New York University (NYU) and then see some of the sites. Plan a day including NYU and three other locations. Tell how you would use the subway system on this day.
   _____
   _____
   _____

2. One of the most popular outdoor observation sites in the world is the deck of the Empire State Building, but the building is not listed on the subway map. Find out where it is located. How would you get there by subway from Columbus Circle?
   _____

3. A favorite activity for visitors and locals alike is walking across the Brooklyn Bridge. You've been told that you will need to get off at one of the nearest subway stops and follow the crowds. If you want to get to the Brooklyn Bridge, how would you do it? What subway stops are closest to the bridge?
   _____
   _____

Word Study
Context Clues

Efficient reading requires the use of various problem-solving skills. For example, it is impossible for you to know the exact meaning of every word you read, but by developing your guessing ability, you will often be able to understand enough to arrive at the total meaning of a sentence, a paragraph, or an essay. Context Clues exercises are designed to help you improve your ability to guess the meaning of unfamiliar words by using context clues. (Context refers to the sentence and paragraph in which a word occurs.) In using the context to decide the meaning of a word, you have to use your knowledge of grammar and your understanding of the author's ideas. Although there is no formula that you can memorize to improve your ability to guess the meanings of unfamiliar words, you should keep the following points in mind.

1. Use the meanings of the other words in the sentence (or paragraph) and the meaning of the sentence as a whole to reduce the number of possible meanings.

2. Use grammar and punctuation clues that point to the relationships among the various parts of the sentence.

3. Be content with a general idea about the unfamiliar word; the exact definition or synonym is not always necessary.

4. Learn to recognize situations in which it is not necessary to know the meaning of the word.

The explanations given on page 12 for each sentence in the example exercise show how context clues can be used to guess the meaning of unfamiliar words.

Example

Each of the sentences in this exercise contains a blank in order to encourage you to look only at the context provided as you attempt to determine the possible meanings of the missing word. Read each sentence quickly, and supply a word for each blank. There is no single correct answer. Use context clues to help you provide a word that is appropriate in terms of grammar and meaning.

1. I removed the _____book_____ from the shelf and began to read.

2. Harvey is a thief; he would _____steal_____ the gold from his grandmother's teeth and not feel guilty.

3. Our uncle was a _____Traveler_____, an incurable wanderer who never could stay in one place.

4. Unlike his brother, who is truly a handsome person, Hogartty is quite _____ugly_____.

5. The Asian _____shampansi_____, like other apes, is specially adapted for life in trees.

6. But surely everyone knows that if you step on an egg, it will _____Break_____.

7. Mary got a new _____car_____ for her birthday. It is a sports model—red with white interior and bucket seats.

Explanation

1. I removed the _____ from the shelf and began to read.

   book
   magazine
   paper
   newspaper

   The number of things that can be taken from a shelf and read is so few that the word *book* probably jumped into your mind at once. Here, the association between the object and the purpose for which it is used is so close that you have very little difficulty guessing the right word.

2. Harvey is a thief; he would _____ the gold from his grandmother's teeth and not feel guilty.

   steal
   take
   rob

   Harvey is a thief. A thief steals. The semicolon (;) indicates that the sentence that follows contains an explanation of the first statement. Further, you know that the definition of *thief* is a person who steals.

3. Our uncle was a _____, an incurable wanderer who never could stay in one place.

   nomad
   roamer
   traveler
   drifter

   The comma (,) following the blank, indicates a phrase in apposition, that is, a word or group of words that could be used as a synonym of the unfamiliar word. The words at the left are all synonyms of *wanderer.*

4. Unlike his brother, who is truly a handsome person, Hogartty is quite _____.

   unattractive
   homely
   plain

   Hogartty is the opposite of his brother, and since his brother is handsome, Hogartty must be ugly. The word *unlike* signals the relationship between Hogartty and his brother.

5. The Asian _____, like other apes, is specially adapted for life in trees.

   gibbon
   monkey
   chimp
   ape

   You probably didn't write *gibbon,* which is the word the author used. Most native speakers wouldn't be familiar with this word either. But since you know that the word is the name of a type of ape, you don't need to know anything else. This is an example of how context can teach you the meanings of unfamiliar words.

6. But surely everyone knows that if you step on an egg, it will _____.

   break

   You recognized the cause-and-effect relationship in this sentence. There is only one thing that can happen to an egg when it is stepped on.

7. Mary got a new _____ for her birthday. It is a sports model, red, with white interior and bucket seats.

   car

   The description in the second sentence gave you all the information you needed to guess the word *car.*

Exercise

In the following exercise, do *not* try to learn the italicized words. Concentrate on developing your ability to guess the meanings of unfamiliar words using context clues. Read each sentence carefully and write a definition, synonym, or description of the italicized word on the line provided.

1. _____ We watched as the cat came quietly through the grass toward the bird. When it was just a few feet from the victim, it gathered its legs under itself and *pounced* (1).

2. _____ Some people have no difficulty making the necessary changes in their way of life when they move to a foreign country; others are not able to *adapt* (2) as easily to a new environment.

3. _____ In spite of the fact that the beautiful *egret* (3) is in danger of dying out completely, many clothing manufacturers still offer handsome prices for their long, elegant tail feathers, which are used as decorations on hats.

4. _____ When he learned that the club was planning to admit women, the colonel began to *inveigh against* (4) all forms of liberalism; his shouting attack began with universal voting and ended with a protest against divorce.

5. _____ The snake *slithered* (5) through the grass.

6. _____ John thought that the other children were defenseless, so he walked boldly up to the oldest and demanded money. Imagine his surprise when they began to *pelt* (6) him with rocks.

7. _____ Experts in *kinesics* (7), in their study of body motion as related to speech, hope to discover new methods of communication.

8. _____ Unlike her *gregarious* (8) sister, Jane is a shy, unsociable person who does not like to go to parties or to make new friends.

9. _____ After a day of skiing, Harold is *ravenous* (9). Yesterday, for example, he ate two bowls of soup, a salad, a large chicken, and a piece of chocolate cake before he was finally satisfied.

10. _____ After the accident, the ship went down so fast that we weren't able to *salvage* (10) any of our personal belongings.

Word Study
Stems and Affixes

Using context clues is one way to discover the meaning of an unfamiliar word. Another way is word analysis, that is, looking at the meanings of parts of words. Many English words have been formed by combining parts of older English, Greek, and Latin words. If you know the meanings of some of these word parts, you can often guess the meaning of an unfamiliar English word, particularly in context.

For example, *report* is formed from *re-*, which means "back," and *-port*, which means "carry." *Scientist* is derived from *sci-*, which means "know," and *-ist*, which means "one who." *Port* and *sci* are called **stems.** A stem is the basic part on which groups of related words are built. *Re* and *ist* are called **affixes,** that is, word parts that are attached to stems. Affixes like *re-*, which are attached to the beginnings of stems, are called **prefixes.** Affixes attached to the end, like *-ist*, are called **suffixes.** Generally, prefixes change the meaning of a word, and suffixes change its part of speech. Here is an example.

Stem	Prefix	Suffix
pay (verb)	*re*pay (verb)	repay*ment* (noun)
honest (adjective)	*dis*honest (adjective)	dishonest*ly* (adverb)

Word analysis is not enough to give you the precise definition of a word you encounter in a reading passage, but often along with context it will help you to understand the general meaning of the word so that you can continue reading without stopping to use a dictionary.

Below is a list of some commonly occurring stems and affixes*. Study their meanings. Your teacher may ask you to give examples of other words you know that are derived from these stems and affixes. Then do the exercises that follow.

Prefixes		
com-, con-, col-, cor-, co-	together, with	*cooperate, connect*
in-, im-, il-, ir-	in, into, on	*invade, insert*
in-, im-, il, ir-	not	*impolite, illegal*
micro-	small	*microscope, microcomputer*
pre-	before	*prepare, prehistoric*
re-, retro-	back, again	*return, retrorocket*
Stems		
-audi-, -audit-	hear	*auditorium, auditor*
-chron-	time	*chronology, chronological*
-dic-, -dict-	say, speak	*dictator, dictation*
-graph-, -gram-	write, writing	*telegraph, telegram*
-log-, -logy	speech, word, study	*biological*
-phon-	sound	*telephone*

---

*For a list of all the stems and affixes that appear in *Reader's Choice*, see Appendix B.

-scrib-, -script-	write	*describe, script*
-spect-	look at	*inspect, spectator*
-vid-, -vis-	see	*video, vision*
Suffixes		
-er, -or	one who	*worker, spectator*
-ist	one who	*typist, biologist*
-tion, -ation	condition, the act of	*action, celebration*

Exercise 1

1. For each item, select the best definition of the italicized word.

    a. He lost his *spectacles.*

        _____ **1.** glasses   _____ **3.** pants

        _____ **2.** gloves   _____ **4.** shoes

    b. He drew *concentric* circles.

        _____ **1.** ⚭   _____ **3.** ⚭

        _____ **2.** ◉   _____ **4.** ⓪

    c. He *inspected* their work.

        _____ **1.** spoke highly of   _____ **3.** examined closely

        _____ **2.** did not examine   _____ **4.** did not like

2. Circle the words where *in-* means *not*. Watch out; there are false negatives in this list.

inject	inside	insane	inspect
invaluable	inflammable	inactive	invisible

3. In current usage, the prefix *co-* is frequently used to form new words (for example, *co-* + *editors* becomes *coeditors*). Give another example of a word that uses *co-* in this way.

_____

4. The prefix *re-* (meaning *again*) often combines with simple verbs to create new verbs (for example, *re-* + *do* becomes *redo*). List three words familiar to you that use *re-* in this way.

_____

Exercise 2

Word analysis can help you to guess the meanings of unfamiliar words. Using context clues and what you know about word parts, write a synonym, description, or definition of the italicized word or phrase.

1. _____ The doctor asked Martin to *inhale* deeply and hold his breath for 10 seconds.

2. _____ Many countries *import* most of the oil they use.

3. _____ Three newspaper reporters *collaborated* in writing this series of articles.

4. _____ Calling my professor by her first name seems too *informal* to me.

5. _____ It is Lee's *prediction* that by the year 2040 most automobiles will be electric powered.

6. _____ Historians use the *inscriptions* on the walls of ancient temples to guide them in their studies.

7. _____ You cannot sign up for a class the first day it meets in September; you must *preregister* in August.

8. _____ After his long illness, he didn't recognize his own *reflection* in the mirror.

9. _____ I *dictated* the letter to my assistant over the phone.

10. _____ I'm sending a sample of my handwriting to a *graphologist* who says he can use it to analyze my personality.

11. _____ The university has a very good *microbiology* department.

12. _____ *Phonograph recordings* of early jazz musicians are very valuable now.

13. _____ At the drugstore, the pharmacist refused to give me my medicine because she could not read the doctor's *prescription*.

14. _____ He should see a doctor about his *chronic* cough.

15. _____ Maureen was not admitted to graduate school this year, but she *reapplied* and was admitted for next year.

16. _____ I recognize his face, but I can't *recall* his name.

17. _____ Ten years ago, I decided not to complete high school; *in retrospect*, I believe that was a bad decision.

18. _____ She uses *audiovisual* aids to make her speeches more interesting.

19. _____ Some people believe it is *immoral* to fight in any war.

20. _____ Babies are born healthier when their mothers have good *prenatal* care.

Exercise 3

Following is a list of words containing some of the stems and affixes* introduced in this unit. Definitions of these words appear on the right. Put the letter of the appropriate definition next to each word.

1. _____ microbe

    a. an instrument used to make soft sounds louder

2. _____ phonology

    b. not able to be seen

3. _____ audience

    c. a group of listeners

4. _____ chronicler

    d. the study of speech sounds

5. _____ chronology

    e. not normal

6. _____ irregular

    f. a person who creates records of events in the order in which they occur

7. _____ microphone

    g. an organism too small to be seen with the naked eye

8. _____ invisible

    h. a listing of events arranged in order of their occurrence

---

*For a list of all the stems and affixes that appear in *Reader's Choice*, see Appendix B.

Sentence Study
Introduction

The exercises in this book provide you with practice in using a number of reading skills and strategies to understand a reading passage. Context Clues, Stems and Affixes, and Dictionary Use exercises provide you with practice in quickly finding specific pieces of information in a passage. Skimming, introduced in this unit, focuses on reading a passage quickly for a general idea of its meaning.

When you have difficulty understanding a passage, just reading further will often make the passage clearer. Sometimes, however, comprehension of an entire passage depends on your being able to understand a single sentence. Sentences that are very long and sentences that contain difficult vocabulary or difficult grammatical patterns often cause comprehension problems for readers. The sentence study exercise that follows as well as similar ones in later units gives you the opportunity to develop strategies for understanding complicated sentences.

Although there is no easy formula that will help you to arrive at an understanding of a difficult sentence, you should keep the following points in mind.

1. Try to determine what makes the sentence difficult:

    a. If the sentence contains a lot of difficult vocabulary, it may be that the sentence can be understood without knowing the meaning of every word. Try crossing out unfamiliar items.

    > The West had sent armies to ~~capture and~~ hold Jerusalem; instead they themselves fell ~~victim~~ to ~~a host of~~ new ideas and ~~subtle~~ influences which left their mark on the development of European literature, ~~chivalry,~~ warfare, ~~sanitation,~~ commerce, political institutions, medicine, ~~and the papacy itself.~~

    b. If the sentence is very long, try to break it up into smaller parts:

    > The West had sent armies to capture and hold Jerusalem. The West fell victim to a host of new ideas and subtle influences. These ideas and influences left their mark on the development of European literature, chivalry, warfare, sanitation, commerce, political institutions, medicine, and the papacy.

    c. Also, if the sentence is very long, try to determine which parts of the sentence express specific details supporting the main idea. Often clauses that are set off by commas, or introduced by words such as *which, who,* and *that,* are used to introduce extra information or to provide supporting details. Try crossing out the supporting details in order to determine the main idea:

    > These ideas, ~~which left their mark on the development of European literature, chivalry, warfare, sanitation, commerce, political institutions, medicine, and the papacy,~~ greatly changed Western culture.

identify for example

> **Be careful! A good reader reads quickly but accurately!**

2. Learn to recognize the important grammatical and punctuation clues that can change the meaning of a sentence:

a. Look for single words and affixes* that can change the entire meaning of a sentence.

> Summery weather is *not un*common.
> The *average* daytime *high* temperature is *approximately* 56°.

b. Look for punctuation clues:

> Wally "sings" at all of his friends' parties.
> Barry said, "George has been elected president?"

Note that all of the italicized words or affixes and the circled punctuation above are essential to the meaning of the sentences; if any of these are omitted, the meaning of the sentences changes significantly.

c. Look for key words that tell you of relationships within a sentence:

> The school has grown *from* a small building holding 200 students *to* a large institute that educates 4,000 students a year.

From… to indicates the beginning and end points of a period of change.

> Many critics have proclaimed Doris Lessing as *not only* the best writer of the postwar generation, *but also* a penetrating analyst of human affairs.

Not only… but also indicates that both parts of the sentence are of equal importance.

> *In order to* graduate on time, you will need to take five courses each semester.

In order to is like *if;* it indicates that some event must occur before another event can take place.

> The West had sent armies to capture and hold Jerusalem; *instead* they themselves fell victim to new ideas and subtle influences.

Instead indicates that something happened contrary to expectations.

> *As a result of* three books, a television documentary, and a special exposition at the Library of Congress, the mystery has aroused considerable public interest.

As a result of indicates a cause-and-effect relationship. The clause that follows *as a result of* is the cause of some event. The three books, television program, and exposition are the *cause;* the arousal of public interest is the *effect*.

> *Because of* the impact of these ideas, *which* had been introduced originally to Europe by soldiers returning from the East, the West was greatly changed.

Because of indicates a cause-and-effect relationship. The West was changed as a result of these ideas. The information between the word *which* and the final comma (,) refers to *these ideas*.

---

*For a list of all stems and affixes that appear in *Reader's Choice,* see Appendix B.

Sentence Study
Comprehension

Read the following sentences carefully. The questions that follow are designed to test your comprehension of complex grammatical structures. Select the *best* answer.

Example

The student revolt is not only a thorn in the side of the prime ministers's newly established government, but it has international implications as well.

Whom or what does the revolt affect?

_____ **a.** the students

_____ **b.** the side of the president's body

_____ **c.** only the national government

_____ **d.** national and international affairs

Explanation

_____ **a.** According to the sentence, the students are the cause of certain events, not among those affected.

_____ **b.** Although you may not have been familiar with the idiom *a thorn in someone's side*, context clues should have told you that this phrase means *a problem* and does not actually refer to the side of the prime minister's body.

_____ **c.** National government is an incomplete answer. The construction *not only... but... as well* should tell you that more than one element is involved. The prime minister's newly established government (the national government) is not the only area affected by the revolt.

___✓___ **d.** The revolt affects both national and international affairs.

1. I disagreed then as now with many of John Smith's judgments but always respected him, and this book is a welcome reminder of his big, honest, friendly, stubborn personality.

    How does the author of this sentence feel about John Smith?

    _____ **a.** He dislikes him but agrees with his ideas.

    _____ **b.** He considers him to be a disagreeable person.

    _____ **c.** He disagrees with his ideas but respects him.

    _____ **d.** He disagreed with him then but agrees with him now.

2. Concepts like *passivity*, *dependence*, and *aggression* may need further research if they are to continue to be useful ways of thinking about human personalities.

What might require more research?

_____ **a.** human thought processes

_____ **b.** certain concepts

_____ **c.** human personalities

_____ **d.** useful ways of thinking

3. In order for you to follow the schedule set by the publisher, your paper must be looked over over the weekend, revised, and handed in in its final form on Monday.

What must you do on Saturday and Sunday?

_____ **a.** meet the publisher

_____ **b.** examine your paper

_____ **c.** hand in a paper

_____ **d.** look over over the weekend

4. The real reason why prices were, and still are too high, is complicated, and no short discussion can satisfactorily explain this problem.

What word or phrase best describes prices?

_____ **a.** complicated

_____ **b.** adequately explained

_____ **c.** too high in the past, but low now

_____ **d.** too high in the past and in the present

5. This is not just a sad-but-true story; the boy's experience is horrible and damaging, yet a sense of love shines through every word.

How does the author of this sentence feel about the story?

_____ **a.** It transmits a sense of love.

_____ **b.** It is just sad.

_____ **c.** It is not true.

_____ **d.** It is horrible and damaging.

6. In the past five years the movement has grown from unorganized groups of poorly armed individuals to a comparatively well-armed, well-trained army of anywhere from 10,000 to 16,000 members.

What is the present condition of this movement?

_____ a. The members are poorly armed.

_____ b. There are only a few poor individuals.

_____ c. There are over 16,000 members.

_____ d. The members are organized and well armed.

7. The financial situation isn't bad yet, but we believe that we have some vital information and, if it is correct, unemployment will soon become a serious problem.

What do we know about the financial situation?

_____ a. It won't change.

_____ b. It will become a serious problem.

_____ c. It is not bad now.

_____ d. It will improve.

8. The general then added, "The only reasonable solution to the sort of problems caused by the current unstable political situation is one of diplomacy and economic measures and not the use of military force."

What type of solution does the general support?

_____ a. economic and diplomatic action

_____ b. diplomatic and economic action if military force fails

_____ c. only diplomatic action

_____ d. military actions in response to political problems

9. Because the supply of natural gas was plentiful in comparison to other choices like coal and fuel oil, and because it burns cleaner, many people changed their heating systems to natural gas, thereby creating shortages.

Why did people prefer natural gas?

_____ a. It was natural.

_____ b. There were no other choices.

_____ c. The other fuels were dirtier and less plentiful.

_____ d. There is, even today, a plentiful supply of it.

Paragraph Reading
Main Idea

In this exercise, you will practice finding the main idea of a short text. Being able to determine the main idea of a passage is one of the most useful reading skills you can develop. It is a skill you can apply to any kind of reading. For example, when you read for enjoyment or to obtain general information, it is probably not important to remember all the details of a selection. Instead, you want to quickly discover the general message—the main idea of the passage. For other kinds of reading, such as reading textbooks or articles in your own field, you need both to determine the main ideas and to understand the way in which these are developed.

The main idea of a passage is the thought that is present from the beginning to the end. In a well-written paragraph, most of the sentences support, describe, or explain the main idea. It is sometimes stated in the first or last sentence of the paragraph. Sometimes the main idea is only implied.

In order to determine the main idea of a piece of writing, you should ask yourself what idea is common to most of the text. What is the idea that relates the parts to the whole? What opinion do all the parts support? What idea do they all explain or describe?

When reading short passages, you need to be able to both recognize the main idea and sometimes to express the main idea in your own words. Read the following short texts to discover the main idea. After each of the first three passages, select the statement that best expresses the main idea. For Passages 4 and 5, you will write a sentence that expresses the main idea. Finally, for Passage 6, which is several paragraphs long, you will move to doing this task on a larger scale; you will be asked to both identify the main idea and create a summary of the entire text.

When you have finished, your teacher may want to divide the class into small groups for discussion. Study the example carefully before you begin.

Example

By the time the first European travelers on the American continent began to record some of their observations about Native Americans, the Cherokee people had developed an advanced culture that probably was exceeded only by the civilisations of the Southwest: Maya and Aztec groups. The social structures of the Cherokee people consisted of a form of clan kinship in which there were seven recognized clans. All members of a clan were considered blood brothers and sisters and were bound by honor to defend any member of that clan from injury or wrongdoing from others. Each clan, the Bird, Paint, Deer, Wolf, Blue, Long Hair, and Wild Potato, was represented in the civil council by a councilor or councilors. Two chiefs were selected from these clans and did not inherit their office from their kinsmen. One served as a Peace chief and one served as a War chief. The Peace chief served when the tribe was at peace, but the minute war was declared, the War chief was in command.

Select the statement that best expresses the main idea of the passage.

_____ a. The Cherokee chief was different in wartime than in peacetime.

_____ b. Before the arrival of the Europeans, the Cherokees had developed a well-organized society.

_____ c. The Maya and the Aztecs were part of the Cherokee tribe.

___✓___ d. Several Native American cultures had developed advanced civilizations before Europeans arrived.

Explanation

_____ **a.** This is not the main idea. Rather, it is one of the several examples the author uses to support his statement that the Cherokee people had developed an advanced culture.

___✓___ **b.** This statement expresses the main idea of the paragraph. All other sentences in the paragraph are examples supporting the idea that the Cherokees had developed an advanced culture by the time Europeans arrived on the continent.

_____ **c.** This statement is false, so it cannot be the main idea.

_____ **d.** This statement is too general. The paragraph describes the social structure of the Cherokee people only. Although the author names other advanced Native American cultures, he does this only to strengthen his argument that the Cherokees had developed an advanced culture.

Passage 1

A remarkable feature of Australian English is its comparative uniformity. Australia, a continent roughly the size of Europe, has almost no regional variation of accent. A citizen of Perth can sound much like a citizen of Adelaide or Sydney, or like a station hand in Alice Springs or Broken Hill. In Britain or the United States, by contrast, even the outsider can probably decide from the local accent whether he or she is in Scotland or Dorset, New England or Louisiana.

Select the statement that best expresses the main idea of the passage.

_____ **a.** Regional accents are remarkably useful in deciding where someone is from.

_____ **b.** In Britain or the United States, there are different accents in different regions.

_____ **c.** English spoken across Australia is not very different from that spoken in Britain and in the United States.

_____ **d.** There are surprisingly few regional differences in Australian English.

Passage 2

At the University of Kansas art museum, investigators tested the effects of different-colored walls on two groups of visitors to an exhibit of paintings. For the first group the room was painted white; for the second, dark brown. Movement of each group was followed by an electrical system under the carpet. The experiment revealed that those who entered the dark brown room walked more quickly, covered more area, and spent less time in the room than the people in the white environment. Dark brown stimulated more activity, but the activity ended sooner. Not only the choice of colors but also the general appearance of a room creates ambiance and influences the behavior of those inside. Another experiment presented subjects with photographs of faces that were to be rated in terms of energy and well-being. Three groups of subjects were used; each was shown the same photos, but each group was in a different kind of room. One group was in an "ugly" room that resembled a messy storeroom. Another group was in an average room—a nice office. The third group was in a tastefully designed living room with carpeting and drapes. Results showed that the subjects in the beautiful room tended to give higher ratings to the faces than did those in the ugly room. Other studies suggest that students do better on tests taken in comfortable, attractive rooms than they do in ordinary-looking or ugly rooms.

Select the statement that best expresses the main idea of the passage.

_____ **a.** People in beautiful rooms tend to give higher ratings to photographs of faces than do people in ugly rooms.

_____ **b.** The color and general appearance of a room influence the behavior and attitudes of the people in it.

_____ **c.** The University of Kansas has studied the effects of the color of a room on people's behavior.

_____ **d.** Beautifully decorated, light-colored rooms make people more comfortable than ugly, dark rooms.

Passage 3

One disagreement in the field of evolutionary biology is between the "creeps" and the "jerks." The creeps (named by the jerks) argue that evolutionary change is gradual, happening slowly and steadily. The jerks (named by the creeps) believe it happens in sudden jumps that are separated by long periods of little change. Their humorous names are the result of a lively dialogue between the two groups.

Select the statement that best expresses the main idea of the passage.

_____ **a.** "Creeps" and "jerks" are biologists who do not believe in evolutionary change.

_____ **b.** There are many theories that evolutionary biologists disagree about.

_____ **c.** Evolutionary biologists don't agree about how quickly evolutionary change happens.

_____ **d.** Evolutionary biologists study how quickly evolutionary change happens.

Passage 4

Have you heard that to stay warm in cold weather you should wear a hat because most of your body heat that is lost when you are in the cold escapes through your head? According to a US Army manual written in the 1970s, you should cover your head in cold weather because "40 to 45 percent of body heat is lost through the head." Researchers at the University of Indiana recently examined available evidence related to this claim. They report that although our head is particularly sensitive to temperature changes, no one body part loses more heat than others. Only about 10% of the body's heat escapes from an uncovered head. The common belief that most heat escapes through the head probably originated from a military survival study in the 1950s. Scientists put hatless subjects in heavy winter clothing and measured their heat loss in very cold temperatures. Today's researchers argue that the only reason those subjects lost so much heat through their heads is that their heads were the only body part exposed.

Write a sentence that expresses the main idea of the passage.

_____

_____

Passage 5

There is widespread fear among policymakers and the public today that the family is disintegrating. Much of that anxiety stems from a basic misunderstanding of the nature of the family in the past and a lack of appreciation for its resiliency in response to broad social and economic changes. The general view of the family is that it has been a stable and relatively unchanging institution through history and is only now undergoing changes; in fact, change has always been characteristic of it.

Write a sentence that expresses the main idea of the passage.

_____

_____

Read Passage 6 to identify the most important ideas.

Passage 6: Main Idea and Prose Summary

Scientists believe they have found the answer to a question that has been puzzling bird lovers and scientists alike. Typically, the common English robin is one of the earliest birds to begin singing at the dawn of each day and the last to stop singing at nightfall. Singing is the way male robins attract a mate. Around some cities, however, it is now not unusual to hear robins singing at night. This phenomenon has been the subject of study by researchers at the University of Sheffield, in the UK, who are interested in the effects of urbanization on biodiversity.

Until recently, urban light pollution was offered as the explanation for why some robins sing at night. The theory was that light from street lamps, large office buildings, and automobiles fooled robins into thinking it was still daylight. According to Richard Fuller, a scientist at the University of Sheffield, there was inadequate research to support this claim. He and his colleagues suspected something else was at play.

In a two-year study, Fuller's research team visited 121 sites in and around the city of Sheffield. At 67 of the sites, they heard robins singing during the day, and at 18 sites, nocturnally. At each site where they heard birds, they measured nighttime light and daytime noise. The nighttime light levels at the sites did have a small effect, but the daytime noise levels were much more strongly related to nighttime singing. They found that in areas where robins sang at night, the noise levels during the day were on average twice as loud as at the other sites, loud enough to make it difficult for the birds' songs to be heard.

That birds' singing is affected by urban noise is supported by several other studies. European researchers showed that birds living in areas with a lot of traffic sing at a higher pitch than similar birds in quieter areas, to be heard over the low-frequency sound of traffic. Another study suggested that nightingales in Germany sing louder in noisy areas. Further studies will be conducted to investigate the effects of nighttime singing on birds. It is possible that the adaptation is harmless; however, it could also tire birds out and take time away from feeding, which could threaten their survival.

1. What was the main finding of Fuller's research?

    _____ **a.** Nighttime singing appears to be dangerous for robins.

    _____ **b.** A loud level of noise in the day appears to cause robins to sing at night.

    _____ **c.** Nighttime singing by robins appears not to be as common as was once thought.

    _____ **d.** English robins do not appear to sing as loudly as German nightingales.

    _____ **e.** Urban light pollution does not appear to affect robins' singing.

2. Imagine you are part of a study group in an ecology class. You have agreed to read this passage and write a one-paragraph summary of Fuller's research for your study group. You will begin your summary with this topic sentence:

    Richard Fuller and his colleagues investigated why some robins living near urban areas sing at night.

Now, choose three more sentences from the choices below to complete your summary. Put a check (✓) next to the three sentences that express the most important ideas about the study. Do not check the sentences that express ideas not found in the passage or ones that are less important ideas for summarizing the research study.

    _____ **a.** They theorized that the main cause was light pollution.

    _____ **b.** They studied places where robins sing at night and places where they do not.

    _____ **c.** They found that most robins sing during the day.

    _____ **d.** They measured light and noise levels at 121 sites.

    _____ **e.** They discovered it was noisier in places where robins sang at night.

    _____ **f.** They found that robins sing louder at night than during the day.

    _____ **g.** They discovered that light pollution had less effect than people had theorized.

    _____ **h.** They proved that nighttime singing threatens the robins' survival.

UNIT 2

Reading Selections 1A–1B
Interdisciplinary Research

Selection 1A Report on Research: History

BEFORE
YOU BEGIN

People's sleep patterns can be quite different. Compare your sleep habits with those of your classmates. Using the following questions, your teacher may want you to interview each other, answer by a show of hands, or have people with similar responses move to similar locations in the room.

- How many hours per night do you think people should sleep?

- How many hours per night do you sleep?

- Do you sleep through the night? If not, how many times and when do you wake up?

The following article describes research on human sleep patterns. When reading, it is helpful to know what your assumptions are so you can compare your expectations to what is in the text. Now that you know something about the current sleep habits of your classmates, let's see what your assumptions are about human sleep patterns over time.

Do you think that human beings have always had the same sleep patterns?

- If so, what are they?

- If not, what would other sleep patterns be like and why would they change?

Read "How We Sleep" to find out about new research on the history of sleep. Your teacher may want you to do Vocabulary from Context Exercise 1 on page 31 before you begin.

How We Sleep

1   Do you ever wake up in the middle of the night and worry that you won't be able to get back to sleep? Are you concerned when you can't sleep for seven or eight hours at one time? Research suggests that "monophasic" sleep, with eight hours of continuous rest, may be unnatural. We overlook both human variation and human history when we assume that it is best for everyone.

2   An experiment in the early 1990s suggested the natural or prehistoric sleep pattern for humans. Psychiatrist Thomas Wehr placed people in darkness for 14 hours every day for a month. By the fourth week, the subjects came to have a clear sleeping pattern. They slept first for four hours, then woke for one or two hours before falling into a second four-hour sleep.

3   Recent historical research has confirmed this pattern, showing that human sleep habits have changed over the centuries. Historian Roger Ekirch, of Virginia Tech University, discovered more than 500 references to a "segmented sleeping pattern" in pre-industrial documents and descriptions—in diaries, court records, medical books, and literature—from the ancient Greeks to an anthropological account of modern tribes in Nigeria. All of these describe a "first sleep" or "deep sleep," which begins about two hours after sundown and lasts until after midnight. After a waking period of one or two hours, a "second sleep" or "morning sleep" lasts until sunup. As Ekirch says, "It's not just the number of references" that tells us that this was the norm, but "it is the way they refer to it, as if it was common knowledge."

4   During the waking period, people were active. In descriptions from pre-industrial Europe, people got up, went to the toilet or smoked tobacco, and some even visited neighbors. Most people stayed in bed, some read, wrote, and often prayed. And these hours weren't spent entirely alone; people often chatted to bedfellows or had sex.

5   In Europe, before the seventeenth century, nighttime was associated with criminals. There was no good reason to go out at night. Historians describe how that gradually changed over the next 200 years. Craig Koslofsky explains that during religious persecution of Protestants or Catholics, people began to meet for religious services in secret. Respectable people began to come out at night. When street lighting became available in cities, and domestic lighting was improved, people of all classes began to socialize at night. There were coffee houses that were open all night. Lying in bed in the middle of the night came to be seen as a waste of time. "People were becoming increasingly time-conscious and sensitive to efficiency, certainly before the 19th century," says Roger Ekirch. "But the industrial revolution intensified that attitude by leaps and bounds."

6   It may be that because of the lightbulb, the entire world is now sleeping unnaturally. Once electricity was widely available, people everywhere started going to bed much later, and once people did get to bed, there was no time to get up again between sleeps. References to segmented sleep stop appearing in the late nineteenth century. At the same time, historian Ekirch begins to find discussions of a sleep problem: "sleep maintenance insomnia," in which people wake during the night and have trouble getting back to sleep.

7   "For most of evolution we slept a certain way," says sleep psychologist Gregg Jacobs. "Waking up during the night is part of normal human physiology. The idea that we must sleep in a single block could be damaging, he says, if it makes people who wake up at night anxious, as this worry can itself make it impossible to sleep.

8   So the next time that you wake in the middle of the night, think of your pre-industrial ancestors and relax.

Comprehension

Answer the following questions according to the article. True/False items are indicated by a T / F preceding a statement.

1. **T / ~~F~~** Science has shown that all humans need eight hours of uninterrupted sleep every night.

2. **T / ~~F~~** Throughout history there are references to people sleeping for eight hours without waking up.

3. **~~T~~ / F** Research shows that people naturally sleep in two four-hour segments.

4. Historical documents show that people generally did the following things between first and second sleeps. Check (✔) all those that apply.

   a. ___✔___ Talk to bed fellows

   b. _____ Check email

   c. ___✔___ Visit neighbors

   d. ___✔___ Smoke

   e. _____ Go to coffee houses

   f. ___✔___ Pray

5. **T / F** If you wake up in the middle of the night, you should see a doctor.

6. Check (✔) the reasons given for why people stopped sleeping in segments.

   a. ___✔___ Street lights made it possible to move around more easily at night.

   b. _____ Sleep doctors wanted to make more money.

   c. ___✔___ Artificial lighting in the home permitted people to stay up later.

   d. ___✔___ It's more stressful to wake up during the night.

   e. ___✔___ Industrialization placed more emphasis on the efficiency of sleeping through the night.

   f. ___✔___ There was religious persecution of people who studied the Bible at night.

   g. ___✔___ An increase in coffee houses gave people a destination and a reason to be out and about at night.

Discussion/Composition

1. Most animals sleep on polyphasic schedules. But social pressure seems to have made humans monophasic sleepers. If you could arrange your day any way that you wanted, what would it look like? Below is one example inspired by the sleep schedule of author Jerzy Kosinski. Notice that the author chooses to have two segmented four-hour periods of sleep.

8:00 am – noon	write
noon – 4:00 pm	do errands
4:00 pm – 8:00 pm	sleep
8:00 pm – midnight	dinner in a café with friends
midnight – 4:00 am	write
4:00 am – 8:00 am	sleep

What would your ideal day look like? You can divide your sleep between sleep segments and naps. How many sleep segments would you have; how long? How many naps would you take; how long? Why would this be your ideal schedule?

2. The monophasic eight-hour sleep has allowed people to spend less time in bed. But what have people lost and gained with that change?

   • Who gains from a more regular and longer work and shopping day?

   • What have people lost in giving up a first and second sleep?

   • Do you think the current pattern of monophasic sleep is a good thing or a bad thing?

Vocabulary from Context

Exercise 1

Both the ideas and the vocabulary in the exercise below are taken from "How We Sleep." Use the context provided to determine the meanings for the italicized words. Write a definition, synonym, or description in the space provided.

1. _____

2. _____

3. _____

4. _____

5. _____

6. _____

7. _____

8. _bad guy_____

9. _____

10. _____

11. _____

12. _____

Research is showing that the regular and repeated ways that humans sleep have not always been the same. These *patterns* (1) of sleep have changed over time. The current *habit* (2) in industrialized society of one long period of sleep may be relatively new. Instead of today's *monophasic* (3) sleep, with only one period of sleep, people in previous centuries slept in *segments* (4), often two *blocks* (5) of sleep with a waking period in between. Historians find mention of these segments in documents written hundreds of years before the end of the nineteenth century. These *references* (6) seem to confirm that human beings used to be *polyphasic* (7) sleepers.

How did things change? When lights came to city streets and homes, the night stopped being associated only with *criminals* (8). Instead of people breaking the law, night became associated with *respectable* (9) people. During periods of religious *persecution* (10) in the seventeenth century, for example, those who were treated badly and felt themselves in danger, met at night. And once lighting at home became better,

13._____

14._____

15._____

16._____

17._____

18._____

19._____

this *improved* (11) *domestic* (12) lighting encouraged people to stay up later. At the same time, the industrial revolution increased the attention to using time well. This *intensified* (13) interest in *efficiency* (14) led to the *attitude* (15) that sleeping longer was inefficient, a *waste of time* (16).

Today, people worry if they are not able to remain asleep throughout the night. Some doctors consider this a health problem called "*sleep maintenance insomnia*" (17). But more recently experts believe that creating harmful *anxiety* (18) about waking in the night causes *damaging* (19) worry and fear.

Exercise 2

This exercise gives you additional clues to determine the meaning of vocabulary in context. In the paragraph of "How We Sleep" indicated by the number in parentheses, find the word or phrase that best fits the meaning given. Your teacher may want to read these aloud as you quickly scan* the paragraph to find the answer.

1. (Paragraph 3) What phrase means *something that most people know*? _Common Knowledge_

2. (Paragraph 5) What phrase means *without others knowing*? _Secret_

3. (Paragraph 5) What phrase means *concerned about time*? _____

4. (Paragraph 5) What phrase means *very quickly*? _____

5. (Paragraph 7) What word is *a branch of biology that deals with the activities of living things*? _____

Vocabulary Review

Exercise 1

Three of the words in each line below are similar in meaning. Circle the word that doesn't belong.

1. segment   block   phase   habit

2. pattern   habit   block   custom

Exercise 2

Are these pairs of words and phrases similar in meaning or opposite in meaning? Circle S if similar; circle O if opposite.

1. **S / O**   efficient   waste of time

2. **S / O**   monophasic   polyphasic

3. **S / O**   criminal   respectable

---

*For an introduction to scanning, see Unit 1.

BEFORE
YOU BEGIN

The previous article, "How We Sleep," describes changes in human sleep patterns over time. These changes suggest that current industrialized sleep patterns may be unnatural, including how long we sleep. But if we can't go back in time, how could biologists find out how "preindustrial" societies slept? How can they find people to study? If you found a "preindustrial" group, who would you compare it to?

Read the following article to see what some researchers were able to do. Read to understand the research and its findings; don't worry about unfamiliar vocabulary.

Access to Electricity is Linked to Reduced Sleep
By Michelle Ma

1   New research comparing traditional hunter-gatherer living conditions to a more modern setting suggests that access to artificial light and electricity has shortened the amount of sleep humans get each night. The research, published online in the *Journal of Biological Rhythms*, is the first study to document this relationship in the field.

2   "Everything we found supports what we had predicted from laboratory or intervention studies, where researchers manipulate certain aspects of light. But this is the first time we've seen this hold true in a natural setting," said lead author Horacio de la Iglesia, a University of Washington biology professor.

3   The researchers compared two communities that were traditionally hunter-gatherers and have almost identical ethnic and sociocultural backgrounds. But they differ in one key aspect—access to electricity. They wanted to see if, all other factors aside, electricity would impact people's sleep during an average week in both the summer and winter.

4   They found this rare scenario in northeastern Argentina, with two Toba/Qom indigenous communities living about 50 kilometers (31 miles) apart. The first has 24-hour free access to electricity and can turn on lights at any time, while the second has no electricity, relying only on natural light.

5   The researchers visited each community for a week during the summer and winter, placing bracelets onto the wrist of each study participant to monitor activity. The activity logger can track slight changes in movement, so a wrist that doesn't move for a longer time implies that a person is sleeping.

6   Participants also kept sleep diaries during the study period, where they recorded what times they went to bed and woke up, as well as any naps throughout the day. This information was mainly used to corroborate data collected from the wristbands.

7   The community with access to electricity slept less than the community without access. In their usual daily routines, the community with electricity slept about an hour less than their counterparts with no electricity. These shorter nights were

mostly due to people who could turn on lights and go to bed later, the researchers found.

8 Both communities slept longer in the winter and for fewer hours in the summer.

9 "Though this study took place in the twenty-first century, the sleep-pattern differences observed between the communities can be seen as an example of how our ancestors likely adapted their sleep behaviors as livelihoods changed and electricity became available," de la Iglesia said.

10 "In a way, this study presents a representation of what happened to humanity as we moved from hunting and gathering to agriculture and eventually to our industrialized society," he said. "All the effects we found are probably an underestimation of what we would see in highly industrialized societies where our access to electricity has tremendously disrupted our sleep."

UW biologist Horacio de la Iglesia puts an activity logger onto a participant's wrist. (Photo credit: U of Washington)

An activity logger is shown next to a wrist watch. (Photo credit: U of Washington)

Comprehension

Answer the following according to the article. True/False items are indicated by a by a T / F preceding a statement.

1. **T**/ **F**   The research reports the effect of artificial light and electricity on sleep time.

2. **T** /**F**   Both of the groups studied are hunter-gatherers.

3. **T** / **F**   Access to electricity was the main difference between the two groups studied.

4. **T**/ **F**   The community with access to electricity slept less than the community without access.

5. **T** / **F**   According to the article, people in the two groups went to sleep at about the same time.

6. **T**/ **F**   According to the article, people in the two groups got up at about the same time.

7. **T** /**F**   Both groups slept less in the winter.

8. **T**/ **F**   The researchers believe that the study shows how people changed their sleep patterns as societies developed.

9. **T** /**F**   The researchers put watches on participants' wrists to see if this had any effect on sleep time.

1. The design of a research study is critical in evaluating it. Answer the following questions about the research study you have just read about.

    a. **T / F**   One group had to pay for electricity.

    b. **T / F**   The researchers studied each group for a month in the winter and summer.

    c. Why are these two elements of the study important? Do the answers for each question make you more or less persuaded by the study?

2. Sometimes brief research descriptions leave out important information. The article says the two groups had "almost identical ethnic and sociocultural backgrounds" and that the key difference between them was access to electricity. What are other ways in which the groups would need to be similar for you to feel that the findings are strong? What additional information would you have liked the summary to provide? Based on the information you are given, how strong do you find the conclusions of this study: (a) very strong, (b) fairly strong, (c) not very strong ? Why did you make this judgment?

Discussion/Composition

1. The research seems to show that access to artificial light and electricity has shortened the amount of sleep humans get each night. Do you think this is (a) a good thing, (b) a bad thing, or (c) of no consequence? Why?

2. Briefly describe the results of the research and why they are important.

Vocabulary from Context

This exercise gives you additional clues to determine the meaning of vocabulary in context. In the paragraph of "Access to Electricity is Linked to Reduced Sleep" indicated by the number in parentheses, find the word or phrase that best fits the meaning given. Your teacher may want to read these aloud as you quickly scan* the paragraph to find the answer.

1. (1) What phrase means *availability of, the ability to use something?* _access to_
2. (1) What phrase means *unnatural/electric light?* _artificial_
3. (1) What phrase means *in a natural setting?* _____
4. (2) What word means, *change, control something in a planned way?* _____
5. (3) What word means *a culture in which people hunt animals and look for plants to eat instead of growing crops and raising animals?* _____

---

*For an introduction to scanning, see Unit 1.

6. (3) What word means *extremely important, essential, fundamental, the main thing*?

_____

7. (3) What word means *things that help produce a result*? _____

8. (4) What word means *situation, setting, context*? Seenario _____

9. (5) What word means *observe, watch for a special purpose*? _____

10. (6) What word means *confirm, support, uphold, show something to be true*?

_____

11. (7) What word means *corresponding groups, groups with a similar function*?

_____

12. (9) What word means *transformed, adjusted, changed to make something useful for a new situation*?

_____

13. (9) What word means *ways to make a living; ways to get the necessities of life*?

_____

14. (10) What word means *an assumption about something that is lower than it really is*?

_____

15. (10) What word means *interrupted, disturbed*? _____

Reading Selection 2
Narrative

Recent world events can make travelers nervous—nervous because of how strangers seem to them, nervous about how they may appear to strangers. "Gate A-4" is variously referred to as narrative prose poetry, a mini-essay, or a tiny story. However you think of it, it is nonfiction—an account of a personal experience.

> **BEFORE YOU BEGIN**

1. Poet Naomi Shihab Nye was in an airport when she heard an announcement that anyone who spoke her father's language should come to Gate 4-A immediately. What emotions do you think you would feel if this happened to you? Check all those you might feel.

   ___✓___ Curious

   ___✓___ Glad you could help

   _____ Nervous (about what?)

   _____ Worried (about what?)

   Other _____ happy.

2. In what ways might your reaction to such an announcement depend on the language you were being asked to speak?

   Read on to discover how Nye's world changed.

Gate A-4

By Naomi Shihab Nye

WANDERING AROUND THE ALBUQUERQUE AIRPORT TERMINAL, after learning my flight had been detained for four hours, I heard an announcement: "If anyone in the vicinity of Gate 4-A understands any Arabic, please come to the gate immediately!"

Well—one pauses these days. Gate 4-A was my own gate. I went there.

An older woman in full traditional Palestinian embroidered dress, just like my grandma wore, was crumpled to the floor, wailing loudly. "Help," said the Flight Service Person. "Talk to her. What is her problem? We told her the flight was going to be late and she did this."

I stooped to put my arm around the woman and spoke to her haltingly. "*Shu do-a, Shu-bid-uck Habibti, Stani schway, Min fadlick, Shu-bit-se-wee?*" The minute she heard any words she knew, however poorly used, she stopped crying. She thought our flight had been cancelled entirely. She needed to be in El Paso for a major medical treatment the next day.

I said, "No, no, we're fine. You'll get there, just late. Who is picking you up? Let's call him."

We called her son and I spoke with him in English. I told him I would stay with his mother until we got on the plane and would ride next to her. She talked to him. Then we called her other sons just for the fun of it. Then we called my dad and he and she spoke for a while in Arabic and found out, of course, they had ten shared friends. Then I thought, just for the heck of it, why not call some Palestinian poets I know and let them chat with her? This all took up about two hours.

She was laughing a lot by then, telling about her life, patting my knee, answering questions. She had pulled a sack of homemade mamool cookies—little powdered sugar crumbly mounds stuffed with dates and nuts—out of her bag and was offering them to all the women at the gate. To my amazement, not a single woman declined one. It was like a sacrament. The traveler from Argentina, the mom from California, the lovely woman from Laredo—we were all covered with the same powdered sugar. And smiling. There is no better cookie.

And then the airline broke out the free beverages from the huge coolers and two little girls from our flight ran around serving us all apple juices and they were covered in powdered sugar too. And I noticed my new best friend—by now we were holding hands—had a potted plant poking out of her bag, some medicinal thing, with green furry leaves. Such an old country traveling tradition. Always carry a plant. Always stay rooted to somewhere.

And I looked around that gate of late and weary ones and thought, "This is the world I want to live in. The shared world." Not a single person in this gate—once the crying of confusion stopped—seemed apprehensive about any other person. They took the cookies. I wanted to hug all those other women too. This can still happen anywhere. Not everything is lost.

Naomi Shihab Nye lives in San Antonio, Texas. Her books include *19 Varieties of Gazelle*, *Sitti's Secrets*, and *Habibi* (a novel for teens).

Exercise 1

Part of the power of this text lies in the carefully chosen details that convey a great deal of information, often indirectly. If one has understood the details, one has understood the tale. Below are excerpts taken from "Gate A-4" with particular details italicized. Indicate why you think the author chose to include these details and what information they convey. Line numbers are in parentheses.

1. [She was] an older woman in full Palestinian embroidered dress, *just like my grandma wore...* (5)

    _____

2. I stooped to put my arm around the woman and spoke to her *haltingly.* (8)

    _____

3. She was laughing a lot by then, telling about her life, *patting my knee,* answering questions. (22–23)

    _____

4. The *traveler from Argentina, the mom from California, the lovely woman from Laredo* — we were *all covered with the same powdered sugar.* (26–28)

    _____

5. *And smiling.* (28)

    _____

6. ...two little girls...*were covered with powdered sugar too.* (29–30)

    _____

7. —by now *we were holding hands*— (31)

    _____

8. And I noticed...[she] *had a potted plant...* (30–31)

    _____

Exercise 2

Naomi Shihab Nye also takes great care to use just the right word. Each of the two sentences below from "Gate A-4" is followed by a list of definitions. Circle the number of the definition(s) that best match the meaning of the italicized word in each sentence. Line numbers from the reading passage are in parentheses.

1. (3) Well—one *pauses* these days.

pause (pôz)
v. **paused, paus·ing, paus·es**
v. *intr.*
1   to cease or suspend an action temporarily.
2   to linger; tarry: *paused for a while under the huge oak tree.*
3   to hesitate: *He paused before replying.*

2. (26) It was like a *sacrament.*

sac·ra·ment [sak-r*uh*-m*uh*nt]
—noun
1   a sacred religious rite; the term in Christianity can refer to a ritual involving bread as a symbol of divine/sacred connection.
2   something regarded as possessing a sacred character or mysterious significance.
3   a sign, token, or symbol.
4   an oath; solemn pledge.

Exercise 3

At the center of this text is the issue of language. The significance of events comes from the language people are using. In each of the conversations listed below, indicate which language(s) the speaker was using. There is not necessarily a single correct response for each situation; be prepared to defend your choices.

1. Naomi Shihab Nye speaking to the older woman _____

2. The older woman speaking to her sons _____

3. Nye speaking with the sons _____

4. Nye speaking to the Palestinian poets _____

5. The older woman speaking to the Palestinian poets _____

6. Nye speaking to her father _____

7. The older woman speaking to Nye's father _____

x

Discussion/Composition

One could argue that the main idea of the essay is captured in the last sentence, "Not everything is lost." What does Nye mean? Your teacher may want you to discuss this with your classmates or write a short essay. Use examples from Nye's memoir and from what you know of the contemporary world to explain your point of view.

Reading Selections 3A–3C
Globalization

BEFORE YOU BEGIN

Have you ever been a tourist? Where did you go? How did you choose your destination(s)?

Reading Selections 3A and 3B, from United Nations publications, report on the globalization of tourism between the turn of the twenty-first century and 2030. The articles and the activities that accompany them provide practice in predicting and in understanding interrelated textual and quantitative information. The first article was written at the turn of the twenty-first century; it reported early data (from 1997) and predicted tourism in 2020. The second article predicts tourism to 2030. See if you can anticipate some of the findings.

y

z

w

Selection 3A United Nations Report

> **BEFORE YOU BEGIN**
>
> Before you read the first article in this section, "The Globalization of Tourism," what is your sense of global tourism?
>
> 1. Which countries do you think were the most popular countries for tourists around the year 2000?
>
> 2. Do you think that has changed? If so, which countries are more popular to visit? Which countries are sending more tourists now?

Comprehension

Read "The Globalization of Tourism" quickly to see if your predictions are confirmed, and then answer the questions that follow. True/False items are indicated by a T / F preceding a statement.

1. **T / F** The purpose of the pair of bar graphs at the top of page 45 is to compare spending on tourism in different years.

2. **T / F** The purpose of the bar graphs at the bottom of page 45 is to show changes in where tourists would be traveling to in the future.

3. **T / F** Tourism was the world's leading industry when this article was written.

4. What does the author say is an effect of the Internet on tourism? _____

5. According to the bar graphs, in what did the United States lead the world in 1998? _____

6. **T / F** The number of travelers to Europe was predicted to decline 45 percent by 2020.

7. Which continent both spent the most on tourism and earned the most from tourism?

   _____

8. **T / F** Germany spent more on tourism than it earned from tourism.

9. **T / F** The United States was predicted to be the most popular tourist destination in 2020.

10. What changes related to tourism were predicted for China by 2020? _____

    _____

11. **T / F** The arrows on the maps on page 43 show all international tourism in 1997 and all international tourism predicted for 2020.

12. **T / F** According to the maps on page 44, fewer tourists from Asia would visit the East Asia/Pacific region in 2020 than visited in 1997.

The globalization of tourism

Americas to Europe: 23.6

Europe to Americas: 19.5

Europe to East Asia/Pacific: 10.4

Asia to Europe: 14.3

Europe to Africa: 6.9

Middle East to Europe: 3.5

Africa to Europe: 1.9

Asia to East Asia/Pacific: 1.3

Asia to Americas: 10.1

Americas to East Asia/Pacific: 6.2

Major intercontinental tourism flows (millions)

1997

2020

Americas to Europe: 44

Europe to East Asia/Pacific: 47

Europe to Americas: 65

East Asia/Pacific to Europe: 47

Europe to Africa: 19

Europe to Asia: 10

Africa to Europe: 11

Europe to Middle East: 22

East Asia/Pacific to Americas: 42

Americas to East Asia/Pacific: 20

Source: World Tourism Organization

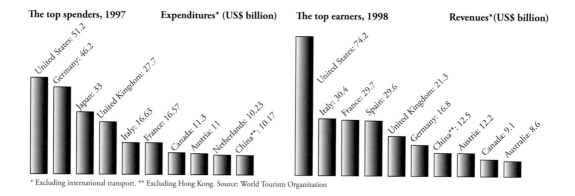

The top spenders, 1997 — Expenditures* (US$ billion)

United States: 51.2
Germany: 46.2
Japan: 33
United Kingdom: 27.7
Italy: 16.63
France: 16.57
Canada: 11.3
Austria: 11
Netherlands: 10.23
China**: 10.17

The top earners, 1998 — Revenues*(US$ billion)

United States: 74.2
Italy: 30.4
France: 29.7
Spain: 29.6
United Kingdom: 21.3
Germany: 16.8
China**: 12.5
Austria: 12.2
Canada: 9.1
Australia: 8.6

* Excluding international transport. ** Excluding Hong Kong. Source: World Tourism Organization

(1) If the World Tourism Organization's forecasts are on target, international tourist arrivals will climb from the present 625 million a year to 1.6 billion in 2020. By this date, travelers will spend over US$2 trillion, (against US$44.5 billion in 1999), making tourism the world's leading industry.

(2) Electronic technology is facilitating this growth by offering access to fare and hotel information and online reservation services. Despite a modest annual growth rate (3.1%), Europe will remain, by far, the most popular destination (it can expect 717 million international arrivals in 2020, double the 1998 figure), though its market share will decline from 59 to 45%. Growth on the continent will be led by Central and Eastern European countries, where arrivals are expected to increase by 4.8% per year. At the same time, almost half the world's tourists will be coming from Europe. Given this dominance, it is not surprising to find that six European countries count among the top ten tourism earners and spenders. The United States holds first place in both categories.

(3) With a 7% per annum growth in international arrivals, the East Asia/Pacific region will overtake the Americas as the second most popular destination, holding a 27% market share in 2020 against 18% by the Americas. But the industry will also be doing its utmost to court the Asian traveller, since East Asia/Pacific is forecast to become the world's second most important generator of tourists, with a 7% annual growth rate, pushing the Americas into third position. China is expected to become the fourth largest source of tourists on the world market, while it was not even among the first twenty in 1999. Both arrivals to and departures from Africa (and especially Southern Africa), the Middle East, and South Asia are expected to grow by about 5% per year.

(4) While France held its place as the top destination throughout the 1990s, it will be dethroned in the next decades, with China (excluding Hong Kong) expected to top the list by 2020 even though it was not even featured on it in 1998. Also making an entry into the top ten are the Russian Federation, Hong Kong, and the Czech Republic.

(5) Despite this growth forecast, tourism is and will remain the privilege of a few: WTO forecasts that only 7% of the world population will travel abroad by 2020.

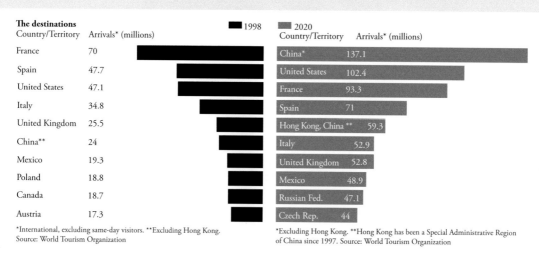

The destinations — 1998

Country/Territory	Arrivals* (millions)
France	70
Spain	47.7
United States	47.1
Italy	34.8
United Kingdom	25.5
China**	24
Mexico	19.3
Poland	18.8
Canada	18.7
Austria	17.3

*International, excluding same-day visitors. **Excluding Hong Kong.
Source: World Tourism Organization

2020

Country/Territory	Arrivals* (millions)
China*	137.1
United States	102.4
France	93.3
Spain	71
Hong Kong, China **	59.3
Italy	52.9
United Kingdom	52.8
Mexico	48.9
Russian Fed.	47.1
Czech Rep.	44

*Excluding Hong Kong. **Hong Kong has been a Special Administrative Region of China since 1997. Source: World Tourism Organization

Critical Reading

It is sometimes the case that the text and the graphics in technical reports aren't completely consistent. Below are two claims made in the text of "The Globalization of Tourism." Does the information in the bar graphs support these statements?

- (Paragraph 3) "the East Asia/Pacific region will overtake the Americas as the second most popular destination."

- (Paragraph 4) China was "expected to top the list [of tourist destinations] by 2020 even though it was not even featured on it in 1998."

When you do research, if you are faced with a discrepancy (difference) in information between the text and graphics in an article, you will probably need to do further study. How might you find additional information that would give you more confidence in the claims made in "The Globalization of Tourism"?

Discussion/Composition

1. From which areas do most tourists come to your home country or region? If you were developing an advertising brochure designed to encourage tourists to visit your home country or region, what kinds of information would you include? What physical and cultural sights should tourists be sure to see? What cultural and historical information would they need? Are there common things that you would want to explain to tourists? Would you mention these in your brochure? After discussing these issues, write a brochure to advertise your locality.

2. If tourism to your home country or region were to double in the next 20 years, would this be a good or a bad thing? Write a letter that could appear in a blog arguing your point of view.

The second article in this section, "Tourism Towards 2030," was published almost 20 years after "The Globalization of Tourism." It made new predictions for 2020 and beyond. We can use the more recent publication to see how accurate the predictions made in the earlier article were and to think about what kinds of events make predicting so difficult.

> **BEFORE YOU BEGIN**

Following is a list of predictions from "The Globalization of Tourism" about what would happen to world tourism "by 2020." Check (✓) all the predictions that you believe will be supported by data published 20 years later.

_____ **1.** By region, Europe will remain the most popular destination in 2020.

_____ **2.** Almost half the world's tourists will be coming from Europe.

_____ **3.** The Asia/Pacific region will become the second most popular destination in 2020.

_____ **4.** By country, China will be the top destination in the world for tourism.

_____ **5.** China will become the fourth largest source of tourists (this is measured in money spent).

Below are figures from "Tourism Towards 2030". Look at these figures to see whether your answers in "Before You Begin" were correct according to more recent predictions for either 2016 or 2020. When you have checked your responses, read "Tourism Towards 2030," and answer the questions that follow.

FIGURE 1

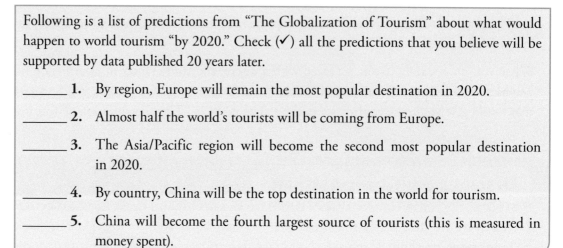

UNWTO Tourism Towards 2030: Actual trend and forecast 1950-2030

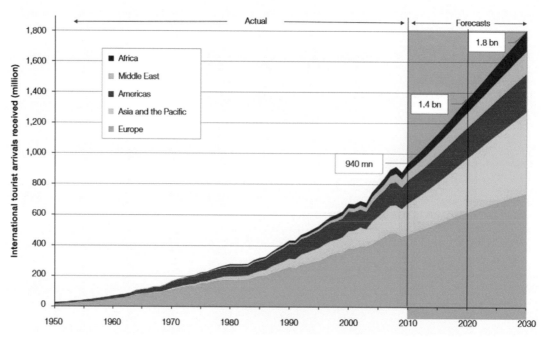

FIGURE 2

	UNWTO tourism towards 2030: International tourism by region of destination											
	International tourist arrivals received (million)					Average increase per year (%)					Share (%)	
	Actual data			Projections		Actual data		Projections				
								2010-'30, of which				
	1980	1995	2010	2020	2030	1980-'95	'95-2010	2010-'30	2010-'20	2020-'30	2010	2030
World	**277**	**528**	**940**	**1,360**	**1,809**	**4.4**	**3.9**	**3.3**	**3.8**	**2.9**	**100**	**100**
to advanced economies	194	334	498	643	772	3.7	2.7	2.2	2.6	1.8	53	43
to emerging economies	83	193	442	717	1,037	5.8	5.7	4.4	4.9	3.8	47	57
By UNWTO regions: Africa	**7.2**	**18.9**	**50.3**	**85**	**134**	**6.7**	**6.7**	**5.0**	**5.4**	**4.6**	**5.3**	**7.4**
North Africa	4.0	7.3	18.7	31	46	4.1	6.5	4.6	5.2	4.0	2.0	2.5
West and Central Africa	1.0	2.3	6.8	13	22	5.9	7.5	5.9	6.5	5.4	0.7	1.2
East Africa	1.2	5.0	12.1	22	37	10.1	6.1	5.8	6.2	5.4	1.3	2.1
Southern Africa	1.0	4.3	12.6	20	29	10.1	7.4	4.3	4.5	4.1	1.3	1.6
Americas	**62.3**	**109.0**	**149.7**	**199**	**248**	**3.8**	**2.1**	**2.6**	**2.9**	**2.2**	**15.9**	**13.7**
North America	48.3	80.7	98.2	120	138	3.5	1.3	1.7	2.0	1.4	10.4	7.6
Caribbean	6.7	14.0	20.1	25	30	5.0	2.4	2.0	2.4	1.7	2.1	1.7
Central America	1.5	2.6	7.9	14	22	3.8	7.7	5.2	6.0	4.5	0.8	1.2
South America	5.8	11.7	23.6	40	58	4.8	4.8	4.6	5.3	3.9	2.5	3.2
Asia and the Pacific	**22.8**	**82.0**	**204.0**	**355**	**535**	**8.9**	**6.3**	**4.9**	**5.7**	**4.2**	**21.7**	**29.6**
North-Last Asia	10.1	41.3	111.5	195	293	9.9	6.8	4.9	5.7	4.2	11.9	16.2
South East Asia	8.2	28.4	69.9	123	187	8.7	6.2	5.1	5.8	4.3	7.4	10.3
Oceania	2.3	8.1	11.6	15	19	8.7	2.4	2.4	2.9	2.0	1.2	1.0
South Asia	2.2	4.2	11.1	21	36	4.3	6.6	6.0	6.8	5.3	1.2	2.0
Europe	**177.3**	**304.1**	**475.3**	**620**	**744**	**3.7**	**3.0**	**2.3**	**2.7**	**1.8**	**50.6**	**41.1**
Northern Europe	20.4	35.8	57.7	72	82	3.8	3.2	1.8	2.2	1.4	6.1	4.5
Western Europe	68.3	112.2	153.7	192	222	3.4	2.1	1.8	2.3	1.4	16.3	12.3
Central/Eastern Europe	26.6	58.1	95.0	137	176	5.3	3.3	3.1	3.7	2.5	10.1	9.7
Southern/Medit. Europe	61.9	98.0	168.9	219	264	3.1	3.7	2.3	2.6	1.9	18.0	14.6
Middle East	**7.1**	**13.7**	**60.9**	**101**	**149**	**4.5**	**10.5**	**4.6**	**5.2**	**4.0**	**6.5**	**8.2**

FIGURE 3

| International tourism arrivals | | | | | |
| Rank | Series | (millions) | | Change (%) | |
		2015	2016	15/14	16/15
1 France	TF	84.5	82.6	0.9	−2.2
2 United States	TF	77.5	75.6	3.3	−2.4
3 Spain	TF	68.5	75.6	5.5	10.3
4 China	TF	56.9	59.3	2.3	4.2
5 Italy	TF	50.7	52.4	4.4	3.2
6 United Kingdom	TF	34.4	35.8	5.6	4.0
7 Germany	TCE	35.0	35.6	6.0	1.7
8 Mexico	TF	32.1	35.0	9.4	8.9
9 Thailand	TF	29.9	32.6	20.6	8.9
10 Turkey	TF	39.5	-	−0.8	-

FIGURE 4

| | International tourism expenditure (US$ billion) | |
Rank	2015	2016
1 China	249.8	261.1
2 United States	114.7	123.6
3 Germany	77.5	79.8
4 United Kingdom	63.3	63.6
5 France	39.3	40.5
6 Canada	30.1	29.1
7 Korea (ROK)	25.3	26.6
8 Italy	24.4	25.0
9 Australia	23.8	24.9
10 Hong Kong (China)	23.1	24.2

Tourism Towards 2030
United Nations World Tourism Organization (UNWTO)

1 A key output of "Tourism Towards 2030" is a set of quantitative projections for international tourism demand over a 20-year period; 2010 is the base year, and the report ends in 2030. The updated forecast has been enriched by qualitative data on the social, political, economic, environmental, and technological factors that have shaped tourism in the past, and which are expected to influence it in the future.

2 According to "Tourism Towards 2030," the number of international tourist arrivals worldwide is expected to increase by an average of 3.3% a year over the period 2010 to 2030.

3 It is expected that the rate of growth will gradually decrease over time, but this is on top of growing base numbers. In absolute numbers, international tourist arrivals will increase by 43 million a year, compared with an average increase of 28 million a year during the period 1995 to 2010. At the projected rate of growth, international tourist arrivals worldwide are expected to reach 1.8 billion by the year 2030.

4 International tourist arrivals in the emerging economy destinations (Asia, Latin America, Central and Eastern Europe, Eastern Mediterranean Europe, the Middle East, and Africa) will grow at double the rate (+4.4% a year) of advanced economy destinations (+2.2% a year). By 2030, 57% of international arrivals will be in emerging economy destinations (versus 30% in 1980) and 43% in advanced economy destinations (versus 70% in 1980).

5 The strongest growth by region is expected to occur in Asia and the Pacific. The Middle East and Africa are forecast to more than double their number of arrivals during this period. Europe and the Americas are projected to grow comparatively more slowly. Thanks to their faster growth, the global market shares of Asia and the Pacific, the Middle East and Africa will all increase. As a result, Europe and the Americas will experience a further decline in their share of international tourism.

Comprehension

Answer the following questions according to the article and Figures 1–4. True/False items are indicated by a T / F preceding a statement.

1. What does it mean that 2010 is "the base year"? _____

2. **T / F** This article is based only on quantitative data.

3. **T / F** The total number of international tourists will continue to increase.

4. **T / F** The rate of growth in international tourism will have risen annually from 2010 to 2030.

5. **T / F** Between 2010 and 2030, the average increase of international tourist arrivals will be 28 million a year.

6. **T / F** The greatest increase in tourist numbers will come in the advanced economies.

7. **T / F** Tourism to Europe will decrease.

8. **T / F** By 2030, the regions with the highest rates of growth in tourism will be the Middle East and Africa.

9. **T / F** By 2030, the world will have 1.8 million international tourists.

10. **T / F** Looking at Figure 2, by 2030, the Americas will have under 14% of world tourists.

11. **T / F** The regions of the world that received most tourists in 2010 will have a smaller share of world tourism in 2030 than they do now.

Critical Reading

1. The following graphic compares tourist arrivals in 2021 to the previous two years (2019, before tourism was affected by Covid-19, and 2020, at the height of the pandemic in most places). In which parts of the world was tourism most negatively affected? What might explain that? Tourism began to recover in 2021. Which areas of the world were recovering fastest? Why do you think that is?

FIGURE 5

2. In what ways do world events (for example, economic cycles, international meetings, political unrest, widespread illness, or terrorist attacks) affect tourism? Are there predictions made in "Tourism Towards 2030" that you believe will not hold true because of recent world events, or events you predict will occur in the future?

Discussion/Composition

If tourism were to double in your home country/community in the next 20 years, would this be a good thing or a bad thing? Write a letter to your local newspaper or community website arguing your point of view.

Selection 3C Essay

The previous articles in this section, "The Globalization of Tourism" and "Tourism Towards 2030," show that over time the number of people traveling the globe has been increasing dramatically. In fact, tourism is becoming the world's leading industry. The author of the next article, "The Politics of Travel," argues that this is a mixed blessing, that tourism brings problems as well as profits.

BEFORE YOU BEGIN

1. What are advantages to regions that become popular tourist attractions?

2. What are problems brought on by tourism?

3. Why do people become tourists? What are the attractions of travel?

Read "The Politics of Travel" to discover the author's perspective, and then answer the questions that follow. Do not be concerned if you don't know the meaning of every word. Your teacher may want you to do Vocabulary from Context Exercise 1 on pages 54–55 before you begin reading.

Excerpt from THE POLITICS OF TRAVEL
By David Nicholson-Lord

1   Tourism has seriously damaged fragile ecosytems like the Alps—the winter skiing playground of Europe—and the trekking areas of the Himalayas. Worldwide, it poses a serious threat to coastal habitats like dunes, mangrove forests and coral reefs. It fuels a booming and usually illegal trade in the products of threatened wildlife, from tortoiseshell and coral to ivory. Its "consumers" inevitably bring their habits and expectations with them—whether it's hot showers and flush toilets or well-watered greens for golfers. In the Himalayas, showers for trekkers often mean firewood, which means deforestation. In Hawaii and Barbados, it was found that each tourist used between six and ten times as much water and electricity as a local. In Goa, villagers forced to walk to wells for their water had to watch as a pipeline to a new luxury hotel was built through their land. Over the past decade golf, because of its appetite for land, water and herbicides, has emerged as one of the biggest culprits, so much so that "golf wars" have broken out in parts of Southeast Asia; campaigners in Japan, one of the chief exponents of golf tourism, have launched an annual World No Golf Day.

2   This is not to say tourism can't do some good— but the cost-benefit equation is complex. Historic monuments, houses and gardens thrive on visitors. Throughout much of the world, but notably in southern and eastern Africa, tourism underpins the survival of wildlife. Why else would small farmers put up with elephants trampling their crops? Whale watching is now a bigger business than whaling. In the uplands of Rwanda, known to millions through the film *Gorillas in the Mist*, the mountain gorilla's salvation lies partly in the income and interest generated by tourists visiting in small groups. In Kenya, a lion's worth is estimated at $7,000 a year in tourist income— for an elephant herd the figure is $610,000. And if large animals, with large ranges, are protected, then so are their habitats—the national parks.

3   Yet none of these gains is unqualified. To get to see your whales and your gorillas, for example, you have to travel, by car, coach or plane. Each time you do so you're effectively setting fire to a small reservoir of gasoline—and releasing several roomfuls of carbon dioxide into the atmosphere. Transport is the world's fastest growing source of carbon dioxide emissions; leisure travel accounts for half of all transport. The cumulative result of such activity is one of the biggest disruptions in the Earth's history—global warming, climate change and rising seas.

4   Some observers now argue that tourism can strengthen local cultures by encouraging an awareness of tradition and the ceremonies and festivals that go with it. But what's the value of tradition if it's kept alive self-consciously, for profit, and bears little relation to real life—which, today, across the world, grows ever more uniform? The pressures of tourism breed a phenomenon often referred to as "Disneyfication," in which culture and history are transformed, the authentic giving way to Disney-like replicas. What's undeniable is that tourism, in one way or another, changes tradition.

5   In truth, there are no easy answers to the dilemmas posed by mass tourism. Awareness, certainly, is a step forward—the knowledge of what it means to be a tourist. With that comes the ability to make better choices, where and how and even whether to travel. An increasing number of nonprofit organizations offer working holidays, in which the economic and social asymmetries that lie at the heart of the holiday industry are somewhat redressed: The tourist takes but also gives. Among the best-known is the research organization Earthwatch.

6   Such initiatives are undoubtedly one of the ways forward for tourism. The world, clearly, is not going to stop taking holidays—but equally clearly we can no longer afford to ignore the consequences. And if one of the major culprits has been the industrialization of travel, a genuinely post-industrial tourism, with the emphasis on people and places rather than product and profits, could turn out to be significantly more planet-friendly.

David Nicholson-Lord, who lives in England, is former environment editor of The Independent on Sunday *and author of* The Greening of the Cities *(Routledge).*

Comprehension

Indicate if each statement below is true (T) or false (F) according to your understanding of the author's point of view.

1. **T / F**   Tourism threatens the environment.

2. **T / F**   Taking a shower in the Himalayas can lead to global warming.

3. **T / F**   Taking an airplane contributes to climate change.

4. **T / F**   The "golf wars" took place between Iraq and Kuwait.

5. **T / F**   There is no good side to tourism.

6. **T / F**   If you kill a lion in Kenya, you can sell it for $7,000.

7. **T / F**   The author is disappointed that whale watching is now a bigger business than whaling.

8. **T / F**   The author believes that tourism can strengthen local culture.

9. **T / F**   Tourism changes tradition.

10. T / F The author believes that by writing articles such as this he can persuade people to stop taking vacations.

11. T / F Working holidays will not help the environment.

12. T / F A major concern of the author is the environment.

Critical Reading

1. Why do you think the author talks about "consumers" instead of "tourists" in Paragraph 1?

2. Why do you think this article is titled "The Politics of Travel"? How is travel political?

Discussion/Composition

1. **Simulation**. You and your classmates are government officials in a nation that very much needs tourist money. However, the beautiful natural and cultural sights that bring tourists will also be threatened if too many people visit. You will have to develop a reasonable tourist policy.

    a. **Groups**. Form groups representing various government groups.

    -   Ministry of the Treasury

        ○ This is the group that must worry about the financial state of the government.

    -   Ministry of the Interior

        ○ This group protects natural and cultural sites.

    -   Ministry of Education

        ○ This group needs money from tourism but also worries about the effects on the younger generation of so many visitors from other cultures.

    -   Ministry of Transportation

        ○ On the one hand, this group hopes that tourist money will help fund new roads, but its members are worried that they can't build roads fast enough to accommodate large numbers of tourists.

    -   Ministry of Health

        ○ This group, too, needs tourist money, but its members also worry that they don't have the resources to take care of tourist health needs.

    Your teacher may decide to have fewer groups, but you must have the final one:
    -   Ministry of Tourism

        ○ This is the group that will be deciding on a final tourist policy for your country.

b. **Statements**. In groups, prepare statements. First, brainstorm (additional) concerns and desires of your ministry. What do you want to see in the tourism policy? What do you want to avoid happening? Now work on preparing a two- to three-minute presentation to representatives from the Ministry of Tourism arguing for a specific tourist policy. You may use your time however you wish; you may have one speaker or more. The following are examples of issues you might want to address.

   • Why should/shouldn't your country encourage tourism?

   • Should there be unlimited tourism in your country? If not, how many tourists should you aim for?

   • Should there be a high cost for a tourist visa? Should there be no tourist visas required?

   • Should you focus your tourist advertising on certain countries?

   • Should some sites be closed to visitors all the time or during some periods of the year?

   • Should some sites limit the number of visitors?

   • Should you increase the cost of admission to cultural sites?

   • How will you protect your environment?

   • How should your tourist dollars be spent?

During this time, the Ministry of Tourism will be meeting to decide what criteria it will be using to make decisions and to see if there are specific questions it would like to ask of the other ministries.

c. **Government hearings**. Sometimes when governments make policy, they hold public "hearings," at which groups make presentations and provide information in an effort to influence government policy. Each group will make its presentation to the Ministry of Tourism.

d. **Rebuttals**. Groups may have one minute to rebut (argue against) statements made by other ministries. Groups may then have one minute to respond to the rebuttals.

e. **Government policy**. The Ministry of Tourism will meet and deliver its policy.

f. **Written statements**. Your teacher may ask each group for a written statement. The Ministry of Tourism would present a tourism policy. The other ministries would present written statements arguing their positions.

2. In the "Before You Begin" section, you considered why people travel. The author addresses this question, too, in a longer version of this article. He argues that people travel to escape their lives. He quotes a Swiss academic, Jost Krippendorf, who believes that people travel because "they no longer feel happy where they are—where they work, where they live. They feel the monotony of the daily routine." The author says that "we need the unknown, what historians of religion call 'otherness,' to lend our lives significance." Do you think this is why people travel? Support your position orally or in writing by presenting reasons and examples.

3. Should you feel guilty when you travel? By and large, is travel a positive or a negative thing for travelers and the places they visit? After reading this article, will you make any different travel decisions?

Vocabulary from Context

Exercise 1

Both the ideas and the vocabulary in the following exercise are taken from "The Politics of Travel." Use the context provided to determine the meanings of the italicized words or phrases. Write a definition, synonym, or description in the space provided.

1. _____

2. _____

3. _____

4. _____

5. _____

6. _____

7. _____

8. _____

9. _____

10. _____

11. _____

12. _____

To attract tourism to one's country was once thought of as an *unqualified* (1) success; there seemed to be no negative aspects to it. However, today we are coming to realize that tourism is a mixed blessing: it has advantages and disadvantages. On the one hand, it can bring money to parts of the world that very much need it. People can earn a great deal through tourism. And this *income* (2) can help to preserve the environment. Anything that helps to protect the *ecosystem* (3), the interrelated community of plants and animals that makes up the Earth, is, of course, positive.

A recent worry, however, is the fact that tourists can cause serious damage to the *fragile* (4) environments they love to visit. Ecosystems are delicate and easily damaged. Around the world, areas are endangered by the large numbers of tourists who visit them. On every continent, tourism *threatens* (5) the environment. Even *trekkers* (6) who take difficult journeys on foot can cause damage.

There are, then, serious dangers that come with the promise of tourism. Every advantage brings with it real disadvantages and vice versa. This *dilemma* (7) makes planning difficult for nations trying to decide what to do. Countries can make a good deal more money from the tourist industry than they need to put into attracting tourists. This financial *profit* (8) can help nations protect *habitats* (9) where endangered animals (and plants) live.

These efforts can assure the *survival* (10) of wildlife that otherwise would not continue to exist. It also may be that tourism can help strengthen local cultures by encouraging awareness of traditions and ceremonies. Historic buildings *thrive on* (11) tourism. These cultural locations enjoy great success with the money and attention and respect brought by tourism.

But there is a downside to all this. Because cultural sites are becoming too crowded, Disneyland-like reproductions are being created. These are not *authentic* (12) cultural sites but copies of something that may or may not have ever really

13. _____

14. _____

15. _____

16. _____

17. _____

18. _____

19. _____

existed. The author says, "what's the value of tradition if it's kept alive for profit, and bears little relation to real life?"

Taken together, the negative effects of tourism grow larger over time. The *cumulative* (13) effects of tourism are great because every time we use cars or planes to travel we contribute to one of the greatest *disruptions* (14) in the history of the planet: global warming and climate change are interrupting what has been the normal climate pattern for centuries.

As people understand the problems of tourism, some are beginning to organize against it through planned actions with particular goals. *Campaigns* (15) in Japan have been *launched* (16) against the sport of golf. Japan is one of the chief *exponents* (17) of golf tourism. Because golf uses so much land and water, campaigners have introduced an annual World No Golf Day.

New approaches to the problem are also being developed. One *initiative* (18) has been the development of tourist opportunities in which the tourists both give and receive through working and studying vacations. This kind of personal, small-scale tourism is meant to be a positive response to the kind of *industrialization* (19) of tourism that has become typical with its large-scale organizing. Working tourism may not be for everyone, but the hope is that some kinds of travel can become more planet friendly.

Exercise 2

This exercise gives you additional practice using context clues to guess the meaning of unfamiliar vocabulary. Give a definition, synonym, or description of each of the words below. The number in parentheses indicates the paragraph of "The Politics of Travel" in which the word can be found. Your teacher may want you to do these orally or in writing.

1. (1) local _____

2. (1) culprits _____

3. (2) monuments _____

4. (2) notably _____

5. (2) trampling _____

6. (4) replicas _____

7. (4) awareness _____

8. (5) redressed _____

9. (6) postindustrial _____

Figurative Language and Idioms

This exercise is designed to give you additional clues to understand the meanings of unfamiliar vocabulary items in context, in this case figurative language and idioms. In the paragraph of "The Politics of Travel" indicated by the number in parentheses, find the word or phrase that best fits the meaning given. Your teacher may want to read these aloud as you quickly scan* the paragraph to find the answer.

1. (1) What phrase means *creates a significant danger?* _____

2. (1) What phrase means *hunger for; need for?* _____

3. (2) What phrase means *relation of advantages to disadvantages, of costs to benefits?* _____

4. (2) What phrase means *rescue/recovery/saving/survival depends on?* _____

5. (4) Which word means *create?* _____

Stems and Affixes

The sentences below were adapted from "The Politics of Travel". Use your knowledge of stems and affixes** and the context to determine the meanings of the italicized words. Your teacher may want you to do this orally or in writing.

1. In the Himalayas, showers for tourists often mean cutting down firewood to make warm water, which leads to *deforestation.*

   _____

2. Because of golf's appetite for land, water, and *herbicides,* people worried about the ecosystem have launched an annual World No Golf Day.

   _____

3. Because tourism brings in money, in southern and eastern Africa, tourism *underpins* the survival of *wildlife.*

   _____

   _____

4. Each time we travel by car, bus, or train, we're effectively setting fire to a small *reservoir* of gasoline.

   _____

---

*For an introduction to scanning, see Unit 1.

**For a list of all stems and affixes that appear in *Reader's Choice*, see Appendix B.

5. Through the Disneyfication of culture, what we think of as "tradition" around the world can come to look more and more *uniform*.

_____

6. Through Disneyfication, authentic culture and history are *transformed* into Disney-like replicas.

_____

7. To give people better travel choices, *nonprofit* organizations offer working holidays that address the economic and social *asymmetries* that are characteristic of many tourist experiences.

_____

_____

Dictionary Study

Many words have more than one meaning. When you use a dictionary to discover the meaning of an unfamiliar word, you need to use the context to determine which definition is appropriate. Use the dictionary entries provided to select the best definition for each of the italicized words in the following sentences. Write the number of the definition in the space provided.

_____ **1.** Tourism *fuels* (1) a *booming* (2) trade in buying and selling products made from threatened

_____ **2.** wildlife, such as the illegal sale of ivory from elephants' tusks.

_____ **3.** If large animals, with large *ranges* (3), are protected, then so are their habitats—the national parks.

fu•el (fyoo′əl) *n.* **1.** Something consumed to produce energy, esp.: **a.** A material such as coal, gas, or oil burned to produce heat or power, **b.** Fissionable material used in a nuclear reactor. **c.** Nutritive material metabolized by a living organism; food. **2.** Something that maintains or stimulates an activity or emotion. — *v.* **-eled, -el•ing, -els** also **-elled, -el•ling, -els.** — *tr.* **1.** To provide with fuel. **2.** To support or stimulate the activity or existence of. — *intr.* To take in *fuel.* [ME *feuel* < OFr. *feuaile* < VLat. **focālia,* neut. pl. of **focālis,* of the hearth < Lat. *focus,* hearth.] — **fu′el•er** *n.*

boom¹ (boom) *v.* **boomed, boom•ing, booms,** —*intr.* **1.** To make a deep resonant sound. **2.** To grow or develop rapidly; flourish. —*tr.* **1.** To utter or give forth a boom. **2.** To cause to boom; boost. — *n.* **1.** A deep resonant sound, as of an explosion. **2.** A time of economic prosperity. **3.** A sudden increase. [ME *bomben,* imit. of a loud noise.]

boom² (boom) *n.* **1.** *Naut.* A spar extending from a mast to hold or extend the foot of a sail. **2.** A long pole extending upward from the mast of a derrick to support or guide objects being lifted or suspended. **3.a.** A barrier composed of a chain of floating logs enclosing other free-floating logs. **b.** A floating barrier serving to contain an oil spill. **4.** A long movable arm used to support a microphone. **5.** A spar connecting the tail surfaces and the main structure of an airplane. [Du., tree, pole < MDu. See **bheuə-*.**]

range (rānj) *n.* **1.a.** Extent of perception, knowledge, experience, or ability, **b.** The area or sphere in which an activity takes place. **c.** The full extent covered: *the range of possibilities.* **2.a.** An amount or extent of variation, **b.** *Mus.* The gamut of tones that a voice or an instrument is capable of producing. **3.a.** The maximum extent or distance limiting operation, action, or effectiveness, as of an aircraft or a sound, **b.** The maximum distance that can be covered by a vehicle with a specified payload before its fuel supply is exhausted. **c.** The distance between a projectile weapon and its target. **4.** A place equipped for practice in shooting at targets. **5.** *Aerospace.* A testing area for rockets and missiles. **6.** An extensive area of open land for livestock. **7.** The geographic region in which a plant or an animal normally lives or grows. **8.** The act of wandering or roaming over a large area. **9.** *Math.* The set of all values a given function may take on. **10.** *Statistics.* The difference or interval between the smallest and largest values in a frequency distribution. **11.** A class, a rank, or an order. **12.** An extended group or series, esp. a row or chain of mountains. **13.** One of a series of double-faced bookcases in a library stack room. **14.** A north-south strip of townships, each six miles square, numbered east and west from a specified meridian in a U.S. public land survey. **15.** A stove with spaces for cooking a number of things at the same time. — *v.* **ranged, rang • ing, rang • es.** — *tr.* **1.** To arrange or dispose in a particular order, esp. in rows or lines. **2.** To assign to a particular category; classify. **3.** To align (a gun, for example) with a target. **4.a.** To determine the distance of (a target). **b.** To be capable of reaching (a maximum distance). **5.** To pass over or through (an area or a region). **6.** To turn (livestock) onto an extensive area of open land for grazing. **7.** *Naut.* To uncoil (a line or rode) along the deck so that it will pay out smoothly. — *intr.* **1.** To vary within specified limits. **2.** To extend in a particular direction. **3.** To extend or lie in the same direction. **4.** To pass over or through an area or a region in or as if in exploration. See Syns at **wander.** **5.** To wander freely; roam. **6.** To live or grow within a particular region. [ME, row, rank < OFr. < *rangier,* to put in a row < *rang, reng,* line, of Gmc. orig. See **sker-²*.**]

UNIT 3

Have you heard the expression, "a picture is worth a thousand words?" Increasingly, researchers and the popular media have relied on the visual presentation of data to clarify and extend texts; efficient readers need to know how to understand these. This exercise is designed to introduce some of the data presentation formats. It provides visual presentations of data along with text on the aging of the world's population.

BEFORE YOU BEGIN

The following paragraph is from an academic journal on aging:

Imagine a world with fewer and fewer children and more and more old people, a world with a shrinking workforce and a declining total population. Countries with older populations such as Japan and Germany are already experiencing these changes. What may be surprising, though, is that a less extreme version of this picture of aging is already beginning to unfold in most developing countries.

1. Why is a world with more and more older people and fewer younger people a problem?

2. How do you think the "graying" of the world population will affect you?

Global and Regional Trends in Population Aging

Worldwide, in 1972, a woman gave birth to an average of 5.6 children over her lifetime. Global population, as a result, was doubling every generation. Citing the trend, a group of intellectuals known as the Club of Rome issued an influential study titled "The Limits of Growth" that told what it all meant. The twenty-first century, said the club, would inevitably be marked by declining standards of living as human population exceeded the "carrying capacity" of the Earth, leading to mass famine and energy shortages.

But in the years since this prediction, a revolutionary change has occurred in human behavior. Around the world, fertility rates are plummeting. Today, women on average have just half the number of children they did in 1972. In 61 countries, accounting for 44 percent of the Earth's population, fertility rates are now at, or below, replacement levels. So the world has a new problem: global aging.

The activities below introduce different formats for data presentation. The figures and texts, from a United Nations report, provide detailed predictions about global aging. Be sure to look at both the figures and the text to answer the questions that follow them. Your teacher may want you to work on these in pairs. It is possible to do these over several different class periods. True/False items are indicated with a T / F preceding the statement.

Line graphs

Line graphs are a simple and powerful way to show changes over time. Multiple lines can compare different data sets.

In most countries, the growth in the absolute number of older persons will occur in a context of low or declining birth rates, leading to increasing shares of older persons in the population. In 2017, one in eight people worldwide was aged 60 or over. In 2050, older persons are projected to account for one in five people globally.

1. What data does this figure show? _____

2. Why are parts of the lines dotted? _____

3. **T / F** The population of people over 60 years of age seems to be growing at approximately the same rate in Latin America/the Caribbean and Asia.

4. Approximately what percentage of the world population is expected to be over 60 years of age in 2050?
    _____

5. In 2017, which area of the world had the highest percentage of older people? _____
    Which region is next? _____ Are these two regions projected to have the highest percentage in 2050? _____

FIGURE 1

Percentage of population aged 60 years or over by region, from 1980 to 2050

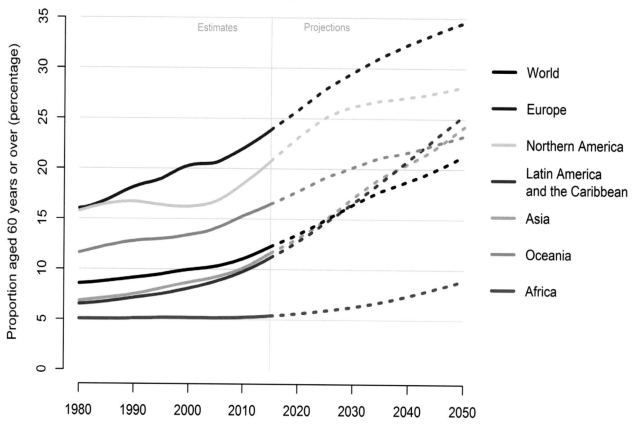

Stacked Area Charts

An area chart, like a line graph, uses lines to show change over time. But in an area chart the goal is to show how much each part contributes to a whole, such as showing the relationship of population growth in some areas of the world to population growth overall. To understand how part-to-whole is displayed, look at Figure 2. The older population of the least developed countries is much smaller than in the less and most developed countries.

The global population aged 60 years and over in 2017 was more than twice as large as in 1980. The number of older people is expected to double again by 2050. But the older population of the less- and least-developed regions is growing much faster than in the more-developed regions. Consequently, the developing regions are home to a growing share of the world's older population. Projections indicate that in 2050, 79 percent of the world's population aged 60 or over will be living in the least-/less-developed regions.

FIGURE 2. Number of persons aged 60 years or older by development group, from 1980 to 2050

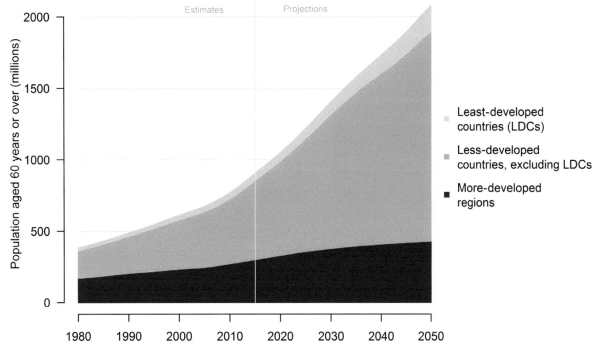

Estimates   Projections

Least-developed
countries (LDCs)

Less-developed
countries, excluding LDCs

More-developed
regions

1. Why is there a vertical line in the middle of the chart? _____
    What year does it represent? _____

2. This chart divides the world into three kinds of countries. What are they?
    _____

    Give an example of one country that you think will be in each of these categories.

    _____

3. In 1980, the least- and less-developed regions were home to slightly more than 50 percent of persons aged
    60 years or over. Circle the area of the chart that tells you this.

4. **T / F** In 2017, more than two thirds of the world's older people lived in the more-developed regions.

5. **T / F** The population of older people is increasing faster in the least- and less-developed countries than in
    the developed countries.

6. **T / F** In 2050, more older people will live in the least-developed countries than in the less-developed
    countries.

7. In one sentence, summarize Figure 2. _____

Bar Charts

Bar charts are one of the most commonly used types of graphs. The heights of the bars are used to compare
different categories of data.

Globally, the number of older persons is growing faster than the number of people in all younger age groups.
The projections also indicate that in 2050 there will be more older persons aged 60 or over than adolescents
and youth at ages 10–24 years (2.1 billion versus 2.0 billion). The number of people at very advanced ages
is increasing too: the global population aged 80 years or over is projected to triple between 2017 and 2050,
increasing from 137 million to 425 million.

FIGURE 3

Global population by broad age group, in 1980, 2017, 2030 and 2050

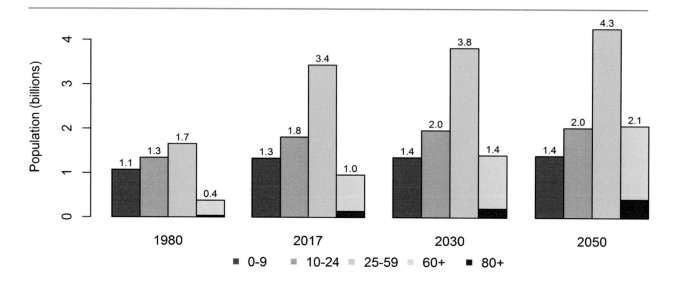

1. What data are included in this chart? _____

2. Which age group is growing fastest? _____

3. **T / F** By 2030 the global population of people over 60 is expected to be approximately the same as that of children under age 10.

4. **T / F** In 2050 there will be more people aged 60 or over than adolescents and youth aged 10–24 years.

Discuss the following two questions with a partner.

5. This chart adds a distinction between people over 60 and people over 80. Why is this distinction significant?

6. The rate of change for the population of people over 60 is higher than for people 25–59, who will have to support them. But the actual number of people 25–59 is still a lot more than people over 60. Should we be worried about the increasing rate of older people? Why or why not?

> ## Tables
> Tables are the most common type of data display. They show data in rows and columns. Tables can give more numeric detail than a chart or a graph.

Over the coming decades, the number of older persons is expected to grow fastest in Africa, where the population aged 60 or over is projected to increase more than 200 percent between 2017 and 2050, from 69 to 226 million. Within the six major geographic regions, the older population is expected to grow most slowly in Europe, with a projected increase of 35 per cent percent between 2017 and 2050 (Figure 4).

FIGURE 4. Number and percentage of persons 60 years or older by region, in 2017 and 2050

	Number of persons aged 60 years or over in 2017 (millions)	Number of persons aged 60 years or over in 2050 (millions)	Percentage change between 2017 and 2050	World percentage of older persons in 2017	World percentage of older persons in 2050
Africa	68.7	225.8	228.5	7.1	10.9
Asia	549.2	1273.2	131.8	57.1	61.2
Europe	183.0	247.2	35.1	19.0	11.9
Latin America & the Caribbean	76.0	198.2	160.7	7.9	9.5
Northern America	78.4	122.8	56.7	8.1	5.9
Oceania	6.9	13.3	92.6	0.7	0.6
WORLD	962.3	2080.5	116.2	100.0	100.0

1. The text says, "Over the coming decades, the number of older people is expected to grow fastest in Africa, where the population aged 60 or over is projected to increase more 200 percent between 2017 and 2050, from 69 to 226 million." Circle the places where you can find this information.

2. What is the projected percentage change in population between 2017 and 2050 where you live?
   _____

3. **T / F** By 2050, Africa will have the largest population of older people.

4. Europe will see the slowest percentage growth of older people between 2017 and 2050. Does that mean it will have the smallest population of people over 60? _____ Will it have the smallest percentage in the world of people over 60 in 2050? _____

5. The region with the smallest percentage of the world's older population has been Oceania. What countries can you name in Oceania? _____

6. When looking at population data, why is both number and percentage of world population important?
   _____

   _____

7. **T / F** The total world population is expected to be approximately 2000 million (i.e., two billion) in 2050.

Bubble Charts

Bubble charts are an effective visual way to show three or more variables. The bubbles in Figure 5 represent individual countries. For each country (Variable 1), the chart shows the growth rate (percentage change) of the older population (Variable 2) and the average income in 2016 (Variable 3). There is also another piece of information given in this chart: colors are used to indicate the region of the world for each country (Variable 4).

Note that the size of a bubble represents the size of the population of older people in the country, not the range of income. For example, if you want to know the average income of the country represented by the largest bubble in Figure 5, just look at the center of the bubble ($8,000/year).

FIGURE 5

Projected change from 2017 to 2050 in the number of persons aged 60 years or over versus gross national income per capita in 2016

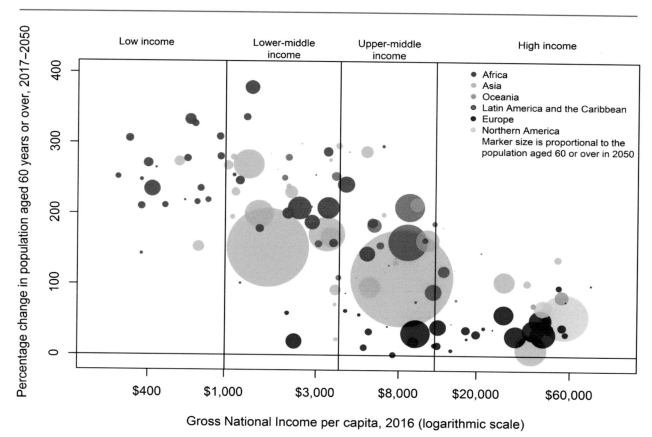

1. What information is provided by the vertical axis of the chart? _____
   What is on the horizontal axis? _____

2. Knowing that the two largest dots are in Asia, what countries do you think they are? _____

3. What region of the world is projected to have the largest percentage change in older population between 2017 and 2050? _____

4. **T / F** In general, the percentage change of older population is growing fastest in the poorest countries.

5. Which region of the world has the least economic diversity? _____

6. **T / F** The average income in the US is projected to be almost $60,000/year in 2050.

7. What does this chart have to say about your country? _____

Critical Reading

1. Why do you think these charts and graphs showing data between 1980 and projected data to 2050 focus on the year 2017?

2. Responding to trends reported here, Neil Howe, an expert on aging, observed, "The developed world at least got rich before it got old. In the Third World the trend is reversed." What does this mean? Why is this a problem?

3. In Figure 2 countries are categorized as "least developed," "less developed," and "more developed." These are terms used by the United Nations and other organizations to categorize countries in terms of such things as their economic and environmental risk, and the education and life expectancy of their populations. Shose Kessi, a social psychologist at the University of Cape Town, has said,

> I dislike the term "developing world" because it assumes a hierarchy between countries. It paints a picture of Western societies as ideal but there are many social problems in these societies as well. It also perpetuates stereotypes about people who come from the so-called developing world as backward, lazy, ignorant, irresponsible.

Do you agree with Kessi? What do you think of these terms?
What are the advantages and disadvantages of having a label that indicates the overall wealth and resources of a country?

Discussion/Composition

1. The UN reports assume that taking care of older retired people will become economically more difficult in the coming years. Two possible ways to address this are to raise the retirement age, so that people work longer than they do now, and raise taxes on working people to provide more money to support retired people.

    a. Which approach would you recommend? What effects would that approach have on both young people and old people?

    b. Another suggestion has been to increase the number of younger people by paying women to have children. Do you think this is a good idea? Why or why not?

2. Who should have the main responsibility for taking care of the elderly? The national government? The local community? Family members? Religious organizations?

3. Imagine you are a community leader in a country where the population is declining. What actions would you recommend that your country take to respond to the crisis of falling population? Prepare a speech or write a position paper in which you make recommendations. You might want to focus your recommendations on one or more of the following aspects of this topic:

    • what role, if any, the government should play in telling people what size family to have

    • the positive and negative effects of immigration on a country

    • whose responsibility it should be to care for the elderly in your country

    • the economic effects of changes in retirement age and tax policies

    • the social effects of changes in retirement age and tax policies

Word Study
Context Clues

Exercise 1

In the following exercise, do not try to learn the italicized words. Concentrate on developing your ability to guess the meanings of unfamiliar words using context clues.* Read each sentence carefully and write a definition, synonym, or description of the italicized word on the line provided.

1. _____ The major points of your plan are clear to me, but the details are still *hazy*.

2. _____ By *anticipating* the thief's next move, the police were able to arrive at the bank before the robbery occurred.

3. _____ All of the palace's laundry, when gathered for washing, formed a *massive* bundle that required the combined efforts of all the servants to carry.

4. _____ "Give me specific suggestions when you criticize my work," said the employee. "*Vague* comments do not help me improve."

5. _____ The apple *appeased* my hunger temporarily, but I could still eat a big dinner.

6. _____ After the workers walked off the job, a committee met to try to discover what could have *provoked* such action.

7. _____ The audience *manifested* its pleasure with hearty laughter.

8. _____ The nation's highway death *toll* has increased every year since the invention of the automobile.

9. _____ The workers' lives were *wretched*; they worked from morning to night in all kinds of weather, earning only enough money to buy their simple food and cheap clothes.

10. _____ In a series of bold moves, government attorneys attacked the *mammoth* computer company, saying that the size of the business endangered the financial freedom of the individual buyer.

---

*For an introduction to using context clues, see Unit 1.

Exercise 2

This exercise is designed to give you practice using context clues from a passage. Use your general knowledge along with information from the entire text below to write a definition, synonym, or description of the italicized word on the line provided. Read through the entire passage before making a decision. Note that some of the words appear more than once; by the end of the passage, you should have a good idea of their meaning. Do not worry if your definition is not exact; a general idea of the meaning will often allow you to understand the meaning of a written text.

Hummingbirds: A Portrait of the Animal World

The hummingbird is truly extraordinary. It is, of course, most famous for its *diminutive* size; even the largest of these little birds weighs barely half an ounce; the tiniest, at barely two inches long, is the smallest of all warm-blooded creatures. But the hummingbird is *notable* for many other reasons. Its ability to *hover*, seemingly motionless, in midair and even to fly upside down is amazing. Its vividly hued iridescent plumage gives it a remarkable appearance. And its specialized feeding habits, its extraordinary migration patterns, and its unusual courtship and mating rituals make it *unique* in the realm of *ornithology*.

diminutive: _____

notable: _____

hover: _____

unique: _____

ornithology: _____

Word Study
Stems and Affixes

Below is a list of some commonly occurring stems and affixes.* Study their meanings and then do the exercises that follow. Your teacher may ask you to give examples of other words you know that are derived from these stems and affixes.

Prefixes		
ante-	before	*anterior, ante meridiem* (a.m.)
circum-	around	*circumference*
contra-, anti-	against	*anti-war, contrast*
inter-	between	*international, intervene*
intro-, intra-	within	*introduce, intravenous*
post-	after	*postgame, postgraduate*
sub-, suc-, suf-, sug-, sup-, sus-	under	*subway, support*
super-	above, greater, better	*superior, supermarket*
trans-	across	*transportation, transgender*
Stems		
-ced-	go, move, yield	*precede*
-duc-	lead	*introduce*
-flect-	bend	*reflect, flexible*
-mit-, -miss-	send	*remit, missionary*
-pon-, -pos-	put, place	*postpone, position*
-port-	carry	*portable*
-sequ-, -secut-	follow	*consequence, consecutive*
-spir-	breathe	*inspiration, conspiracy*
-tele-	far	*telegraph, telephone*
-ven-, -vene-	come	*convene, convention*
-voc-, -vok-	call	*vocal, revoke*
Suffixes		
-able, -ible, -ble	capable of, fit for	*trainable, defensible*
-ous, -ious, -ose	full of, having the qualities of	*poisonous, anxious, verbose*

*For a list of all stems and affixes that appear in *Reader's Choice*, see Appendix B.

Exercise 1

For each item, select the best definition of the italicized word or phrase or answer the question.

1. The first thing Jim did when he arrived at the airport was look for a *porter.*

   _____**a.** person who sells tickets

   _____**b.** taxi cab

   ✓_____**c.** person who carries luggage

   _____**d.** door to the luggage room

2. No matter what Fred said, Noam *contradicted him.*

   ✓_____**a.** said the opposite

   _____**b.** yelled at him

   _____**c.** laughed at him

   _____**d.** didn't listen to him

3. The doctor is a specialist in the human *respiratory* system. She is an expert on…

   _____**a.** bones.

   ✓_____**b.** lungs.

   _____**c.** nerves.

   _____**d.** the stomach.

4. He *circumvented* the problem.

   _____**a.** described

   _____**b.** solved

   ✓_____**c.** went around, avoided

   _____**d.** wrote down, copied

5. Which is a postscript?

   a. _____

   b. _____

   c. ✓_____

   d. _____

   Dear J,
   _ _ _ _ _ _ _ _
   _ _ _ _ _ _ _ _
   Sincerely,
   P.
   P.S. _ _ _ _

   Mr. John Smith
   _ _ _ _ _ _ _ _
   _ _ _ _ _ _ _
   _ _ · _ _

6. Use what you know about stems and affixes to explain how the following words were derived.

   a. telephone _something Far away , hear Far away._

   b. telegram _____

   c. television _Its shows everything far away from you. Far for watching_

7. When would a photographer use a telephoto lens for their camera? _____

8. Use word analysis to explain what *support* means.

   _____

9. What is the difference between *interstate commerce* and *intrastate commerce?*

   One Interstate are between States Intraste are within States

10. At one time, many European towns depended on the system of aqueducts built by the Romans for their water supply. What is an aqueduct?

    _____

11. If a person has a *receding* hairline, what do they look like? _their going bald_

12. The abbreviation *AM* (as in 10:30 AM) stands for *ante meridiem*. What do you think *PM* (as in 10:30 PM) stands for?

P is the middel

13. Consider these sentences.

    a. She *subscribes* to *Time* magazine.

    b. She subscribes to the theory that the moon is made of green cheese.

    Explain how these meanings of *subscribe* developed from the meanings of *sub* and *scribe*.

Exercise 2

Word analysis can help you to guess the meanings of unfamiliar words. Using context clues and what you know about word parts, write a synonym, description, or definition of the italicized word or phrase.

1. _____ Despite evidence *to the contrary*, Mark really believes that he can pass an exam without studying.

2. _____ I haven't finished the report you asked for yet; let's *postpone* our meeting until next Tuesday.

3. *Boss* _____ Ask your *supervisor* if you can take your vacation next month.

4. _____ Please *remit* your payment in the enclosed envelope.

5. *numbers* _____ Something must be wrong with this machine. It doesn't always type *superscripts* correctlxy: 2 $x2 \quad x_2 \quad x^2$ x

6. _____ *Antibiotics*, such as penicillin, help the body fight bacterial but not viral infections.

7. _____ Nowadays, very little mail is *transported* by train.

8. _____ Don't invite Frank again; his behavior tonight was *inexcusable*.

9. _____ Scientists study the *interaction* between parents and their babies to better understand how infants learn.

10. *Send* _____ After the plane crash, the pilot had to fix his radio before he could *transmit* his location.

11. _____ The committee decided to stop working at noon and to *reconvene* at 1:30.

12. *Canceld* _____ The state of Texas *revoked* his driver's license because he had had too many accidents.

13. _____ This material is very useful because it is strong yet *flexible*.

14. _____ Barbara wanted to buy a *portable* heater.

15. _____ The Portuguese sailor Magellan set out to *circumnavigate* the world.

16. _____ The king imposed a heavy tax on his people to pay for his foreign wars.

Exercise 3

Following is a list of words containing some of the stems and affixes introduced in this unit and the previous one. Definitions of these words appear on the right. Put the letter of the appropriate definition next to each word.

1. _b_ anteroom
2. _d_ antecedent
3. _a_ vociferous
4. _c_ vocation
5. _e_ subsequent
6. _h_ subscript
7. _j_ superscript
8. _k_ intervene
9. _g_ introspection
10. _f_ convene
11. _i_ consequence

a. characterized by a noisy outcry or shouting

b. a room forming an entrance to another one

c. the career one believes oneself is called to; one's occupation or profession

d. something that happened or existed before another thing

e. following in time, order, or place

f. the observation or examination of one's own thought processes

g. a letter or symbol written immediately below and to the right of another symbol

h. a logical result or conclusion; the relation of effect to cause

i. a letter or symbol written immediately above and to the right of another symbol

j. to come between people or points in time

k. to come together as a group

Sentence Study
Comprehension

Read each sentence carefully.* The questions that follow are designed to test your comprehension of complex grammatical structures. Select the best answer.

1. My discovery of Tillie Olsen was a gift from a friend; years ago she gave me her copy of *Tell Me a Riddle* because she liked the stories and wanted to share the experience.

   What do we know about Tillie Olsen?

   _____ **a.** She is a friend.

   _____ **b.** She likes stories.

   _____ **c.** She gives gifts.

   _____ **d.** She is an author.

2. A few government officials even estimate that the flood has created more than half a million refugees who need immediate food, clothing, and shelter.

   Exactly how many refugees are there?

   _____ **a.** half a million

   _____ **b.** over half a million

   ___✓___ **c.** We don't know exactly.

   _____ **d.** Only a few government officials know the exact figure.

3. The Green Tiger Press believes that the relatively unknown works of great children's illustrators are sources of ~~vast~~ beauty and power and is attempting to make these treasures more easily available.

   What is the goal of this printing company?

   _____ **a.** to publish more children's books

   _____ **b.** to develop powerful stories

   ___✓___ **c.** to make children's illustrations more easily available

   _____ **d.** to encourage artists to become children's illustrators

4. Although he calls the $100,000 donation "a very generous amount, especially in these times," the president expresses hope that the project will attract additional funds from companies and other sources so that it can continue beyond this first year.

   What does the president know about the project?

   _____ **a.** It will cost only $100,000.

   _____ **b.** It is very special.

   _____ **c.** Special sources will support it.

   ___✓___ **d.** It cannot continue without additional funding.

5. Any thought that this new custom will remain unchanged—or in Europe will remain uniquely English—is ridiculous.

   What does the author believe about the new custom?

   _____ **a.** It will remain limited.

   ___✓___ **b.** The custom will change.

   _____ **c.** Acceptance of the custom is ridiculous.

   _____ **d.** The custom will remain in Europe.

---

*For an introduction to sentence study, see Unit 1.

6. Robust and persistent sailors gathered from all the sea-faring nations set out on voyages that laid foundations for great empires with no other power than sail and oar.

Why were these voyages important?

_____ a. Sailors came from many countries.

_____ b. The voyages laid the foundations for sea-faring nations.

_____ c. The foundations for empires were established.

_____ d. Sea-faring nations lost their power.

7. Young people need to develop the values, attitudes, and problem-solving skills essential to their participation in a political system that was designed, and is still based, on the assumption that all citizens would be so prepared.

What is the basic assumption of this political system?

_____ a. All people will be capable of participation.

_____ b. All people participate in the system.

_____ c. All people should have the same values and attitudes.

_____ d. Most people cannot develop the skills to participate in the system.

8. While we may be interested in the possibilities of social harmony and individual fulfillment to be achieved through nontraditional education, one cannot help being cautious about accepting any sort of one-sided educational program as a cure for the world's ills.

How does the author feel about nontraditional education?

_____ a. He believes that it has no possibility of success.

_____ b. He doubts that it can cure the world's ills.

_____ c. He feels that it is a cure for the world's ills.

_____ d. He believes that it will bring social harmony.

9. The complexity of the human situation and the injustice of the social order demand far more fundamental changes in the basic structure of society itself than some politicians are willing to admit in their speeches.

What is necessary to correct the problems of society?

_____ a. basic changes in its structure

_____ b. fewer political speeches

_____ c. honest politicians

_____ d. basic changes in political methods

Sentence Study
Restatement and Inference

Each sentence below is followed by five statements.* The statements are of four types.

1. Some of the statements are restatements of the original sentence. They give the same information in a different way.

2. Some of the statements are inferences (conclusions) that can be drawn from the information given in the original sentence.

3. Some of the statements are false based on the information given.

4. Some of the statements cannot be judged true or false based on the information given in the original sentence.

Put a check (✓) next to all restatements and inferences (types 1 and 2). Note: do not check a statement that is true of itself but cannot be inferred from the sentence given.

Example

Heavy smokers and drinkers run a fifteen times greater risk of developing cancer of the mouth and throat than nonsmokers and nondrinkers.

_____ a. Cancer of the mouth and throat is more likely to occur in heavy smokers and drinkers than in nonsmokers and nondrinkers.

_____ b. People who never drink and smoke will not get mouth or throat cancer.

_____ c. Heavy drinkers who run have a greater risk of developing cancer than nondrinkers.

_____ d. People who don't smoke and drink have less chance of getting cancer of the mouth and throat than those who smoke and drink heavily.

_____ e. People would probably be healthier if they did not drink and smoke too much.

Explanation

___✓___ a. This is a restatement of the original sentence. If heavy smokers and drinkers run a greater risk of developing cancer than those who do not drink or smoke, then cancer is more likely to occur in heavy smokers and drinkers.

_____ b. It is not true that people who never smoke and drink will never get mouth or throat cancer. We only know that they are *less likely* to get this kind of cancer.

___✓___ c. The word *run* in the original sentence is part of the phrase to run a risk, which means *to be in danger*. The sentence does not tell us anything about heavy drinkers who enjoy the sport of running.

---

*For an introduction to sentence study, see Unit 1.

_✓___ **d.** This is a restatement of the original sentence. If people who drink and smoke heavily have a greater chance of getting mouth and throat cancer than those who don't, then it must be true that those who don't smoke and drink heavily have less chance of developing this kind of cancer.

_✓___ **e.** This is an inference that can be drawn from the information given. If people who smoke and drink heavily run a high risk of developing cancer, then we can infer that people probably would be healthier if they didn't smoke and drink too much (heavily).

1.   Nine out of ten doctors responding to a survey said they recommend our product to their patients if they recommend anything.

_____ **a.** Nine out of ten doctors recommend the product.

_____ **b.** Of the doctors who responded to a survey, nine out of ten doctors recommend the product.

_____ **c.** If they recommend anything, nine out of ten doctors responding to a survey recommend the product.

_____ **d.** Most doctors recommend the product.

_____ **e.** We don't know how many doctors recommend the product.

2.   This organization may succeed marvelously at what it wants to do, but what it wants to do may not be all that important.

_____ **a.** The organization is marvelous.

_____ **b.** The organization may succeed.

_____ **c.** Although the organization may reach its goals, the goals might not be important.

_____ **d.** What the organization wants is marvelous.

_____ **e.** The author questions the goals of the organization.

3.   This book contains a totally new outlook that combines the wisdom of the past with scientific knowledge to solve the problems of the present.

_____ **a.** Problems of the past and present are solved in this book.

_____ **b.** In this book, current knowledge and past wisdom are combined to solve current problems.

_____ **c.** Only by using knowledge of the past and present can we solve problems.

_____ **d.** None of today's problems can be solved without scientific knowledge.

_____ **e.** This book is different because it combines the wisdom of the past with scientific knowledge.

4.   Like other timeless symbols, flags have accompanied humankind for thousands of years, gaining ever wider meaning, yet losing none of their inherent and original force.

_____ **a.** Despite losing some of their original force, flags are a timeless symbol that has accompanied humankind for thousands of years.

_____ **b.** Flags have existed for thousands of years.

_____ **c.** Timeless symbols typically gain wider meaning while not losing their inherent force.

_____ **d.** Thousands of years ago flags accompanied humankind, but through time they have lost their force.

_____ **e.** Because flags are considered a timeless symbol, they have gained continually wider meaning without losing their inherent original force.

5. When there is an absence of reliable information about drugs, the risks involved in using them are greatly increased.

   _____ **a.** There is no reliable information about drugs.

   _____ **b.** Using drugs is more dangerous when we don't know what effects and dangers are involved.

   _____ **c.** The risks involved in using drugs have increased.

   _____ **d.** People should try to find out about drugs before using them.

   _____ **e.** There are no risks involved in using drugs if we have reliable information about them.

6. The project of which this book is the result was first suggested in the summer of 2019, in the course of some leisurely conversations at the foot of and (occasionally) on top of the Alps of western Austria.

   _____ **a.** This book was written in 2019.

   _____ **b.** This book was written in Austria.

   _____ **c.** This book is a collection of conversations held in 2019.

   _____ **d.** This book is the end result of a project.

   _____ **e.** This book is about western Austria.

7. Los Angeles's safety record with school buses is generally a good one, but of course this record is only as good as the school bus drivers themselves.

   _____ **a.** Despite a generally good safety record for their school buses, Los Angeles school bus drivers are not very good.

   _____ **b.** If school bus drivers are not very good, the town's school bus safety record will not be very good either.

   _____ **c.** If cities wish to maintain good safety records with school buses, they should hire good school bus drivers.

   _____ **d.** With better school buses, drivers will be able to maintain better safety records.

   _____ **e.** Los Angeles's safety record with school buses has improved because better bus drivers have been hired.

8. Taxes being so high, the descendants of the wealthy class of the nineteenth century were being forced to rent out their estates to paying guests.

   _____ **a.** In the nineteenth century, the wealthy class rented out its estates.

   _____ **b.** Because of high taxes, families that once were rich had to rent out their estates.

   _____ **c.** Guests paid high taxes when they rented old estates.

_____ **d.** Some families that were once wealthy had trouble paying their taxes.

_____ **e.** High taxes changed the lives of some of the old wealthy families.

9. According to the definition of Chinese traditional medicine, acupuncture is the treatment of disease—not just the alleviation of pain—by inserting very fine needles into the body at specific points called loci.

_____ **a.** The author believes some people do not know that acupuncture can be used to treat illness.

_____ **b.** Finely pointed needles called loci are used in acupuncture.

_____ **c.** In Chinese traditional medicine, acupuncture is known to treat disease and alleviate pain.

_____ **d.** Those using acupuncture treat disease by placing needles into the body at specific points.

_____ **e.** Only those who practice traditional Chinese medicine use acupuncture.

10. It would be difficult to overpraise this book.

_____ **a.** This is a difficult book.

_____ **b.** This book deserves much praise.

_____ **c.** It is difficult not to overpraise this book.

_____ **d.** It is difficult to praise this book.

_____ **e.** The author of this sentence thinks this is an excellent book.

Paragraph Reading
Main Idea

This exercise is similar to one in Unit 1. Read the following passages. Concentrate on discovering the main idea.

After each of the first two passages, select the statement that best expresses the main idea. After Passages 3, 4, and 5, write a sentence that expresses the main idea in your own words. For Passage 6 you will be asked to read several paragraphs, identify the main idea, and create a summary. When you have finished, your teacher may want to divide the class into small groups for discussion.

Passage 1

At one time it was the most important city in the region—a bustling commercial center known for its massive monuments, its crowded streets and commercial districts, and its cultural and religious institutions. Then, suddenly, it was abandoned. Within a generation most of its population departed and the once magnificent city became a ghost town. This is the history of a pre-Columbian city called Teotihuacán (the Aztec word for "the place the gods call home"), once a metropolis of as many as 200,000 inhabitants 30 miles northeast of present-day Mexico City and the focus of a far-flung empire that stretched from the arid plains of central Mexico to the mountains of Guatemala. Why did this city die? A number of theories have been proposed. Some archaeologists point to a period of drought that peaked at the time of the decline of the city, which could have caused crop failures, famine, and disease. Others have suggested that the city fell to raiding bands of invaders. Still others believe it more likely that it was Teotihuacános themselves who burned their temples and some of their other buildings, perhaps as a revolt against leaders or in anger at their gods, and then abandoned their city.

Select the statement that best expresses the main idea of the passage.

_____ **a.** Teotihuacán, once the home of 200,000 people, was the center of a large empire.

_____ **b.** Many archaeologists are fascinated by the ruins of a pre-Columbian city called Teotihuacán.

_____ **c.** Teotihuacán, once a major metropolitan area, was destroyed by an invasion.

_____ **d.** A still unsolved mystery is why the people of Teotihuacán suddenly abandoned their city.

Passage 2

In any archaeological study that includes a dig, the procedures are basically the same: (1) selecting a site (2) hiring local workers (3) surveying the site and dividing it into sections (4) digging trenches to locate levels and places to excavate (5) mapping architectural features (6) developing a coding system that shows the exact spot where an object is found (7) and recording, tagging, cleaning and storing excavated materials. Neilson C. Debevoise, writing on an expedition to Iraq in the early 1930s, described the typical "route" of excavated pottery. Workers reported an object to staff members before removing it from the ground. The date, level, location and other important information were written on a piece of paper and placed with the object.

At noon the objects were brought in from the field to the registry room where they were given a preliminary cleaning. Registry numbers were written with waterproof India ink on a portion of the object previously painted with shellac. The shellac prevented the ink from soaking into the object, furnished a good writing surface, and made it possible to remove the number in a moment. From the registry room objects were sent to the drafting department. If a clay pot, for example, was of a new type, a scale drawing was made on graph paper. Measurements of the top, greatest diameter, base, height, color of the glaze, if any, the quality and texture of the body, and the quality of the workmanship were recorded on paper with the drawing. When the drafting department had completed its work, the materials were placed on the storage shelves, grouped according to type for division with the Iraq government, and eventually shipped to museums. Today, the steps of a dig remain basically the same, although specific techniques vary.

Select the statement that best expresses the main idea of the passage.

_____ a. For a number of years, archaeologists have used basically the same procedure when conducting a dig.

_____ b. Neilson C. Debevoise developed the commonly accepted procedure for organizing a dig.

_____ c. Archaeologists take great care to assure that all excavated objects are properly identified.

_____ d. A great deal of important historical and archaeological information can be provided by a dig.

Passage 3

A summit is not any old meeting between two heads of state. Potentates have been visiting each other since the beginning of time. The Queen of Sheba came to visit King Solomon and exchanged riddles with him. Mark Antony came to visit Cleopatra and stayed on. Royalty, presidents, and prime ministers of allied nations have sometimes gotten together after a victorious war to divide the spoils, as they did at the Congress of Vienna in 1814 and then at Paris after World War I. But a summit, in the sense in which Winston Churchill introduced the word into the language when he called for one in 1950, is something quite different and quite specific: it is a meeting between the leaders of two or more rival enemy Great Powers trying to satisfy their mutual demands and head off future conflict.

Write a sentence that expresses the main idea of the passage.

_____

_____

Passage 4

Through most of the time we are growing from infancy to adulthood, we are told that we have to do certain things: "You have to go to school," "You have to go to bed now." Most people seem to spend the rest of their lives thinking that they "have to" do the things that they do: "I have to go to work," "I have to go to the dentist." Initially, it may seem like mere rhetoric, but you don't have to do anything. Next time you find yourself on the verge of saying "I have to…," try replacing it by "I choose to…," "I want to…," "I've decided to." It's incredibly liberating! Reminding yourself that you do things by choice gives you the sense that you are in control of your life.

Write a sentence that expresses the main idea of the passage.

_____

_____

Passage 5

The police and emergency service people fail to make a dent. The voice of the pleading spouse does not have the hoped-for effect. The woman remains on the ledge—though not, she threatens, for long.

I imagine that I am the one who must talk the woman down. I see it, and it happens like this.

I tell the woman about a man. He was a wealthy man, an industrialist who was kidnapped and held for ransom. It was not a TV drama; his wife could not call the bank and, in twenty-four hours, have one million dollars. It took months. The man had a heart condition, and the kidnappers had to keep the man alive.

Listen to this, I tell the woman on the ledge. His captors made him quit smoking. They changed his diet and made him exercise every day. They held him that way for three months.

When the ransom was paid and the man was released, his doctor looked him over. He found the man to be in excellent health. I tell the woman what the doctor said then—that the kidnap was the best thing to happen to that man.

Maybe this is not a come-down-from-the-ledge story. But I tell it with the thought that the woman on the ledge will ask herself a question, the question that occurred to the kidnapped man. He wondered how we know that what happens to us isn't good.

Passage 5 is a parable; a short story designed to illustrate or teach a lesson about life. This lesson is the main idea of the parable. Write a sentence that expresses the main idea of this passage.

_____

_____

If you are having trouble identifying the main idea, try answering these comprehension questions about the story.

1. **T / F**   The woman on the ledge thinks her life is going badly.

2. **T / F**   People think that being kidnapped is a bad thing to happen to someone.

3. **T / F**   Being kidnapped was bad for the man in the story.

Read the passage below to identify the most important ideas.

Passage 6: Main Idea and Prose Summary

Recent research led by Andrew Whiten, a scientist at the University of St Andrews in Scotland who studies primate behavior, provides evidence suggesting that chimpanzees, like humans, desire to conform to the behavior of others in their social group. Whiten, with British and American colleagues, studied three groups of captive chimpanzees at the Yerkes National Primate Research Centre in Atlanta, Georgia, USA. They investigated the ways in which the chimpanzees learned to use a tool to get food trapped behind a blockage in a network of pipes called "pan-pipes."

The scientists presented the same problem to two high-ranking females from two different groups of chimpanzees. Food they wanted was placed just out of reach, behind a blockage, within pan-pipes. The females were each taught a different way to solve the problem. Erika was taught to use a stick to lift the blockage so the food would fall towards her. Georgia was taught to use a stick to poke the blockage until it pushed the food backwards, rolled down another pipe and out into her hand.

When they had mastered their lessons, Erika and Georgia rejoined their own groups of chimpanzees, which were kept separate from each other. Each of the two females demonstrated what she had learned to the other chimpanzees in her group, who gathered around her to observe what she was doing. Most chimpanzees in each of these groups soon began using the particular technique they had been shown, either lifting or poking.

Unexpectedly, some of the members of the first two groups did independently learn how to extract the food using the technique used by the other group. That is, some in Erika's group taught themselves the poking technique and some in Georgia's, the lifting technique. However, according to Whiten, when the pan-pipes were taken away for two months and then re-introduced to the two groups of chimps, all the chimps in each group reverted to their group's normal way of doing things. They conformed to tradition. This was true even for the animals in the lifting group, some of whom gave up the poking technique, which is actually a more natural movement for chimpanzees than is lifting.

The researchers are intrigued by this evidence of members of a non-human species conforming to a group norm, even when they are capable of using an alternative technique that is typical for another group. They believe this suggests that the tendency of humans to conform to others in their social group, which is the hallmark of culture, may have ancient origins and that further research into primate culture could provide insights into why people prefer to do one thing rather than another simply because their colleagues are doing it.

1. Imagine you are part of a study group in a psychology class. You have agreed to read this passage and write a one-paragraph summary of it for your study group. You will begin your summary paragraph with a sentence that is the main idea of the entire passage that you have read. Circle the letter next to the sentence below that expresses the main idea.

   a. Recent research shows that female chimpanzees play an important role in teaching members of their social group.

   b. Findings of an international team of primatologists provide evidence that some groups of chimpanzees are more intelligent than others.

c. Primate researchers have found that it is difficult to teach chimpanzees new methods to solve problems when they already have a method that works.

d. A recent study suggests that chimpanzees, like humans, want to behave like others in their social group.

2. Now, you will continue your summary. First, however, check your answer to Question 1 with your classmates. Use the answer to Question 1 as the first sentence of your paragraph. Choose six more sentences from the choices below to complete your summary. Put a check (✔) next to the six sentences that express the most important ideas from the passage. Do not check sentences that express ideas not found in the passage or ones that present minor ideas.

_____ **a.** Two chimpanzees, Erika and Georgia, were taught two different methods to solve a single problem.

_____ **b.** Chimpanzees cannot learn different ways to get food that is trapped in pipes.

_____ **c.** Chimpanzees like using tools.

_____ **d.** Erika and Georgia taught the others in their social groups how to get the trapped food.

_____ **e.** Most chimpanzees in each group used the method they had learned from their female leader.

_____ **f.** Some chimpanzees in each group taught themselves the method used by the other group.

_____ **g.** After some time passed, however, all chimps in Erika's group used her method and all chimps in Georgia's group used her method.

_____ **h.** Erika's lifting method is not a natural motion for chimpanzees.

_____ **i.** Research shows that chimpanzees are intelligent and can use tools.

_____ **j.** This study suggests that humans' interest in conformity may have ancient origins.

Paragraph Analysis
Reading for Full Understanding

The previous exercise and the one in Unit 1 require you to determine the main idea of a passage. This exercise and the one in Unit 7 require much more careful reading. Each selection is followed by a number of questions. The questions are designed to give you practice in:

1. determining the main idea

2. understanding supporting details

3. drawing inferences

4. guessing vocabulary items from context

5. using syntactic and stylistic clues to understand selected portions of the paragraphs

Read each passage carefully. Try to determine the author's main idea while attempting to remember important details. For each of the multiple-choice questions below, select the best answer. You may refer to the passage to answer the questions.

Example

1	It is not often realized that women held a high place in southern European societies in the tenth
2	and eleventh centuries. As a wife, the woman was protected by the setting up of a dowry or
3	decimum. Admittedly, the purpose of this was to protect her against the risk of desertion, but
4	in reality its function in the social and family life of the time was much more important. The
5	decimum was the wife's right to receive a tenth of all her husband's property. The wife had the
6	right to withhold consent in all transactions the husband would make. And more than just a right:
7	the documents show that she enjoyed a real power of decision, equal to that of her husband. In no
8	case do the documents indicate any degree of difference in the legal status of husband and wife.
9	The wife shared in the management of her husband's personal property, but the opposite was not
10	always true. Women seemed perfectly prepared to defend their own inheritance against husbands
11	who tried to exceed their rights, and on occasion they showed a fine fighting spirit. A case in point
12	is that of María Vivas, a Catalan woman of Barcelona. Having agreed with her husband Miró to
13	sell a field she had inherited, for the needs of the household, she insisted on compensation. None
14	being offered, she succeeded in dragging her husband to the scribe to have a contract duly drawn
15	up assigning her a piece of land from Miró's personal inheritance. The unfortunate husband was
16	obliged to agree, as the contract says, "for the sake of peace." Either through the dowry or through
17	her determination, the Catalan wife knew how to win herself, within the context of the family, a
18	powerful economic position.

1. A *decimum* was…

    _____ **a.** the wife's inheritance from her father.

    _____ **b.** the gift of money to the new husband.

    _____ **c.** an alternative to a dowry.

    _____ **d.** the wife's right to receive one-tenth of her husband's property.

2. In the society described in the passage, the legal standing of the wife in marriage was…

    _____ **a.** higher than that of her husband.   _____ **c.** the same as that of her husband.

    _____ **b.** lower than that of her husband.   _____ **d.** higher than that of a single woman.

3. What compensation did María Vivas get for the field?

    _____ **a.** some of the land Miró had inherited   _____ **c.** money for household expenses

    _____ **b.** a tenth of Miró's land   _____ **d.** money for Miró's inheritance

4. Could a husband sell his wife's inheritance?

    _____ **a.** No, under no circumstances.   _____ **c.** Yes, if she agreed.

    _____ **b.** Yes, whenever he wished to.   _____ **d.** Yes, if his father-in-law agreed.

5. Which of the following is *not* mentioned as an effect of the dowry system?

    _____ **a.** The husband had to share the power of decision in marriage.

    _____ **b.** The wife was protected from desertion.

    _____ **c.** The wife gained a powerful economic position.

    _____ **d.** The husband was given control over his wife's property.

Explanation

1. (d) This is a restatement of a part of the passage. If you did not remember the definition of the word *decimum*, you could have scanned* for it quickly and found the answer in Lines 4 and 5.

2. (c) This is the main idea of the passage. The high place of women in the society is introduced in the first sentence. In lines 6 and 7 the author states that a woman enjoyed a legal power of decision equal to that of her husband. The last sentence tells us that, within the context of the home, women held a powerful economic position.

3. (a) This tests your understanding of details. In Lines 14, 15, and 16, the author states that María Vivas forced her husband to agree to a contract giving her a piece of land from his inheritance.

4. (c) This is an inference. In Lines 6 and 7 the author states that the wife could refuse to agree to any business agreements the husband might want to make. Thus, we can infer that a husband could only sell his wife's inheritance if she agreed. Furthermore, in Lines 12 and 13 the fact that María Vivas allowed her husband to sell a field she had inherited indicates that her agreement was necessary.

---

*For an introduction on scanning, see Unit 1.

5. (d) Items a, b, and c serve as a summary of the ideas of the passage.

   (a) Lines 7 and 8 tell us that wives enjoyed a real power of decision; Lines 9 and 10 state that a wife shared in the management of her husband's estate.

   (b) Lines 3 and 4 state that the purpose of the dowry was to protect wives from desertion.

   (c) The final sentence states that, within the context of the family, the wife was able to win a powerful economic position.

   (d) Nowhere does it state that a husband was given control over a wife's property, and in several instances the opposite is stated (see Questions 3 and 4).

Passage 1

    1   Linguists believe that the languages of about one-third of the human race all developed from one
    2   Indo-European language. But who were the speakers of this ancient language? Linguistic detective
    3   work offers some clues. It is sometimes said that you can deduce a people's history from the words
    4   they use. Study of some fifty ancient vocabularies has led to a reconstruction of the lifestyle of
    5   the first Indo-Europeans, a vanished people. From the words they used, it seems likely that they
    6   lived a half-settled, half-nomadic existence. They had horses, oxen, and sheep. They plowed,
    7   planted, worked leather, and wove wool. They worshipped gods who are clear ancestors of Indian,
    8   Mediterranean, and Celtic deities. However, exactly who the original Indo-Europeans were and
    9   when they lived remains a hotly debated mystery. According to an early theory, they lived in
   10   Mesopotamia, but this idea was exploded by nineteenth-century archaeology. Today, some argue
   11   for the Krugan culture of the Russian steppes, others for the farming culture of the Danube valley.
   12   The most widely accepted theory locates the Indo-Europeans in a cold, northern climate where
   13   common words for snow and wolf were important. None of these prehistoric languages had a
   14   word for the sea. From this, and from our knowledge of nature, it is clear that the Indo-Europeans
   15   must have lived somewhere in northern central Europe.

---

1. What would be a good title for this passage?

    _____ a. In Search of Ancient Indo-Europeans   _____ c. Prehistoric Lifestyles in Europe

    _____ b. The Mistakes of Early Archaeologists   _____ d. Prehistoric Vocabularies

2. According to the author, what has helped us understand the lifestyle of the original Indo-Europeans?

    _____ a. studying their writings   _____ c. studying their gods

    _____ b. studying prehistoric languages   _____ d. studying ancient climate data

3. None of the prehistoric languages studied had a word for sea. According to the passage, what kind of information about the Indo-Europeans does this provide?

    _____ a. information about where they lived

    _____ b. information about how they traveled

    _____ c. information about when they lived

    _____ d. information about what gods they worshipped

4. What does *exploded* mean in Line 10?

_____ **a.** developed   _____ **c.** explained

_____ **b.** strengthened   _____ **d.** disproved

5. According to the passage, what was one thing that nineteenth-century archaeology showed?

_____ **a.** that the Krugan culture began in Mesopotamia

_____ **b.** that the first Indo-Europeans did not live in Mesopotamia

_____ **c.** that the earliest Indo-Europeans lived in Mesopotamia

_____ **d.** that there was a disastrous explosion in ancient Mesopotamia

6. What do some people think that the Krugan culture might be?

_____ **a.** a tribe that lived in Mesopotamia   _____ **c.** the original Indo-Europeans

_____ **b.** a farming culture in the Danube valley   _____ **d.** a tribe that lived near a sea

7. Where do you think this passage probably appeared?

_____ **a.** in an article meant for a general audience   _____ **c.** in an article for specialists in archaeology

_____ **b.** in an article meant for linguists   _____ **d.** in an article for specialists in history

Passage 2

1 Fifty volunteers were alphabetically divided into two equal groups, Group A to participate in
2 a seven-week exercise program, and Group B to avoid deliberate exercise of any sort during those
3 7 weeks. On the day before the exercise program began, all 50 men participated in a step-test. This
4 consisted of stepping up and down on a 16-inch bench at 30 steps per minute for 5 minutes. One
5 minute after completion of the step-test, the pulse rate of each subject was taken and recorded. This
6 served as the pretest for the experiment. For the next 7 weeks, subjects in the experimental group
7 (Group A) rode an Exercycle (a motor-driven bicycle-type exercise machine) for 15 minutes each
8 day. The exercise schedule called for riders to ride relaxed during the first day's ride, merely holding
9 on to the handlebars and foot pedals as the machine moved. Then, for the next 3 days, they rode
10 relaxed for 50 seconds of each minute, and pushed, pulled, and pedaled actively for 10 seconds of
11 each minute. The ratio of active riding was increased every few days, so that by the third week it
12 was half of each minute, and by the seventh week the riders were performing 15 solid minutes of
13 active riding.
14   At the end of the seven weeks, the step-test was again given to both groups of subjects, and
15 their pulses taken. The post-exercise pulse rates of subjects in the experimental group were found
16 to have decreased an average of 30 heart beats per minute, with the lowest decrease 28 and the
17 highest decrease 46. The pulse rates of subjects in the control group remained the same or changed
18 no more than 4 beats, with an average difference between the initial and final tests of zero.

1. How many people were in each group?

_____ **a.** 100   _____ **b.** 50   _____ **c.** 25   _____ **d.** 15

2. The step-test was given…

_____ **a.** after each exercise period.

_____ **b.** at the beginning and at the end of the seven-week period.

_____ **c.** only once, at the beginning of the seven-week period.

_____ **d.** twice to the men in Group A and once to the men in Group B.

3. When were pulse rates taken?

_____ **a.** after each exercise period

_____ **b.** every day

_____ **c.** after the step-tests

_____ **d.** every time the ratio of active riding was increased

4. The exercise schedule was planned so that the amount of active riding…

_____ **a.** increased every few days.

_____ **b.** varied from day to day.

_____ **c.** increased until the third week and then was kept constant.

_____ **d.** increased every exercise period.

5. What did Group A do in their program?

_____ **a.** They stepped up and down on a bench each day.

_____ **b.** They pushed and pulled on exercise handles every day.

_____ **c.** They rode on an Exercycle every day.

_____ **d.** They refrained from any exercise.

6. The post-exercise pulse rates of Group B were found on the average to have…

_____ **a.** not changed.   _____ **c.** gone down 30 beats per minute.

_____ **b.** gone down 28 beats per minute.   _____ **d.** gone down 4 beats per minute.

7. This passage implies that…

_____ **a.** most people do not get enough exercise.   _____ **c.** regular exercise can strengthen your heart.

_____ **b.** a high pulse rate is desirable.   _____ **d.** everyone should exercise 15 minutes a day.

Passage 3

1   It is often said that women are more talkative than men. This widely-held view appeared to gain
2   scientific support several years ago with the publication of the best-selling book, *The Female*
3   *Brain*. The author, Dr. Louann Brizendine of the University of California at San Francisco, wrote
4   that, on average, a man speaks about 7,000 words a day while a woman speaks about 20,000,
5   nearly three times as many. This statistic was widely reported in newspapers and magazines and
6   on radio and television.

7   A year later, an article published in the journal *Science* challenged the stereotypes of the talkative
8   woman and the silent man. The authors had heard Brizendine's claim but could find no prior
9   research to support it. They realized they already had collected data that could be used to examine
10 whether the 7,000–20,000 figures were accurate. As part of another project, they had recorded
11 natural conversations of 396 college students. Small microphones placed on the students recorded
12 their speech periodically throughout the day for a number of days. The students did not know
13 when the recorders were running. From this sample, the researchers estimated how many words
14 each student used in a day.

15 The researchers were surprised by their findings. They had always doubted there was a
16 difference as large as Brizendine claimed, but they expected to find that women talk more than
17 men. However, they found no statistically significant difference. The men averaged 15,669 words
18 a day and the women 16,215. The three most talkative people were men, one who spoke 47,000
19 words a day. The least talkative was a man who used 700. In part because of this study, Brizendine
20 has omitted the 7,000–20,000 statistic from newer editions of *The Female Brain*.

Use the information from the paragraphs to complete the table below. The first row of the first section has been filled in as an example.

Are women more talkative than men?	
Example: What many people believe	*Women speak more than men*
1. What Brizendine believed when she wrote *The Female Brain*	
2. What the researchers believed BEFORE they did their study	
3. What the researchers believed AFTER they did their study	
4. What Brizendine believed AFTER the study published in Science	
How did the researchers conduct their study?	
5. Whom did they record?	
6. Why did they record them?	
7. How did they record them?	
8. How did they calculate the number of words spoken each day? (Hint: What does *sample* mean?]	

Passage 4

1   Recently, researchers at the Karolinska Institute in Stockholm, Sweden conducted an experiment
2   to study one aspect of the relationship between memory and how we breathe. Two dozen healthy
3   male and female volunteers, ages 19 to 25, inhaled 12 different scents from small vials held to their
4   noses. Six of the smells were familiar, such as strawberry, while the other six were obscure, such
5   as 1-butanol. The participants were told to remember each scent. The same people went through
6   this "training session" twice, with different scents in each training session. The first time, after
7   they sniffed the scents, they sat quietly for an hour with their noses clipped shut to force them to
8   breathe through the mouth. The second time, after they sniffed the scents, they sat for an hour
9   with tape over their mouths forcing them to breathe through the nose.

10   After each hour, the participants were exposed to the same scents they had sniffed first, mixed
11   in with 12 new scents (6 familiar and 6 unfamiliar). For each scent, they then had to say whether
12   or not they had sniffed it earlier in the training session. The men and women were consistently
13   much better at recognizing smells from the training session if they had breathed through the
14   nose during the quiet hour. They had more incorrect answers when tested after the hour of
15   breathing through their mouth. The researchers report that nasal breathing, as compared to
16   mouth breathing, appears to enhance memory of odors. Whether this is true for other types of
17   memories remains to be investigated.

Answer the following questions. For items preceded by T / F / N, indicate if the statement is true, false, or there is not enough information to know.

1. What was the main purpose of this study?

    _____ **a.** to investigate which types of smells are remembered most easily

    _____ **b.** to investigate how breathing affects memory of smells

    _____ **c.** to investigate whether men or women have better senses of smell

    _____ **d.** to investigate whether men or women have better memories

2. What does obscure (in the first paragraph) mean?

    _____ **a.** chemical   _____ **b.** strong   _____ **c.** unpleasant   _____ **d.** unfamiliar

3. **T / F / N** Each participant smelled more than 24 scents.

4. **T / F / N** After an hour, participants were better at recognizing familiar scents they had sniffed earlier than unfamiliar scents they had sniffed earlier.

5. **T / F / N** Breathing through their mouths for an hour after "training" seemed to help participants remember smells better.

6. **T / F / N** Women and men participants in this study performed the same way.

7. **T / F / N** We can infer that how we breathe affects how well we remember sounds as well as smells.

UNIT 4

> **BEFORE YOU BEGIN**
>
> Before you read the article below about cities, explore your own ideas about cities by answering the following questions and sharing your ideas with your classmates.

Selection 1A Science Journal

1. How would you describe life in a big city? Put a check (✓) next to all the words that you think describe life in a large city.

   _____ Crowded

   _____ Exciting

   _____ Frightening

   _____ Dangerous

   _____ Full of opportunities (to study and to work)

   _____ Noisy

   _____ Dirty

   _____ Relaxing

   _____ "Green" (good for the environment)

   _____ Expensive

   _____ Lonely

   _____ Modern

   _____ Fashionable

2. In general, do you have a positive or negative attitude toward cities?

3. Did you grow up in a large city or in a small town or in the countryside? What about your grandparents? Where do you think most people in future generations will live?

The article below is taken from a special issue of the journal *Scientific American* about cities. The issue explores global changes in the way we live and changes in how we feel about cities. Read the article, and then do the exercises that follow. Your teacher may want you to do Vocabulary from Context Exercise 1 on pages 95–96 before you begin reading.

Cities: Smarter, Greener, Better
By The Editors

1 It's impossible to know the precise moment it happened. For thousands of years, people lived in the countryside. They worked on farms or in villages and knew little of the world beyond their immediate families and neighbors. Slowly, they began to congregate. It happened in Mesopotamia and Egypt, later in Greece and Rome, and also in Europe and the Americas. More recently, we've seen fast growth in Africa and, even faster growth in Asia. And then, by 2008, according to the United Nations, the number of people who inhabit the world's cities became the majority, for the first time ever.

2 The milestone itself isn't nearly as significant as the trend. In the twentieth century cities grew more than 10-fold, from 250 million people to 2.8 billion. In the coming decades, the UN predicts, the number of people living in cities will continue to rise. By 2050 the world population is expected to surpass nine billion and urban dwellers to surpass six billion. Two in three people born in the next 30 years will live in cities.

3 Not so long ago, many philosophers, architects, and politicians tended to think of cities as centers of poverty, crime, pollution, congestion and poor health. In recent years, though, the thinking has shifted. Many experts have come to realize that people are better off when they live in a city. This is not to dismiss the problems of urban life; cities, particularly fast-growing ones in the poorer parts of Asia and Africa, can be places of great human suffering. But even a city slum has benefits that you won't find on the farm or in the village. The move from the country leads, for instance, to dramatic changes for many women. Kavita N. Ramdas of the Global Fund for Women has written that in the village, there is little opportunity for a woman to do anything besides preparing food and caring for her family. Ramdas says, "If she moves to town, she can get a job, start a business, and get education for her children."

4 Indeed, the city has come to look less like a source of problems than as an opportunity to fix them. Investments in sanitation and water have turned many cities in the developed world from places of disease into centers of health. City folk are at lower risk of death from motor vehicle accidents and suicide by firearms. Cities also make the problem of climate change seem easier to manage. Because city residents rely less on cars and live in more compact dwellings than suburbanites, they tend to leave smaller carbon footprints. The challenge is to extend the efficiency of the urban center to the areas around it. Although climate change is bigger than any one solution, how we build our cities, and how efficiently we live in them, is going to play a large part in our response.

5 The most hopeful impact of city life may be its effect on the mind. Humans are social animals; we draw stimulation from other minds close at hand. Plato and Socrates both lived in fifth-century B.C. Athens, a city-state. Galileo and Michelangelo lived in Renaissance Florence. Steve Jobs and Steve Wozniak grew up in a western US urban area that includes Silicon Valley. The young, creative minds at work on the next Big Thing are probably tweeting—they live in a kind of digital meta city. Chances are, they are living in a physical city, too. Technology is reshaping city life and making it more intellectually productive, but it will not soon replace the easy interchange of ideas that comes from living near our neighbors, the heart of city life.

Comprehension

Answer the following questions according to your understanding of "Cities: Smarter, Greener, Better". Your teacher may want you to answer the questions orally, in writing, or by underlining appropriate parts of the text. True/False items are indicated by a T / F preceding a statement.

1. In the first sentence of this passage, the authors say that no one knows when "it" happened. What do they mean by "it?" _____

2. **T / F**   The proportion of people living in cities is expected to increase.

3. **T / F**   It is predicted that 9 million people will live in cities in 2050.

4. **T / F**   Two-thirds of the world's population will live in cities in 2050.

5. **T / F**   According to the article, cities are viewed more positively by leading thinkers now than they were in the past.

6. What are two advantages of city living for individuals; what are two advantages for society as a whole?

    _____

    _____

7. **T / F**   Kavita N. Ramdas moved from a village to a city to find a job.

8. **T / F**   People living in suburbs have smaller carbon footprints than people living in central cities.

9. What do Plato, Socrates, Galileo, Michelangelo, Steve Jobs, and Steve Wozniak have in common?

    _____

10. What do the authors mean (in paragraph 5) by "the next Big Thing"? _____

11. **T / F**   The authors believe that people are more likely to come up with new ideas when they are living in cities than when they are living in the country.

Discussion/Composition

1. Consider the descriptions you checked in Before You Begin. Were most of them positive or negative? Do you think that most people today have a positive or negative attitude toward cities? Use ideas from the passage and from your experience to support your opinion.

2. The authors of "Cities: Smarter, Greener, Better" mention the comments of Kavita N. Ramdas to argue that living in cities is better for women than living in rural areas. Do you agree? Why or why not?

3. Recently, while campaigning in a rural area in the United States, a candidate for President said his opponent had "New York values." What do you think he meant by that? Why do you think he said that?

4. In "Cities: Smarter, Greener, Better" you read, "Not so long ago, many famous philosophers, architects, and politicians tended to think of cities as centers of poverty, crime, pollution, congestion and poor health." John Lindsay, a former mayor of New York City, wrote in a book about US attitudes toward cities:

In one sense, we can trace all the problems of the American city back to a single starting point: we Americans don't like our cities very much.

That seems impossible. After all, more than three-fourths of us now live in cities, and more are moving to them every year. Nonetheless, it is historically true: in the American psychology, the city was not to be trusted; it was filled with the dishonesty and immorality of Europe. Much of the theory supporting freedom in America was related to the availability of land and the perfectibility of human beings outside the bad influences of the city.

Using information from "Cities: Smarter, Greener, Better" and your own experience, write a letter to Mayor Lindsay and explain to him how attitudes have changed.

Vocabulary from Context

Exercise 1

Both the ideas and the vocabulary in the exercise below are taken from "Cities: Smarter, Greener, Better." Use the context provided to determine the meanings of the italicized words and phrases. Write a definition, synonym, or description in the space provided.

1. _____

2. _____

3. _____

4. _____

5. _____

6. _____

7. _____

8. _____

No one knows the *precise* (1) number of people that live in cities today. Although they don't know the exact number, experts estimate that it is more than 3 billion. Not long ago, most people on earth lived in small towns or rural areas. But now the *majority* (2) of the world's population lives in cities. This is a significant event in the development of civilization. But this *milestone* (3) is not as significant as the *trend* (4), the general direction of change, toward urbanization.

In many cities, housing and roads are now badly overcrowded. This *congestion* (5) can make everyday life difficult for city dwellers. Many people today are excited about benefits that cities can offer our society, but they don't put the problems that cities have out of their mind. They don't *dismiss* (6) urban problems like poverty, congestion, and crime. They know these problems cause great pain, illness, and sadness to many city dwellers and that it will be difficult to end this *suffering* (7).

They know that there is much work needed to make life better for the cities' very poorest citizens, who live in crowded, dirty neighborhoods. There is no easy solution that will make life better for those who live in *slums* (8).

Cities will have to spend money to create a better future, to improve the public health conditions for the poor. Cities in developing countries that have made *investments* (9) in a clean water supply, and other *sanitation projects* (10) have made their cities healthier places than the countryside.

9. _____

10. _____

11. _____

12. _____

13. _____

14. _____

15. _____

Compared to living in the suburbs, living in the city can be better for the environment. People in cities have smaller *dwellings* (11); these more *compact* (12) homes take less energy to heat and cool than large suburban houses. Also, city dwellers can walk to work and shop, or use public transportation, instead of driving miles in their own cars every day.

This means that people who live in cities have smaller *carbon footprints* (13) than people in the suburbs—they put less carbon dioxide into the environment because of their daily activities. So, cities may play an important role in fighting global warming. They can play an important part in our efforts to reduce the amount of carbon dioxide we release into the atmosphere.

An important effect of city life is its *impact* (14) on creative minds. Cities make it easy for people to exchange ideas with each other. They offer an environment filled with excitement and interest that encourages new ideas—an environment that is a *stimulation* (15) for creativity.

Exercise 2

This exercise gives you additional clues to the meaning of vocabulary in context. In the paragraph of "Cities: Smarter, Greener, Better" indicated by the number in parentheses, find the word that best fits the meaning given. Your teacher may want to read these aloud as you quickly scan* the paragraph to find the answer.

1. (1) Which word means *come together; gather*? _____

2. (1) Which word means *live in*? _____

3. (2) Which word means *ten times; 1000%*? _____

4. (2) Which word means *ten-year period of time*? _____

5. (2) Which word means *be greater than; be larger than; exceed; go beyond*? _____

6. (3) Which word in the first half of the paragraph means *changed*? _____

7. (5) Which word means *sharing* or *exchanging*? _____

_____

*For an introduction to scanning, see Unit 1.

Answer the following questions according to the information in the graphic. True/False items are indicated by a T / F preceding a statement. Your teacher may want to read the questions aloud as you scan* to find the answers.

1. At the time of the most recent figures, which continent had the highest percentage of its population living in cities? _____

2. **T / F**   At the time of the most recent figures, Osaka is the 2nd largest city in the world.

3. **T / F**   Shanghai is growing faster than Mumbai.

4. **T / F**   According to the infographic, New York's population decreased between 1975 and 2022.

5. **T / F**   In 2050, Los Angeles and New York will probably be the only US cities among the world's 10 largest cities.

6. Between 1975 and 2009, which cities grew so much that they became one of the 10 largest cities? _____

7. In 2022, how many cities in Africa had a population of more than 10 million? _____

8. Which cities are predicted to appear in the top 10 for the first time in 2050? _____

9. **T / F**   In 2022, the 10 largest urban areas all had a population of at least 10 million.

10. In 2022, which continent was home to more than half of the world's 10 largest cities? _____

11. Which two continents will have the lowest fraction of their population living in cities in 2050? _____

12. **T / F**   The growth of cities is important to a country's economic growth.

13. How are Tokyo and Mexico City unlike all the other cities shown on the map? _____

14. **T / F**   By 2050, every continent will have more people living in cities than outside cities.

15. In areas you are familiar with, can you identify some of the cities indicated by green dots? _____

16. Why do you think so many of the large cities are on, or close to, water? _____

---

*For an introduction to scanning, see Unit 1.

The growth of cities is a global phenomenon. The infographic on pages 98–99 presents information about the world's largest cities and their patterns of population growth.

> **GETTING ORIENTED**

Skim* "Flocking to Urban Spaces: The Global Growth of Cities" to get an understanding of what information is presented. Then answer the questions below.

1. How does the infographic distinguish between cities and countries on the map?

   _____

2. What do the colors mean in the circles on the map?

3. **T / F** In 1975 the population of Paris was larger than that of Moscow.

_____

*For an introduction to skimming, see Unit 1.

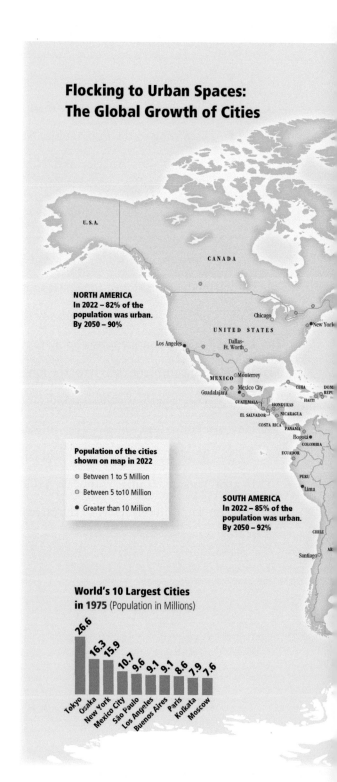

Flocking to Urban Spaces: The Global Growth of Cities

NORTH AMERICA
In 2022 – 82% of the population was urban.
By 2050 – 90%

Population of the cities shown on map in 2022
- Between 1 to 5 Million
- Between 5 to 10 Million
- Greater than 10 Million

SOUTH AMERICA
In 2022 – 85% of the population was urban.
By 2050 – 92%

World's 10 Largest Cities in 1975 (Population in Millions)

26.6 Tokyo
16.3 Osaka
15.9 New York
10.7 Mexico City
9.6 São Paulo
9.1 Los Angeles
9.1 Buenos Aires
8.6 Paris
7.9 Kolkata
7.6 Moscow

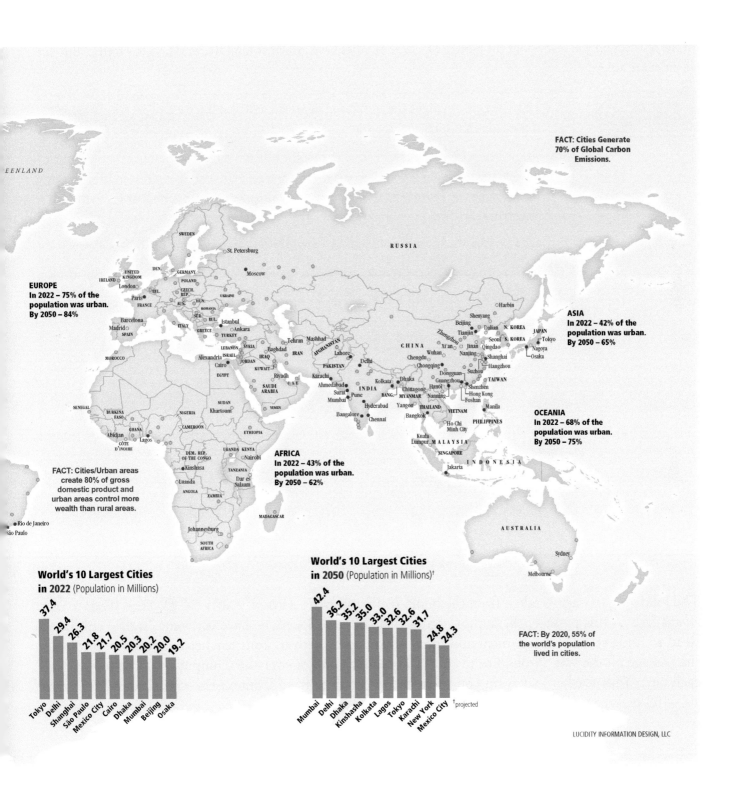

FACT: Cities Generate 70% of Global Carbon Emissions.

EUROPE
In 2022 – 75% of the population was urban.
By 2050 – 84%

ASIA
In 2022 – 42% of the population was urban.
By 2050 – 65%

OCEANIA
In 2022 – 68% of the population was urban.
By 2050 – 75%

AFRICA
In 2022 – 43% of the population was urban.
By 2050 – 62%

FACT: Cities/Urban areas create 80% of gross domestic product and urban areas control more wealth than rural areas.

World's 10 Largest Cities in 2022 (Population in Millions)

City	Population
Tokyo	37.4
Delhi	29.4
Shanghai	26.3
São Paulo	21.8
Mexico City	21.7
Cairo	20.5
Dhaka	20.3
Mumbai	20.2
Beijing	20.0
Osaka	19.2

World's 10 Largest Cities in 2050 (Population in Millions)†

City	Population
Mumbai	42.4
Delhi	36.2
Dhaka	35.2
Kinshasha	35.0
Kolkata	33.0
Lagos	32.6
Tokyo	32.6
Karachi	31.7
New York	24.8
Mexico City	24.3

† projected

FACT: By 2020, 55% of the world's population lived in cities.

LUCIDITY INFORMATION DESIGN, LLC

Reading Selection 2
Sociology

In the last section you read about the growth of cities. As cities have grown around the world, so has traffic. But not all cities are alike.

> **BEFORE YOU BEGIN**

1. Have you ever thought that drivers in another city or country were "crazy?" What is it that made you think so?

2. Below is a list of traffic behaviors. If you are a driver, circle the number that indicates how often you do each one (1 = never, 4 = always). (If you are not a driver, fill this out for someone you know well.) When you are finished, compare your answers with your classmates'.

   a. 1, 2, 3, 4 Flash your headlights at other drivers when they are going too slowly.

   b. 1, 2, 3, 4 Stop for pedestrians when you can see that they are about to cross the street.

   c. 1, 2, 3, 4 Flash your headlights at drivers at night to remind them to turn on their headlights.

   d. 1, 2, 3, 4 Honk your horn at friends when you see them on the street.

   e. 1, 2, 3, 4 Drive above the speed limit.

   f. 1, 2, 3, 4 Go through a red light.

   g. 1, 2, 3, 4 Go through a stop sign without first coming to a full and complete stop.

   h. 1, 2, 3, 4 Drive slowly in the passing lane on the highway.

   i. 1, 2, 3, 4 Honk your horn when traffic isn't moving.

   j. 1, 2, 3, 4 As you approach a traffic signal, speed up when the light turns from green to yellow.

3. Why do you think traffic is different in different cities?

The following passage is taken from the book *Traffic: Why We Drive the Way We Do (and What it Says About Us)*. In this passage, the author argues that different locations have different "traffic cultures." Read to understand this argument and to see if you agree with it. Your teacher may want you to read the passage all the way through or to read it in sections and answer the Comprehension questions for each part. Your teacher may want you to do the Vocabulary from Context Exercises 1 and 2 on pages 107–109 before you begin.

Excerpt from **Traffic as Culture**
By Tom Vanderbilt

1 One of the first things that a visitor notices in a new country is the traffic. This happens in part because foreign traffic, like foreign money or language, represents a different standard. The cars look odd, the road widths may feel unusual, the traffic may drive on the other side of the road, the speed limits may be higher or lower than one is used to, and one may struggle to understand traffic signs that look somewhat familiar but still are difficult to interpret.

2 What is difficult is the *traffic culture*. This is how people drive, how people cross the street, how power relations work in those interactions, what sorts of patterns emerge from the traffic. Traffic is a secret window into the inner heart of a place, a form of cultural expression as vital as language, dress, or music. Traffic culture is the reason a horn in Rome does not mean the same thing as a horn in Stockholm, why flashing your headlights at another driver is understood one way on the German autobahn and quite another way on the freeway in Los Angeles, why people jaywalk constantly in New York and hardly at all in Copenhagen.

3 But what explains this traffic culture? Where does it come from? Why did I, a New Yorker, find the traffic in Delhi, India, so hard to understand? Why does Belgium, a country for all intents and purposes quite similar to neighboring Netherlands, have comparatively riskier roads? Is it the quality of the roads, the kinds of cars driven, the education of the drivers, the laws on the books, the mindset of the people? The answer is complicated. It may be a bit of all of these things. But first, there are two things to understand about traffic.

Traffic Culture is Relative

4 The first thing to recognize is that traffic culture is *relative*, what is crowded in one place is normal in another. One reason Delhi traffic feels intense to outsiders is simple population density: The metropolitan area of Delhi has five times the people in the same space as New York City, a place that already feels pretty crowded. More people, more traffic, more interactions. Another reason Delhi seems so chaotic (to me, at least) is the overwhelming number of vehicle types, all moving at different speeds and in different ways. The forty-eight kinds of transport in Delhi are very different from New York City, which has roughly five: cars, trucks, bicycles, pedestrians, and motorcycles or scooters (with a few horse-drawn carriages and bicycle rickshaws used by tourists). Many places in the United States have only two modes: cars and trucks.

5 According to Geetam Tiware, a professor of civil engineering at the Indian Institute of Technology in Delhi, what may look like anarchy actually has a logic all its own. Far from creating gridlock, she suggests, the system that developed in Delhi can actually move more people at the busiest times than more familiar traffic engineering models would imply. When traffic is moving quickly on two- and three-lane roads, bicycles tend to form an impromptu bike lane in the curb lane; the more bikes, the wider the lane. But when traffic begins to get congested, when the flows approach 2,000 cars per lane per hour and 6,000 bikes per lane per hour, the system undergoes a change. The bicyclists (and motorcyclists) start to integrate, filling in the gaps between cars and buses. Cars slow dramatically, bikes less so. The slowly moving queues grow not only lengthwise but laterally, creating extra capacity from the roads.

6 Delhi challenges expectations. In a study of various locations around Delhi, Tiwarie and a group of researchers found that the sites that had a low conflict rate—that is, fewer places where people are trying to be in the same space—tended to have a high fatality rate, and vice versa. In other words, the seeming chaos functioned to create safety. More conflicts meant lower speeds, which meant fewer chances for fatal crashes. The higher the speeds, the better the car and truck traffic flowed, the worse it was for the bicycles and pedestrians.

Traffic Culture can be More Important than Traffic Laws

7 The second point to understand about traffic is that traffic culture can be more important than laws or infrastructure in determining how local traffic works. In a study a few years ago, a group of researchers examined a number of intersections in Tokyo and a number of comparable intersections in Beijing. Physically, the intersections were essentially the same. But those in Tokyo handled up to *twice* as many vehicles in an hour. What was the difference? The researchers had several ideas. One was that Tokyo had more new and higher-quality vehicles, which could start and stop more quickly. Another was that by contrast with Tokyo, Beijing had many more bicycles. Bicycles, the researchers noted, were often not separate from the main traffic flow, and so weaving bikes caused traffic to slow down.

8 The most important difference had nothing to do with the quality or composition of Beijing's traffic flow; it concerned the behavior of its participants. In Tokyo, signal compliance by cars and pedestrians was, like Japanese culture itself, formal and polite. In Beijing, the researchers observed, drivers (and cyclists and pedestrians) were much more likely to violate traffic signals. People not only entered the intersection after the light had changed, the researchers found, but before.

Traffic Creates its own Culture

9 One key to understanding traffic culture is that laws themselves can explain only so much. As important, if not more so, are the cultural norms, or the accepted behavior of a place. Even when laws are the same, norms help explain why traffic can feel so different in different places. Norms may be cultural, but traffic can also create its own culture. Consider the case of jaywalking in New York City and Copenhagen. In both places, jaywalking, or crossing against the light, is against the law. In both places, people have been ticketed for doing it. But a visitor to either city today will witness a shocking study in contrasts. In New York City, where the term jaywalking was popularized, waiting for the signal is now the sign of someone who doesn't know what they are doing. By contrast, the average Copenhagen resident seems to have an inborn aversion to crossing against the light. Early on a freezing Sunday morning in January, not a car in sight, and they'll refuse to jaywalk.

10 One might think that cultural stereotypes would explain these differences (New Yorkers don't follow rules, people in Copenhagen do). But as we sat in the Copenhagen office of urban planner Jan Gehl, he disagreed with this explanation. His company had recently completed a study of London. "We found it was completely complicated to get across any street. We found that only twenty-five percent of the people actually did what the traffic planner suggested to do," he said. The more you make things difficult for pedestrians, Gehl argued, "the more they start to take the law into their own hands." I thought back to New York City. Was it New York's traffic system, and not New Yorkers themselves, that made the city the jaywalking capital of the United States? Jaywalking helps relieve overcrowded clusters at intersections, Michael King, a traffic engineer in New York City, told me.

11   Worldwide, traffic engineers agree that the longer pedestrians have to wait for a signal to cross, the more likely they are to cross against the signal. The jaywalking tipping point seems to be about thirty seconds. Jake Desyllas, an urban planner, pointed out that on certain streets in London the proportion of people who crossed only during the green light would be 75 percent, but on a neighboring street, the number would be drastically lower. It was not that the culture of people waiting to cross the street changed as they walked one block, but rather that one street-crossing made pedestrians wait much longer than the other. Not surprisingly, the places with signals that made pedestrians wait longer to get across had more people crossing against the light. Between the two London streets, the traffic culture hadn't changed, the infrastructure had.

Where do Traffic Norms Come From? The Litter Experiment

12   Where do traffic norms come from? The simplest answer may be that Romans drive the way they do because *other Romans do*. This idea was expressed in a series of experiments by the psychologist Robert Cialdini. In one study, flyers were placed on windshields of cars in a parking garage; the garage was sometimes clean and sometimes filled with litter. Then a nearby experimenter either littered or simply walked through the garage. They did this when the garage was filled with litter and when it was clean. The researchers found that people, upon arriving at their cars, were less likely to litter when the garage was clean. They also found that subjects were more likely to litter when they observed someone else littering, but *only* if the garage was already dirty.

13   What was going on? Cialdini argues there are two different norms at work: an *injunctive norm*, or the idea of what people should do (the *ought* norm), and a *descriptive norm*, or what people actually do (the *is* norm). While injunctive norms can have an effect, it was the descriptive norm that was clearly guiding behavior here: People littered if it seemed like most other people did. If only one person was seen littering in a clean garage, people were *less* likely to litter—perhaps because the other's act was so clearly violating the injunctive norm.

14   *Who* is violating a norm is also important: Studies of pedestrians have found that walkers are more likely to cross against the light when a "high-status" (i.e., well-dressed) person first does so; they're less likely to cross when that same person doesn't. "Low-status" violators don't influence people either way.

Conclusion

15   Traffic is filled with injunctive norms, telling drivers what to do and what not to do. But the descriptive norm is often saying something else—and saying it louder. Most traffic laws around the world are remarkably similar. Many places have relatively similar roads and traffic markings. But the norms of each place are subtly different, and norms are powerful things.

16   In traffic, norms represent some kind of subtle dance with the law. Laws explain what we ought to do; norms explain what we actually do. The relationship between the two helps us understand why traffic behaves the way it does in different places.

Answer the following questions according to your understanding of the passage. True/False items are indicated by a T / F preceding a statement.

Introduction (paragraphs 1–3)

1. **T / F** Foreign traffic seems foreign because it represents a different standard.

2. Underline the sentence in which the author defines traffic culture.

3. **T / F** The author doesn't believe that traffic culture is as important as cultural expressions like language and music.

4. At this stage in the article, check (✓) those explanations the author says may help to explain traffic culture.

   _____ **a.** The quality of the roads

   _____ **b.** The religion of the drivers

   _____ **c.** The mindset of the people

   _____ **d.** Driver's education

   _____ **e.** How crowded the roads are

   _____ **f.** The kinds of cars driven

Traffic Culture is Relative (paragraphs 4–6)

5. **T / F** Driving in the Netherlands is more dangerous than driving in Belgium.

6. What are two reasons why traffic in Delhi seems "intense" to the author?

   _____

7. **T / F** Geetam Tiware describes traffic in Delhi as anarchy.

8. **T / F** Tiware describes that at the busiest times, the heavy traffic in Delhi creates gridlock.

9. **T / F** When traffic is not too busy in Delhi, bicycles form their own lane.

10. **T / F** Traffic is considered congested in Delhi when there are 2,000 cars per lane per hour.

11. What do bicycles do when the traffic is congested? _____

12. Underline the definition of a "low conflict rate."

13. **T / F** When there is a high conflict rate, there is a high fatality rate.

Traffic Culture can be More Important than Laws (paragraphs 7–8)

14. **T / F** Intersections in Tokyo and Beijing are physically very different.

15. **T / F** Similar intersections in Tokyo handle more vehicles than in Beijing.

16. **T / F** The large number of bicycles in Beijing is the most important difference between traffic there and in Tokyo.

17. How is the traffic culture in Japan different from the traffic culture in China?

_____

_____

Traffic Creates its own Culture (paragraphs 9–11)

18. T / F Cultural norms are less important than traffic laws.

19. T / F In New York jaywalking is against the law.

20. T / F New Yorkers think that jaywalkers don't know what they are doing.

21. T / F Differences in traffic behavior between New Yorkers and people in Copenhagen can be explained by cultural stereotypes.

22. T / F A study in London found that the more difficult things were for pedestrians, the more they violated the law.

23. T / F The jaywalking tipping point of 30 seconds is only true in New York.

Where do Traffic Norms Come From? (paragraphs 12–14)

24. Check (✓) all those statements below that describe the experiment by Robert Cialdini.

_____ **a.** He put flyers on the windshields of cars in a parking garage.

_____ **b.** An experimenter always littered near those cars.

_____ **c.** People were always more likely to litter if they saw someone else litter.

25. Cialdini argues that two kinds of norms explain traffic behavior, the *injunctive norm* and the *descriptive norm*. Below are statements describing these two norms. In the space provided, put I if the statement describes the injunctive norm, D if it describes the descriptive norm.

_____ **a.** What people should do

_____ **b.** What people actually do

_____ **c.** The *is* norm

_____ **d.** The *ought* norm

26. T / F The descriptive norm was more important than the injunctive norm in explaining people's behavior in the littering experiment.

27. T / F In another experiment, pedestrians were less likely to cross against a light if a low-status person did so.

Conclusion (paragraphs 15–16)

28. T / F Traffic cultures differ because traffic laws around the world are so different.

Critical reading

In a text that cites many experts, it is important to be able to tell which generalizations are the author's and which are the experts'. Below is a list of generalizations from the passage. The number in parentheses indicates the paragraph in which the statement can be found. Scan* to see whether one of the experts or the author provided the information. If an expert, write E; if the author, write A.

1. _____ (1) One of the first things that strikes a visitor to a new country is the traffic.

2. _____ (2) [Traffic culture is] how people drive, how people cross the street, how power relations work in those interactions…

3. _____ (5) What may look like anarchy [in Delhi] actually has a logic all its own.

4. _____ (6) Delhi challenges preconceptions.

5. _____ (6) Sites that had a low conflict rate… tended to have a high fatality rate.

6. _____ (7) Traffic culture can be more important than laws or infrastructure in determining how local traffic works.

7. _____ (9) Traffic can also create its own culture.

8. _____ (11) The more you make things difficult for pedestrians… the more they start to take the law into their own hands.

9. _____ (13) There are two different norms at work: an injunctive norm… and a descriptive norm.

10. _____ (16) The relationship between norms and laws explains traffic.

Discussion/Composition

1. Describe situations you have observed in which traffic laws say one thing, but people do something else (that is, where injunctive norms and descriptive norms are different). How would you explain the differences?

2. Describe the different traffic cultures of two different places you are familiar with. Why do you think they are different?

*For an introduction to scanning, see Unit 1.

Vocabulary from Context

Exercise 1: Traffic Vocabulary

All the vocabulary in the exercise below, from "Traffic as Culture," is on the topic of traffic. Use the context provided to determine the meanings of the italicized words. Write a definition, synonym, or description in the space provided.

1. _____
2. _____
3. _____
4. _____
5. _____
6. _____
7. _____
8. _____
9. _____
10. _____
11. _____
12. _____
13. _____
14. _____
15. _____
16. _____
17. _____
18. _____

John likes to walk to work. He likes being a *pedestrian* (1), but he is a *jaywalker* (2). He always steps off the *curb* (3) and crosses in the middle of the street, instead of at the *intersection* (4), and always crosses against the *signal* (5). If the traffic light is red, you will see John crossing the street.

Mary loves to drive fast. She always drives above the speed limit. Because she *violates* (6) the law, the police often stop her for *speeding* (7). They give her a very expensive ticket. But even though she is often *ticketed* (8), Mary still doesn't *comply* (9) with the law. She continues to drive too fast.

Mary doesn't take very good care of her car. When a rock fell on her front window, she never fixed her *windshield* (10). Last year her car broke down on a four-lane highway. Police came with their lights *flashing* (11). They had to stop traffic on two of the *lanes* (12) in order to get her car off the road. Traffic was backed up for so long that some people thought someone had died. Luckily there were no *fatalities* (13), just Mary being careless.

Our town has so much traffic that it is often difficult for cars to move. Although it is often *congested* (14), this is not true all the time. Sometimes traffic is able to move and it *flows* (15) quite easily. But sometimes the situation is even worse. When cars cannot move at all, the *gridlock* (16) can keep people in their cars for a long time. Some drivers become quite angry; one can hear lots of car *horns* (17), even though there is nothing anyone can do. Some people believe that if we improved our travel *infrastructure* (18) things would improve. But others say that building more and better roads will only bring more cars.

Exercise 2

Both the ideas and the vocabulary in the exercise below are taken from "Traffic as Culture." Use the context provided to determine the meanings of the italicized words. Write a definition, synonym, or description in the space provided.

1. _____

2. _____

3. _____

4. _____

5. _____

6. _____

7. _____

8. _____

9. _____

10. _____

11. _____

12. _____

13. _____

14. _____

Traffic behavior can differ greatly from one place to another. What seems *intense* (1) to someone from one culture doesn't cause strong feelings or seem extreme to someone from another. That's because different places have different *standards* (2): different things seem normal and acceptable.

Different locations have different traffic cultures with different *patterns* (3). The way that things are regularly done, the regular system, can be quite different from place to place.

For example, the traffic in small towns seems light, easy to understand and deal with, while the huge number of cars in big cities can seem *overwhelming* (4). It takes a while for a newcomer to see what is going on. But after a while patterns *emerge* (5), norms appear and become known.

Most confusing, it could be argued, are situations where there are no visible signs or official rules to follow. In such cases the patterns seem to be unplanned and unconscious on the part of the participants. Such *impromptu* (6) variations in traffic patterns are completely mysterious for the newcomer.

It isn't known why places can be so different. Why is one place more dangerous, having *riskier* (7) roads? Does it have to do with the cars, the roads?

Could it be the *mindset* (8) of the people, the customary way they think about things?

The answers to these questions are *complicated* (9); there are no simple answers.

While it may appear that there are no rules at all to the traffic in a place that is new to us, the situation is far from *anarchy* (10).

That is, the situation is not without its rules, it is just that the observer is not used to it. What appears to be *chaos* (11) and confusion is local reasoning and ways of thinking.

And this local *logic* (12) can be difficult to understand.

But even though these alternate ways of doing things might seem very unusual for traffic engineers who work in more typical *models* (13), local systems and patterns can be effective and efficient.

One example is India, which *challenges* (14) expectations; it calls into question what a visitor might be expecting. The traffic can seem very intense to a visitor, and it's hard to imagine how bicycles can share the streets with so many cars.

15. _____

16. _____

17. _____

18. _____

19. _____

20. _____

21. _____

22. _____

23. _____

24. _____

25. _____

26. _____

27. _____

But a pattern emerges. When traffic gets very crowded, the bikes begin to *integrate* (15) themselves into the traffic, moving in between the cars and buses.

The lines of cars and bikes begin to slow down. These *queues* (16) grow both lengthwise and *laterally* (17) allowing more bikes to fit in the same space, creating more *capacity* (18) on the road.

Surprisingly, the largest number of serious accidents do not occur at these times when many cars and bikes are trying to be in the same place, with a great deal of *conflict* (19) over who can be where.

Things work differently in Beijing. There the bikes move in and out, moving around the cars. *Weaving* (20) bikes cause problems in the traffic patterns.

In Denmark people hate to break the rules; they seem to have an *aversion* (21) to crossing against the light.

In New York pedestrians don't like to wait for a traffic light to change. But like people all over the world they will wait for a small amount of time. There can be small increases in how long people will wait. But as in many parts of the world, behavior changes, that is, the *tipping point* (22) seems to be about 30 seconds. Once that waiting time is reached, people cross against the light.

Thus, although it seems that jaywalking has no rules, research shows that it does. While traffic norms are difficult to notice and more difficult to describe, they represent *subtle* (23) understandings on the part of the local community.

One group of researchers did an experiment to study when people violated norms and when they followed the law. They watched people walk through a clean garage or a garage filled with *litter* (24).

When people saw small bits of garbage like paper and cans and bottles on the floor and saw someone else *littering* (25), they were more likely to throw things on the ground themselves.

Seeing what other people did seemed to affect and direct what people did. What other people did seemed to *guide* (26) behavior.

It also mattered who did the behavior. If people saw a well-dressed person who seemed to have a high position, they were more likely to do what the high-*status* (27) person did.

Exercise 3: Quantitative Vocabulary

"Traffic as Culture" includes vocabulary that is commonly used in texts that describe numerical data. Use the context provided to determine the meanings of the italicized words. Note that a word may appear more than once in a paragraph. Be sure to read each paragraph through. Then write a definition, synonym, or description in the space provided.

1. _____

2. _____

3. _____

4. _____

5. _____

6. _____

7. _____

Kristin was able to enjoy her dinner in *relative* (1) quiet. She could still hear some traffic noise when she closed the windows, but compared to having the windows open, her apartment was much less noisy. Many cities are trying to reduce the density of traffic in the central business district. They want to reduce problems caused by so many cars in so little space. They are encouraging people to use busses and trains. Reducing the *density* (2) of traffic will mean fewer traffic jams and less air pollution.

Traffic planners don't know exactly how long people will wait to cross an intersection, but they say it is *roughly* (3) seconds.

It doesn't always happen, but drivers *tend to* (4) slow down when it's raining heavily.

My cousin Vinny enjoys testing the law. He knows that the police will not stop you if you are within 5 miles per hour (mph) of the speed limit, so he drives through town at speeds *approaching* (5) 40 mph! Because the speed limit is 35mph, he knows he will not get a ticket.

The number of people riding bicycles to work rose *dramatically* (6) in just 5 years.

In 2017, there were only about 200 bike commuters. Then the city built special bike lines, and by 2022 there more than 3,000 people riding to work. Florida police give traffic tickets at a *rate* (7) ten times greater than Montana police. For example, over a recent holiday weekend they handed out 100 tickets, compared to Montana, where police gave out 10 tickets.

Figurative Language and Idioms

This exercise is designed to give you additional clues to understand the meanings of vocabulary in context, in this case figurative language and idioms. In the paragraph in "Traffic as Culture" indicated by the number in parentheses, find the phrase that best fits the meaning given. Your teacher may want to read these aloud as you quickly scan* the paragraph to find the answer.

1. (2) What word means *important, necessary?* _____

2. (3) What phrase means *in effect, in practice, in truth, for all practical purposes?*_____

3. (3) What phrase means *official, formal, written down?*_____

4. (9) What phrase means *cannot explain everything?*_____

5. (9) What word means *see, observe, notice?* _____

6. (9) What phrase means *an example of difference?*_____

7. (10) What phrase means *don't follow the law, violate/disobey the law?*_____

8. (10) What phrase means *the city with the most jaywalkers?*_____

9. (11) What word means *extremely, dramatically?*_____

Vocabulary Review

In each line, circle the word that is not similar in meaning.

1. danger	logic	risk	
2. easily	shockingly	dramatically	
3. relatively	dramatically	drastically	
4. roughly	laterally	approximately	
5. gridlock	congestion	capacity	crowding
6. anarchy	tipping point	chaos	disorder
7. standard	norm	model	aversion
8. pattern	model	density	system

---

*For an introduction to scanning, see Unit 1.

Reading Selections 3A–3B
Psychology

BEFORE YOU BEGIN

Taking multiple-choice tests is part of every student's life. Here is a one-question test of your knowledge about how to take such tests. After you answer the question, your teacher may want you to compare your answer with your classmates' and discuss the reasons you answered as you did.

1. You are taking a difficult multiple-choice test. You finish the test and there is still some time left, so you check your answers. For the last test question, you chose "b" as the answer. But now that you look again, you are not sure "b" is correct. "c" seems like a better answer, but you are not completely sure about that either. What should you do?

   a. Do not change your answer to "c" because your first guess is usually correct.

   b. Change your answer to "c" because "c" is the best guess in multiple-choice questions.

   c. Change your answer to "c" because it now looks like a better answer than "b."

   d. Change your answer to "a" because you can't decide between "b" and "c."

Selection 3A   Textbook

The following selection from a college psychology textbook discusses research on how to take multiple-choice tests. Your teacher may want you to do Vocabulary from Context Exercise 1 on pages 115–116 before you begin.

Myth or Reality? When Taking Tests, Stick with Your First Instinct

1   Double-check your answers, but only change an answer if you misread the question or found something in the test that indicates your first answer was incorrect. Otherwise stick with your first guess because research shows it's usually the right answer (Hutton, 2009; *Education.com*, 2009).

2   Does this advice sound familiar? Many websites that offer test-taking tips give similar advice: If you're unsure about your initial answer, "stick with your first instinct." In other words, if you change answers, you're more likely to switch a right answer to a wrong one than a wrong answer to a right one. Most students and many instructors agree with this claim: They believe that changing answers will more likely lower than raise exam scores (Kruger et al., 2005).

What Happens When Students Switch Answers?

3   In 1929, C.O. Mathews analyzed almost 40,000 answers that college students marked on multiple-choice and true-false tests. Of the answers students had changed, switching from wrong to right was far more common (59 percent of switches) than switching from right to wrong (27 percent of switches).

The remaining switches were from one wrong answer to another wrong answer. Decades later, psychologists reviewed 33 studies on this topic and concluded that in every study "(a) the majority of answer changes are from incorrect to correct and (b) most students who change their answers improve their test scores" (Benjamin et al., 1984).

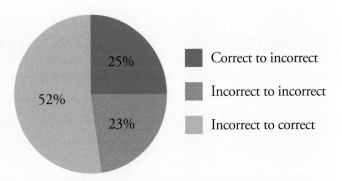

FIGURE 1. Changing answers on multiple-choice tests
Researchers analyzed the eraser marks on 6,412 exams taken by introductory psychology students. Contrary to popular wisdom, changing one's answer was twice as likely to result in gaining points than in losing points. Source: Based on Kruger et al., 2005

4 More recently, psychologists Justin Kruger, Derrick Wirtz, and Dale Miller (2005) obtained similar findings in a study of 1,561 college students. By a 2:1 ratio, more changed answers went from wrong to right than from right to wrong, and by nearly a 3:1 ratio more students who changed answers ended up with higher rather than lower exam scores (Figure 1). Yet most students still believed that as a general test-taking strategy, changing answers was harmful. Kruger et al. called this "the first instinct fallacy."

Conclusions

5 Based on available evidence, "stick with your first instinct" appears to be more myth than reality. If upon reflection you have doubts about an initial exam answer and think that another answer is more likely to be correct, don't be afraid to change it. This doesn't guarantee that on any single exam, or even over the long haul, you'll be better off switching answers. Guarantees like that don't exist. Odds are that being willing to switch answers will benefit you in the long run, but some students do obtain lower scores by switching. What you can do is gather your own evidence from several exams. Act like a scientist. For exam items you were unsure about, note whether you "stayed" or "switched." How often did each strategy help or hurt your score? Keep a tally of the outcomes, and then you'll have some personal evidence to guide your future test-taking strategy.

Comprehension

Answer the following questions according to information in the textbook selection. True/False items are indicated by a T / F preceding a statement.

1. **T / F** "Myth or Reality" (in the title) is similar in meaning to "True or False."

2. What is the "first instinct fallacy?"

_____

3. Textbooks often summarize the views and findings of many different researchers and writers. Below is a list of people and sources mentioned in this reading selection. Put an X in the appropriate column to show what each of them believes, according to this textbook.

	If you are not sure about your answer, it is best to stick with your first answer.	If you are not sure about your first answer, don't be afraid to change it.
Hutton		
Many test-taking websites		
Mathews		
Benjamin et al.		
Kruger, Wirtz, & Miller (2005)		
Most students		
Many teachers		

4. **T / F** Research conducted after 1929 showed that Mathews' research findings were wrong.

5. **T / F** There have been more than 30 studies on what happens when students change their answers on tests.

6. How did Kruger et al. know which test questions students had changed their answers to?

_____

7. **T / F** Kruger et al. found that changing a correct answer to an incorrect answer happened only about half as often as changing an incorrect answer to a correct answer.

8. **T / F** The authors of this textbook only summarize the research of others; they do not say what they believe about how to take a test.

9. **T / F** The test-taking tips on *Education.com* are based on research findings.

Discussion/Composition

1. **a.** If it is a myth that changing an answer to a test question is bad, why do you think so many people believe this myth?

   b. Read the explanation below, offered by researchers Kruger et al. Does this explanation make sense to you? Do the evidence and reasoning convince you?

   Imagine you are looking at the results of a test you took:

   Question #1: You got this one wrong. During the test, you thought about changing your answer—to the right answer— but you didn't. You stayed with your first answer and got the question wrong.

   Question #2: You got this one wrong, too. The first answer you chose was correct, but you changed it to the wrong answer. You changed your first answer and got the question wrong.

   Which would make you feel worse?

   Kruger et al. (2005) found that many students would feel worse about what happened with Question 2. It was painful and frustrating to them to think they had a question right until they changed their answer.

These negative feelings can affect how we remember. They make us remember the times we changed to wrong answers more clearly than we remember the times we changed to right answers. Remembering one thing more than another is a type of memory bias. It leads us to wrongly conclude that changing answers is a bad idea. We believe the myth. This explanation for the first instinct fallacy is illustrated below.

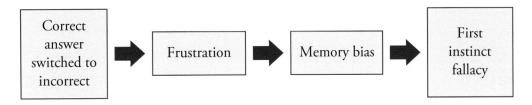

2. Will you take tests differently after reading this textbook selection? Why or why not?

Vocabulary from Context

Exercise 1

Both the ideas and the vocabulary in the exercise below are taken from "Myth or Reality?" Use the context provided to determine the meanings of the italicized words or phrases. Write a definition, synonym, or description in the space provided.

1. _____ Many people believe that money brings happiness, but this is a *myth* (1).

2. _____ Andy suggested that his family try a new restaurant for dinner, but they said they wanted to *stick with* (2) their favorite one.

3. _____ Their *initial* (3) plan was to go swimming, but when it rained, Katie and Eric decided to go to a movie instead.

4. _____ I like to sit next to the window of the plane but my seat is on the aisle. Would you be willing to *switch* (4) seats with me?

5. _____ John gave me advice on how to buy a car; his *tips* (5) saved me a lot of time and money.

6. _____ Amanda doesn't spend a lot of time thinking about what to do; she just follows her *instincts* (6).

7. _____ Many people believe that swimming right after eating is dangerous, but this is a *fallacy* (7).

8. _____ Rising sea levels, warming oceans, and strong storms are *evidence* (8) of global warming.

9. _____ I thought I made a good decision when I took this job, but then I thought about it some more. *Upon reflection* (9), I think I should have stayed in school.

10. _____   All Computer Universe stores *guarantee* (10) that they have the lowest prices for laptop computers. They promise to give you your money back if you find the same computer for a lower price at another store.

11. _____   The chances of winning the lottery are very small. Even if you buy 1000 tickets, *odds* (11) are that you will lose.

12. _____   The coach made a *tally* (12) of the players' votes to find out who they elected as captain of the team.

13. _____   The result was a surprise. No one expected that *outcome* (13).

Exercise 2

This exercise gives you additional clues to determine the meaning of vocabulary in context. In the paragraph of "Myth or Reality?" indicated by the number in parentheses, find the word or phrase that best fits the meaning given. Your teacher may want to read these aloud as you quickly scan* the paragraph to find the answer.

1. (1) Which word means *if not*? _____

2. (3) Which word means *tens of years*?_____

3. (4) Which word means *results*?_____

4. (4) Which word means *plan, approach*? _____

5. (5) Which two phrases mean *after a lot of time passes, in the future, in the end*? _____

6. (Figure 1) Which phrase means *opposite of* or *unlike common belief; different from what most people think*?

_____

Vocabulary Review

Are these pairs of words and phrases similar in meaning or opposite in meaning? Circle S if similar; circle O if opposite.

1.	**S / O**	fallacy	myth
2.	**S / O**	switch	stick with
3.	**S / O**	over the long haul	in the long run
4.	**S / O**	findings	outcome

---

*For an introduction to scanning, see Unit 1.

BEFORE
YOU BEGIN

Why do people help others? When do they help? What are the factors that contribute to their decision to help or not help?

These are questions that psychologists and sociobiologists attempt to answer. Consider the following situations:

1. You are about to cross a busy street. An elderly woman with a cane is also beginning to cross, but you do not think she will be able to make it before the light changes. What do you do?

   a. Continue on your way.

   b. Look to see if someone else is going to help her.

   c. Ask her if she would like assistance.

   d. Offer her your arm and help her across the street.

2. You are passing a playground and you see a group of teenagers pushing and shoving a smaller boy. He is yelling and crying. What do you do?

   a. Continue on your way.

   b. Yell at the boys to stop.

   c. Call the police.

   d. Pull the boys apart.

Researchers use questions like these to try to understand why people help others. The following passage, taken from a psychology textbook, summarizes research on "prosocial behavior"—behavior in which one individual helps another, also known as *altruism*. You will notice that the authors are building an argument and providing examples and evidence to support their position. Read the passage to understand the main argument. Your teacher may want you to do the Vocabulary from Context Exercise 1 on page 121 before you begin.

When Do People Help?

Prosocial Behavior: Helping Others

1   Helping other people, or *prosocial behavior*, comes in many forms, from performing heroic acts of bravery to tutoring a classmate. Acts of violence are often in the headlines, but we should not lose sight of the mountains of good deeds performed around the world each day.

2   Biological, psychological, and environmental factors all play a role in prosocial behavior (Dovidio et al., 2006). Let's examine a few of these factors.

Evolution and Prosocial Behavior

3   Prosocial behavior occurs throughout the animal world. Evolutionary psychologists and sociobiologists (biologists who study social behavior in humans and other animals) propose that helping behavior has a genetic basis shaped by evolution (Hamilton, 1964). According to the principle of *kin selection*, organisms are most likely to help others with whom they share the most genes, namely, their offspring and genetic relatives. By protecting their kin, prosocial individuals make it more likely that their genes will survive across later generations, and the gene pool of the species increasingly represents the genes of its prosocial members (West et al., 2002). In this manner, over the course of evolution, helping becomes a biologically predisposed response to certain situations. Sociobiologists note that identical twins are more similar in helpfulness than are fraternal twins or non-twin siblings (Rushton, 1989).

Psychological Aspects of Prosocial Behavior

4   But what accounts for the help that humans display toward friends and strangers and that some animal species display toward non-kin (Clutton-Brock, 2002)? Sociobiologists propose the concept of *reciprocal altruism*: helping others increases the odds that they will help us or our kin in return, thereby increasing the chances of the survival of our genes (Trivers, 1971).

5   In some cases kin selection and reciprocal altruism do not explain why people and other animals cooperate. Sociobiologists say that genetic factors only predispose us to act in certain ways. Experience also shapes helping behavior.

Social Learning and Cultural Influences

6   Beginning in childhood, we see helpful models and are taught prosocial norms. The *norm of social responsibility* states that people should help others and contribute to the welfare of society (De Cremer & van Lange, 2001). We receive approval for following these norms, and disapproval when we do not follow them, and we observe other people receiving praise for following these norms. Eventually, we internalize prosocial norms and values as our own.

7   Studies in Europe, Asia, and North America show that socialization matters. Children are more likely to act prosocially when they have been raised by parents who are altruistic, encouraging their children to develop empathy—the ability to put themselves in other people's shoes. However, there are also cross-cultural differences in beliefs about when and why we should help. For example, researchers found that Hindu children and adults in India believe that one has a moral obligation to help friends and strangers, whether their need is serious or mild (Miller et al., 1990). In contrast, when a person's need for assistance is mild, American children and adults view helping as more of a choice than an obligation.

References

Batson, C. D. 1991. *The altruism question: Toward a social-psychological answer.* Hillsdale, NJ: Erlbaum.

Batson, C. D. 2006. "Not all self-interest after all:" Economics of empathy-induced altruism. In D. De Cremer, D. M. Zeelenberg, & J. K. Murnighan (Eds.), *Social psychology and economics.* Mahwah, NJ: Erlbaum.

Cialdini, R.B. 2008. *Influence: Science and practice* (5th ed.). Boston: Allyn & Bacon.

Clutton-Brock, 2002. Breeding together: Kin selection and mutualism in cooperative vertebrates. *Science* 2, 96, 69–72.

Dovidio, J., Piliavin, J., Schroeder, D., & Penner, L. 2006. *The social psychology of prosocial behavior.* Mahwah, NJ: Lawrence Erlbaum.

De Cremer, D. & van Lange, P.A. 2001. Why prosocials exhibit greater cooperation than proselfs: The roles of social responsibility and reciprocity. *European Journal of Personality*, 15, 5–18.

Hamilton, W. D. 1964. "The evolution of social behavior." *J. Theor. Biol,* 7:1–52.

Miller, J. G., Bersoff, D. M., & Harwood, R.L. 1990. Perceptions of social responsibility in India and in the United States: Moral imperatives or personal decisions? *Journal of Personality and Social Psychology,* 58, 33–47.

Rushton, J. P. 1989. Genetic similarity, human altruism, and group selection. *Behavioral and Brain Sciences*, 12, 503–559.

Trivers, R. 1971. The evolution of reciprocal altruism. *Quarterly Review of Biology*, 46, 35–57.

West, S.A., Pen, I., & Griffin, A.S. 2002. Cooperation and competition between relatives. *Science*, 296, 72–75.

Comprehension

Answer the following questions according to your understanding of the passage. True/False items are indicated by a T / F preceding a statement. Some questions may have more than one correct answer. Others require an opinion. Be prepared to defend your choices.

1. What is "human behavior?" _____

2. The authors mention three types of factors that play a role in motivating prosocial behavior. What are they?

   _____   _____

   _____

3. **T / F** Prosocial behavior is observed only in humans.

4. **T / F** Prosocial behavior is passed from generation to generation.

5. **T / F** Research shows that prosocial behavior is found only in Asia.

6. In the text, underline the definition of *reciprocal altruism*.

7. **T / F** If a family regularly helps others, the children are more likely to grow up helping others.

8. Consider this situation: I hear that a friend has broken his leg and needs help with meals, shopping, etc. I decide to help, thinking, "I'd better help out, because one day I may need him to help me." Which factor do you think this shows?

   _____ Genetic   _____ Psychological   _____ Cultural

Critical Reading

Answer the following questions according to your understanding of the passage and your own experience. Be prepared to defend your choices. True/False items are indicated by a T / F preceding a statement.

1. **T / F**   The authors believe that prosocial behavior is a good thing.

2. Which of the following would you consider prosocial behavior?

    _____ Helping a friend get the correct answers during an exam.

    _____ Stopping a fight in a parking lot.

    _____ Reporting suspicious behavior to the police.

    _____ Refusing to lend money to a friend who wants to buy drugs.

    _____ All of the above.

3. Examine the research reported in the passage and answer the following questions.

    a. Why do the authors provide a list of references?

    b. The authors give different perspectives on how to explain altruism.

    • Did any of these convince you more than the others?

    • Did the authors say things that you wanted more information about?

    • Circle statements in the text that you think should have been supported with references to research.

    c. When was the research reported in this passage conducted? What conclusions do you draw from the dates of the references?

    d. How many of the studies are reported in articles? In books? Do you think the difference in publication type is important?

    e. If you were to pick one article to read about the genetics of prosocial behavior from the Reference section of this passage, which one would you choose? Why?

4. Did you enjoy this reading? Did you learn anything valuable from it? If not, to whom should you complain?

Vocabulary from Context

Exercise 1

Both the ideas and vocabulary in the exercise below are taken from "When Do People Help?" Use the context provided to determine the meanings of the italicized words. Write a definition, synonym, or description in the space provided. When more than one form of a word is given, define the last one.

1. _____

2. _____

3. _____

4. _____

5. _____

6. _____

7. _____

8. _____

9. _____

10. _____

11. _____

12. _____

When we try to understand actions such as prosocial behavior we need to take into account many things—the individual's biological and social history and details of the situation itself, for example. These are important *factors* (1) that researchers study.

Friends come and go, but family is always with us. We cannot walk away from *kin* (2) when they are in trouble.

Our families are our first teachers—as we grow up we learn what is expected of us, how to behave, what is considered *normal* (3) in daily behavior and thinking. For example, do we take off our hats or our shoes when we enter a house—or neither? Do we say a prayer before eating? Do we shake hands or kiss when we meet others? These *norms* (4) are what guide us as we grow up.

If helping others is something that your parents and grandparents did, then you are far more likely to help others. You may not even know why you feel the need to help others; that's just the way it is. In such families, everyone is just predisposed to help others.

Some scholars believe that all important aspects of behavior can be explained by biology, by discovering the genetic make-up that is passed down from parents to child. They believe that if we understand the basic biological building blocks of an individual, their *genes* (5), we will understand their behavior.

There are many reasons for prosocial behavior, and not all of them come from your genes. Sometimes it makes sense to help others, because you know at some point you may need help from them. This awareness of the *reciprocal* (6) benefits of altruism may be an important explanation for the frequency of good acts. If you do what others want you to do, you are rewarded. If you do not, you are punished. This is the reason for following the rules of society, rather than *violating* (7) them.

Parents and teachers hope that children will learn the lessons they are taught in school, but they cannot be certain that this will happen. The children will not learn exactly what they are taught. Just as a sculptor *shapes* (8) the clay toward a statue, the best adults can hope for is that they will be able to *shape* (9) the learning and behavior of young people toward the goals of the lesson.

The problem with this sort of research is that the questions are many but the answers are not always clear. Researchers agree that many animals behave in prosocial ways, but they do not agree on the reasons. Because the results are often *ambiguous* (10) we are left with more questions than answers.

How we are raised by our parents and our society also shapes our behavior. Through this process of *socialization* (11) researchers say that we learn to help others from the people we grow up around.

Animals develop over time. We have evolved over the centuries, so if we are going to understand prosocial behavior we need to study humans from our past. But *evolution* (12) by itself will not explain everything. We need to look at biological and sociological factors.

Exercise 2

This exercise gives you additional clues to the meaning of vocabulary in context. In the paragraph of "When Do People Help?" indicated by the number in parentheses, find the word or phrase that best fits the meaning given. Your teacher may want to read these aloud as you quickly scan* the paragraph to find the answer.

1. (2) What word means *something that is done; acts or action*? _____

2. (3) What word means *children*? _____

3. (3) What phrase means *all the genetic information of a particular species*? _____

4. (6) What word means *to take into ourselves, to make something the way you think or behave, to make an idea an important part of who you are*? _____

5. (7) What word means *responsibility or duty, something that is expected of you*? _____

Discussion/Composition

The cartoon below shows one artist's view of human behavior. What is this cartoonist saying about society today? Do you agree or disagree? Give reasons and examples to support what you believe.

---

*For an introduction to scanning, see Unit 1.

Video Clip: Baby Left in Car: Social Experiment

Consider this situation:

It is a hot day in the city. You pass a parked car and hear a baby crying. You stop and look in the window of the car. A baby is alone in the car, strapped into a car seat. What would you do?

The US television program "What Would You Do?" did an experiment to find out. Watch the video to see what they found. Use your smart phone to read the QR code, or access the video with the url:

https://www.youtube.com/watch?v=YwZjhUI81Pw

Comprehension

Answer the following questions according to your understanding of the video clip. True/False items are indicated by a T / F preceding a statement. Some questions may have more than one correct answer. Others require an opinion. Be prepared to defend your choices. Your teacher may want you to answer the questions on your own or in pairs or groups.

1. **T / F**   The baby was never in danger.

2. What was the purpose of the experiment? _____

3. Why didn't the police come when the bystanders called? _____

4. What reasons did people give for not stopping to do something? _____

5. What reasons did they give for doing something? _____

6. What do you think you would have done if you had seen the baby? _____

7. How might the authors of "When do People Help?" explain why some people tried to help the baby: biological, psychological, or social factors? _____

8. At one point, a man helps and then others join him. Do you think the others would have helped if they hadn't seen someone help first? How might the authors of "When do People Help?" explain this?

    _____

    _____

9. How would you have felt if you had been fooled by the experiment? _____

10. Do you believe that the answers to these questions differ for different cultures? _____

UNIT 5

Nonprose Reading

Survey Results

How much does the average person understand about science and technology? Researchers in many countries have surveyed adults to try to find out, asking them questions about "basic ideas of science." The results of some of these surveys, reported on page 125, may surprise you.

> **BEFORE YOU BEGIN**

Before you read about what the researchers discovered, test your own knowledge of general science by answering the questions below. True/False items are indicated by a T / F preceding a statement.

1. **T / F**   The center of the Earth is very hot.

2. **T / F**   The continents have been moving their location for millions of years and will continue to move.

3. Does the Earth go around the Sun, or does the Sun go around the Earth?

4. **T / F**   All radioactivity is made by humans.

5. **T / F**   Electrons are smaller than atoms.

6. **T / F**   Lasers work by focusing sound waves.

7. **T / F**   The universe began with a huge explosion.

8. **T / F**   It is the father's gene that decides whether a baby is a boy or a girl.

9. **T / F**   Antibiotics kill viruses as well as bacteria.

10. **T / F**   Human beings, as we know them today, developed from earlier species of animals.

Compare your answers with those of your classmates. Then, check the answers you see printed upside down below.

		10. T
9. F	8. T	7. T
6. F	5. T	4. F
3. Earth around Sun	2. T	1. T

Do you think most people in the United States would get these questions right? What about people in other countries? After you make your predictions, read on to see what the researchers discovered in their surveys.

What We Know

Researchers in many countries have been conducting surveys for a number of years to investigate people's general scientific knowledge. Though the surveys are not identical to each other, some of the same questions do appear in many of them. Table 1, below, shows how adults surveyed in various countries/regions did in answering the questions you answered in Before You Begin. The numbers in Table 1 represent the percentage of adults surveyed who answered each question correctly.

Skim* Table 1 to get a general idea of what information is presented and how it is organized; then answer the comprehension questions.

TABLE 1. Percentage of correct answers to factual knowledge questions in physical and biological sciences, by region or country: Most recent year

Question	United States (2016)	Canada (2013)	China (2015)	EU (2005)	India (2004)	Israel (2016)	Japan (2011)	Malaysia (2014)	Russia (2003)	South Korea (2004)	Switzerland (2016)
1 *The center of the Earth is very hot.* (True)	85	93	47	86	57	86	84	75	NA	87	NA
2 *The continents have been moving their location for millions of years and will continue to move.* (True)	81	91	51	87	32	86	89	62	40	87	80
3 *Does the Earth go around the Sun, or does the Sun go around the Earth?* (Earth around Sun)	73	87	NA	66	70	86	NA	85	NA	86	NA
4 *All radioactivity is man-made.* (False)	70	72	41	59	NA	76	64	20	35	48	NA
5 *Electrons are smaller than atoms.* (True)	48	58	22	46	30	60	28	35	44	46	39
6 *Lasers work by focusing sound waves.* (False)	45	53	19	47	NA	67	26	30	24	31	NA
7 *The universe began with a huge explosion.* (True)	39	68	NA	NA	34	64	NA	NA	35	67	NA
8 *It is the father's gene that decides whether the baby is a boy or a girl.* (True)	59	NA	49	64	38	72	26	45	22	59	60
9 *Antibiotics kill viruses as well as bacteria.* (False)	51	53	24	46	39	53	28	16	18	30	56
10 *Human beings, as we know them today, developed from earlier species of animals.* (True)	52	74	68	70	56	63	78	NA	44	64	NA

NA = not available; question not asked.

EU = European Union.

Note(s)

EU data include Austria, Belgium, Cyprus, Czech Republic, Denmark, Estonia, Finland, France, Germany, Greece, Hungary, Ireland, Italy, Latvia, Lithuania, Luxembourg, Malta, the Netherlands, Poland, Portugal, Slovakia, Slovenia, Spain, Sweden, and the United Kingdom but do not include Bulgaria and Romania.

---

*For an introduction to skimming, see Unit 1.

Comprehension

Use information from Table 1 and from the section above titled "What We Know" to answer the following questions. For statements preceded by T / F / N, circle T if the statement is true, F if the statement is false, and N if there is not enough information given in the chart to tell whether the statement is true or false. Be prepared to defend your choices.

1 **T / F / N** The questionnaire was given to high school students.

2. **T / F / N** The questionnaire was answered by people in more than 11 countries.

3. **T / F / N** Table 1 shows all of the questions asked in these surveys.

4. **T / F / N** Several thousand people in each country/region were given these surveys.

5. **T / F / N** All the people surveyed had the same number of years of education.

6. **T / F / N** The same survey was used in all these countries/regions.

7. **T / F / N** People in the EU did much better than people in the US.

8. **T / F / N** One country/region was consistently more knowledgeable about basic science facts than all the others.

9. **T / F / N** South Korea started surveying people about their science knowledge before Canada did.

10. **a.** Which question was easiest for people in the US? _____

    b. Which question was most difficult for them? _____

    c. If you are from one of the other countries/regions shown, which question was easiest for people in your home country/region? _____ Which was most difficult? _____

11. Which of the following statements are inferences or conclusions that can be drawn from Table 1? Check (✓) all the correct inferences.

    _____ **a.** Many people in these countries/regions don't understand some basic ideas about science.

    _____ **b.** In general, people in the countries/regions mentioned in Table 1 know more about science than people in many other countries.

    _____ **c.** These research studies were well designed.

Discussion/Composition

1. Is it important that nonscientists understand basic ideas of science? Give reasons and examples from your reading and personal experience to support your opinion.

2. The purpose of these questionnaires was to help researchers measure people's scientific knowledge. Do you think questionnaires like the ones used in these research studies are a good way to measure people's basic scientific knowledge? Why or why not?

3. What do you think it is important to know about science? If you were making up a quiz about important ideas of science, what questions would you include? Make up a quiz like this and test your classmates.

4. For more than 60 years, educators and scientists have used the term *scientific literacy* to describe the knowledge and skills related to science that all adults should have. In the survey you just read about, it was knowledge of scientific facts that was emphasized. Is there more to *scientific literacy* than facts?

Below is a list of some definitions that have been proposed for scientific literacy. Put a check (✓) next to the three that you think are most important for *scientific literacy*. Circle the letter next to the single one that you think best expresses what it means to be scientifically literate. Be prepared to defend your answers.

_____ **a.** Knowledge of basic facts and important concepts of physical and biological science

_____ **b.** The ability to "do" science yourself

_____ **c.** The ability to think scientifically

_____ **d.** The ability to understand articles about science presented in the popular media and to discuss with other people whether they are true

_____ **e.** The ability to tell the difference between science and pseudo-science

_____ **f.** The ability to use scientific knowledge in problem solving

_____ **g.** The knowledge and understanding of scientific concepts and processes required for personal decision making, participation in civic and cultural affairs, and economic productivity

_____ **h.** The ability to evaluate the quality of scientific information based on where it came from, and the methods used to create it

_____ **i.** The ability to express opinions that are scientifically informed

_____ **j.** Appreciating and feeling comfortable with science, and approaching it with wonder and curiosity

Word Study
Context Clues

Exercise 1

In the following exercise do not try to learn the italicized words. Concentrate on developing your ability to guess the meanings of unfamiliar words using context clues.* Read each sentence carefully and write a definition, synonym, or description of the italicized word on the line provided.

1. _____ It is difficult to list all of my father's *attributes* (1) because he has so many different talents and abilities.

2. _____ Mary, the president of the family council, *conferred* (2) upon Robert the title of vice president, because she thought he would do a good job.

3. _____ The main character in the movie was tall, fat, and middle-aged. The supporting actor was older, almost as *plump* (3), and much shorter.

4. _____ When Mark was in one of his *pedantic* (4) moods, he assumed the manner of a distinguished professor and lectured for hours, on minute, boring topics.

5. _____ Many members of the old wealthy families in society held themselves *aloof* (5) from Gatsby, refusing even to acknowledge his existence.

6. _____ I became angrier and angrier as Don talked, but I *refrained* (6) from saying anything.

7. _____ Mr. Doodle is always busy in an *ineffectual* (7) way; he spends hours running around accomplishing nothing.

8. _____ Laura was proud of the neat rows of *chrysanthemums* (8) in her flower beds, which she tended with great care.

9. _____ Most dentists' offices are *drab* (9) places, but Emilio's new office is a bright, cheerful place.

10. _____ The inner and outer events of a plant are interdependent; but this isn't saying that the *skin, cortex, membrane* (10), or whatever you want to call the boundary of the individual, is meaningless.

---

*For an introduction to using context clues, see Unit 1.

Exercise 2

This exercise is designed to give you practice using context clues from a passage. Use your general knowledge along with information from the entire text below to write a definition, synonym, or description of the italicized word on the line provided. Read through the entire passage before making a decision. Note that some of the words appear more than once; by the end of the passage you should have a good idea of their meaning. Do not worry if your definition is not exact; a general idea of the meaning will often allow you to understand the meaning of a written text.

Babies Sound Off: The Power of Babble

There is more to the *babbling* of a baby than meets the ear. A handful of scientists are picking apart infants' utterances and finding that not only is there an ordered *sequence* of vocal stages between birth and the first words, but in *hearing-impaired* babies a type of *babbling* thought to signal an emerging capacity for speech is delayed and distorted.

"The traditional wisdom [among developmental researchers] is that deaf babies *babble* like hearing babies," says linguist D. Kimbrough Oller of the University of Miami (Fla.) "This idea is a *myth*." Oller reported his findings on hearing and deaf infants at a National Institutes of Health seminar in Bethesda, Md. He and his colleagues demonstrated some years ago that hearing babies from a variety of language communities start out by cooing and gurgling; at about seven months of age, they start to produce *sequences* of the same syllables (for instance, "da-da-da" or "dut-dut-dut") that are classified as *babbling* and can be recorded and acoustically measured in the laboratory, with words or wordlike sounds appearing soon after one year of age. *Babbling*—the emitting of identifiable consonant and vowel sounds—usually disappears by around 18 to 20 months of age.

In a just-completed study, Oller and his co-workers found that repeated *sequences* of syllables first appeared among 21 hearing infants between the ages of 6 and 10 months; in contrast, these vocalizations emerged among nine severely to profoundly deaf babies between the ages of 11 and 25 months. In addition, deaf babies *babbled* less frequently than hearing babies, produced fewer syllables, and were more likely to use single syllables than repeated *sequences*.

babbling: _____

sequence: _____

hearing-impaired: _____

myth: _____

Word Study
Stems and Affixes

Below is a list of some commonly occurring stems and affixes.* Study their meanings, and then do the exercises that follow. Your teacher may ask you to give examples of other words you know that are derived from these stems and affixes.

Prefixes		
a-, an-	without, lacking not	atypical, apolitical
bene-	good	benefit, benefactor
bi-	two	bicycle, binary
mis-	wrong	misspell, mistake
mono-	one, alone	monarch, monopoly
poly-	many	polynomial, polytechnic
syn-, sym-, syl-	with, together	symphony, sympathy
Stems		
-anthro-, -anthropo-	human	anthropology
-arch-	first, chief, leader	patriarch, monarch, archbishop
-fact-, -fect-	make, do	affect, benefactor, factory
-gam-	marriage	monogamy, polygamous
-hetero-	different, other	heterosexual, heterogeneous
-homo-	same	homogenized milk
-man-, -manu-	hand	manually, manage
-morph-	form, structure	polymorphous
-onym-, -nomen-	name	synonym, nomenclature
-pathy-	feeling, disease	sympathy, telepathy, pathological
-theo-, -the-	god	theology, polytheism
Suffixes		
-ic, -al	relating to, having the nature of	comic, musical
-ism	action or practice, theory or doctrine	Buddhism, communism
-oid	like, resembling	humanoid

---

*For a list of all stems and affixes that appear in *Reader's Choice*, see Appendix B.

Exercise 1

For each item, select the best definition of the italicized word, or answer the question.

1. The small country was ruled by a *monarch* for 500 years.

   _____ a. king or queen   _____ c. group of the oldest citizens

   _____ b. single family   _____ d. group of the richest citizens

2. He was interested in *anthropology*.

   _____ a. the study of apes   _____ c. the study of royalty

   _____ b. the study of insects   _____ d. the study of humans

3. Some citizens say the election of William Blazer will lead to *anarchy*.

   _____ a. a strong central government   _____ c. the absence of a controlling government

   _____ b. a government controlled by one person _____ d. an old-fashioned, outdated government

4. If a man is a *bigamist*, he…

   _____ a. is married to two women.   _____ c. has two children.

   _____ b. is divorced.   _____ d. will never marry.

5. Which of the following pairs of words are *homonyms*?

   _____ a. good bad   _____ b. Paul Peter   _____ c. lie die   _____ d. two too

6. Which of the following pairs of words are *antonyms*?

   _____ a. sea see   _____ b. wet dry   _____ c. read read   _____ d. Jim Susan

7. The reviewer criticized the poet's *amorphous* style.

   _____ a. unimaginative   _____ c. stiff, too ordered

   _____ b. unusual   _____ d. lacking in organization and form

8. Dan says he is an *atheist*.

   _____ a. one who believes in one god   _____ c. one who believes in many gods

   _____ b. one who believes there is no god _____ d. one who is not sure if there is a god

9. There was a great *antipathy* between the brothers.

   _____ a. love   _____ b. difference   _____ c. dislike   _____ d. resemblance

10. Which circle is *bisected*?

    a.   b.   c.   d.

11. This design is symmetric:

    Which of the following designs is *asymmetric*?

    a.   b.   c.   d.

12. Consider these sentences:

Many automobiles are *manufactured* in Detroit.

The authors must give the publisher a *manuscript* of their new book.

How are the meanings of *manufacture* and *manuscript* different from the meanings of the stems from which they are derived?

_____

_____

Exercise 2

Word analysis can help you to guess the meanings of unfamiliar words. Using context clues and what you know about word parts, write a synonym, description, or definition of the italicized word.

1. _____ Doctors say that getting regular exercise is *beneficial* to your health.

2. _____ He's always *mislaying* his car keys, so he keeps an extra set in the garage.

3. _____ Because some of our patients speak Spanish and some speak English, we need a nurse who is *bilingual*.

4. _____ My parents always told me not to *misbehave* at my grandparents' house.

5. _____ Some people prefer to remain *anonymous* when they call the police to report a crime.

Exercise 3

Following is a list of words containing some of the stems and affixes introduced in this unit and the previous ones. Definitions of these words appear on the right. Put the letter of the appropriate definition next to each word.

1. _____ *archenemy*   a. care of the hands and fingernails
2. _____ *archetype*   b. the saying of a blessing
3. _____ *anthropoid*   c. resembling humans
4. _____ *benediction*   d. one who performs good deeds
5. _____ *benefactor*   e. a chief opponent
6. _____ *manicure*   f. the original model or form after which a thing is made
7. _____ *monotheism*   g. made up of similar parts
8. _____ *polytheism*   h. belief in one god
9. _____ *polygamy*   i. the practice of having one marriage partner
10. _____ *monogamy*   j. the practice of having several marriage partners
11. _____ *heterogeneous*   k. consisting of different types; made up of different types
12. _____ *homogeneous*   l. belief in more than one god

Sentence Study
Comprehension

Read these sentences carefully.* The questions that follow are designed to test your comprehension of complex grammatical structures. Select the *best* answer.

1. Like physical anthropology, orthodontics (dentistry dealing with the irregularities of teeth) tries to explain how and why people are different; unlike anthropology, it also tries to correct those differences for functional or aesthetic reasons.

   How does orthodontics differ from physical anthropology?

   _____ a. Physical anthropology is concerned with aesthetics; orthodontics is not.

   _____ b. Physical anthropology deals with the irregularities of teeth.

   _____ c. Orthodontics tries to explain why people are different, anthropology does not.

   _____ d. Anthropology does not try to correct differences among people; orthodontics does.

2. What is most obvious in this book are all those details of daily living that make Mary Richards anything but common.

   According to this statement, what kind of person is Mary Richards?

   _____ a. She is very obvious.   _____ c. She is anything she wants to be.

   _____ b. She is an unusual person.   _____ d. She is quite ordinary.

3. A third island appeared gradually during a period of volcanic activity that lasted over four years. Later, the 1866 eruptions, which brought to Santorini those volcanologists who first began archaeological work there, enlarged the new island through two new crater vents.

   What enlarged the third island?

   _____ a. the eruptions of 1866

   _____ b. a four-year period of volcanic activity

   _____ c. the activities of the people who came to study volcanoes

   _____ d. archaeological work, which created two new crater vents

4. Just before his tenth birthday Juan received a horse from his father; this was the first of a series of expensive gifts intended to create the impression of a loving parent.

   Why did Juan receive the horse?

   _____ a. because he was ten   _____ b. because his father loved him

   _____ c. because his father wanted to seem loving

   _____ d. because his father wouldn't be able to give him expensive gifts in the future

---

*For an introduction to sentence study, see Unit 1.

5. Since industry and commerce are the largest users of electrical energy, using less electricity would mean a reduced industrial capacity and fewer jobs in the affected industries and therefore an unfavorable change in our economic structure.

   According to this sentence, decreasing the use of electricity…

   _____ a. must begin immediately.   _____ c. will cause difficulties.

   _____ b. isn't important.   _____ d. won't affect industry.

6. The medical journal reported that heart attack victims who recover are approximately five times as likely to die within the next five years as those people without a history of heart disease.

   What did this medical journal say about people who have had a heart attack?

   _____ a. They are more likely to die in the near future than others.

   _____ b. They will die in five years.

   _____ c. They are less likely to die than people without a history of heart disease.

   _____ d. They are likely to recover.

7. Few phenomena in history are more puzzling than this one: that men and women with goals so vague, with knowledge so uncertain, with hopes so foggy still would have risked dangers so certain and tasks so great.

   What historical fact is puzzling?

   _____ a. that people had such vague goals

   _____ b. that people took such great risks

   _____ c. that people had foggy hopes and uncertain knowledge

   _____ d. that people completed such great tasks

8. Next he had to uncover the ancient secret—so jealously guarded by the ancients that no text of any kind, no descriptive wall painting, and no tomb inscriptions about making papyrus are known to exist.

   What secret did this man want to discover?

   _____ a. how to understand wall paintings   _____ c. how to read the ancient texts

   _____ b. how to read tomb inscriptions   _____ d. how to produce papyrus

9. Alexis, ruler of a city where politics was a fine art, concealed his fears, received the noblemen with extravagant ceremonies, impressed them with his riches, praised them, entertained them, bribed them, made promises he had no intention of keeping—and thus succeeded in keeping their troops outside his city walls.

   Why did Alexis give money and attention to the noblemen?

   _____ a. because they praised him

   _____ b. in order to prevent their armies from entering the city

   _____ c. in order to impress them with his riches

   _____ d. because they were his friends

Sentence Study
Restatement and Inference

This exercise is similar to the one found in Unit 3.* Each sentence below is followed by five statements. The statements are of four types.

1. Some of the statements are restatements of the original sentence. They give the same information in a different way.

2. Some of the statements are inferences (conclusions) that can be drawn from the information given in the original sentence.

3. Some of the statements are false based on the information given.

4. Some of the statements cannot be judged true or false based on the information given in the original sentence.

Put a check (✓) next to all restatements and inferences (types 1 and 2). Note: Do not check a statement that is true of itself but cannot be inferred from the sentence given.

1. A favorite definition of joking has long been the ability to find similarity between dissimilar things—that is, hidden similarities.

    _____ a. Joking is the ability to find similarity in dissimilar things.

    _____ b. It takes a long time to develop the ability to tell good jokes.

    _____ c. This definition of joking is a new one in literary theory.

    _____ d. Many people define joking as the ability to find similarity in dissimilar things.

    _____ e. The author agrees with this definition.

2. Although women still make up the majority of volunteer groups, male participation is reported on the rise nationwide as traditional distinctions between men's work and women's work fade.

    _____ a. As traditional societal roles change, more men are becoming members of volunteer groups.

    _____ b. Most members of volunteer groups are women.

    _____ c. In the past, volunteer work was done mainly by women.

    _____ d. Male participation in volunteer groups is increasing in all cities.

    _____ e. The author believes there is a relationship between the changing societal roles and the increasing willingness of men to do work previously done by females.

---

*For an introduction to sentence study, see Unit 1.

3. The overall picture of this very early settled Peruvian population is that of a simple, peaceful people living in a small cultivable oasis by the sea; fishing; raising a few food crops; living in small, simple, nonmasonry houses, and making the objects necessary for their economic and household life, with slight attention to art.

_____ a. This early Peruvian population had all the basic necessities of life available to it.

_____ b. We can assume that art only exists in very advanced societies.

_____ c. This society moved many times during the year.

_____ d. Because the people worked so hard they had no time for art.

_____ e. The author believes this society provides nothing of interest for historians.

4. Only a small number of scholars can be named who have entered at all deeply into the problem of jokes.

_____ a. Only a few scholars have studied jokes.

_____ b. The area of jokes is so complex that only a small number of people have been able to study it.

_____ c. Few scholars have studied the problem of jokes at all deeply.

_____ d. The author cannot remember the names of scholars who have studied jokes.

_____ e. It is not possible to name all those who have studied jokes at all deeply.

5. There is a question about the extent to which any one of us can be completely free of a prejudiced view in the area of religion.

_____ a. Probably all people are prejudiced in their views on religion.

_____ b. Any one of us can be free of prejudice in the area of religion.

_____ c. To some extent we can never be free of prejudice in the area of religion.

_____ d. A prejudiced view in the area of religion is undesirable.

_____ e. Because we can't be free of prejudice in the area of religion, we should not practice a religion.

6. Although the November election may significantly change the face of the county Board of Commissioners, the group will still have to confront the same old problems.

_____ a. The November election may give the Board of Commissioners a new building.

_____ b. The Board of Commissioners consists of several members.

_____ c. The November election may change the membership of the Board of Commissioners.

_____ d. Although board members may change, the problems will remain the same.

_____ e. The author does not believe that this election will change the difficulties facing the commissioners.

7. If this book begins with a familiar theme—the Native American experience of the last 150 years—the author brings to it great power and deep understanding.

     _____ a. This book was written 150 years ago.

     _____ b. The Native American experience of the last 150 years is a familiar experience, and nothing new can be written about it.

     _____ c. The book lacks understanding of the Native American experience.

     _____ d. The book begins with a familiar theme.

     _____ e. The author of this sentence likes the book.

8. In this part of the world, the political and social changes of the past 20 years have by no means eliminated the old upper class of royalty and friends and advisers of royalty, the holders of state monopolies, the great landlords and lords of commercial fiefs, and tribal and village leaders.

     _____ a. In this part of the world, political and social changes have eliminated great landlords, lords of commercial fiefs, and village leaders.

     _____ b. In this part of the world, the upper class and their friends and advisers have not been eliminated by political and social change.

     _____ c. No means can eliminate the old upper class of royalty in this part of the world.

     _____ d. The upper class of royalty has not changed in the past 20 years in this part of the world.

     _____ e. In this part of the world, village leaders hold as much power as the advisers of royalty.

9. People should and do choose their elected representatives partly on the basis of how well they believe these representatives, once in office, can convince them to do or support whatever needs to be done.

     _____ a. It is the author's belief that people should choose representatives whom they believe will convince them to take action.

     _____ b. People choose representatives on the basis of whether or not they believe the representatives can be convinced to do what needs to be done.

     _____ c. Although people should choose representatives whom they believe will convince them to take action, often they do not.

     _____ d. People choose representatives whom they believe will convince them to take action.

     _____ e. Representatives are elected only on the basis of their ability to take action.

Paragraph Reading
Restatement and Inference

Each passage is followed by five statements. The statements are of four types.

1. Some of the statements are restatements of ideas in the original passage. They give the same information in a different way.

2. Some of the statements are inferences (conclusions) that can be drawn from the information given in the passage.

3. Some of the statements are false based on the information given.

4. Some of the statements cannot be judged true or false based on the information given in the original passage.

Put a check (✔) next to all restatements and inferences (types 1 and 2). Note: Do not check a statement that is true of itself but cannot be inferred from the passage.

Example

Often people who hold higher positions in a given group overestimate their performance, while people in the lowest levels of the group underestimate theirs. While this may not always be true, it does indicate that often the actual position in the group has much to do with the feeling of personal confidence a person may have. Thus, members who hold higher positions in a group or feel that they have an important part to play in the group will probably have more confidence in their own performance.

_____ a. If people have confidence in their own performance, they will achieve high positions in a group.

_____ b. If we let people know they are an important part of a group, they will probably become more self-confident.

_____ c. People who hold low positions in a group often overestimate their performance.

_____ d. People in positions of power in a group may feel they do better work than they really do.

_____ e. People with higher positions in a group do better work than other group members.

Explanation

_____ a. This cannot be inferred from the paragraph. We know that people who hold high positions have more self-confidence than those who don't. However, we don't know that people with more confidence will achieve higher status. Confidence may come only after one achieves a higher position.

__✔__ b. This is an inference that can be drawn from the last sentence in the paragraph. We know that if people feel they have an important part to play in a group, they will probably have more self-confidence. We can infer that if we let people know (and therefore make them feel) that they have an important part to play, they will probably become more self-confident.

_____ c. This is false. The first sentence states that the people in the lowest levels of a group underestimate, not overestimate, their performance.

___✓___ d. This is a restatement of the first sentence. People who hold higher positions tend to overestimate their performance: they may feel they do better work than they really do.

_____ e. We do not know this from the paragraph. We know that people who hold higher positions often think they do better work than others in a group. (They "overestimate their performance.") We do not know that they actually do better work.

Passage 1

First Light tells the story of astronomers at the Palomar Observatory in the Palomar Mountains of California who peer through the amazing Hale Telescope into deep space, attempting to solve the riddle of the beginning of time. "Science is a lot weirder and more human than most people realize," Preston writes in his foreword to this revised and updated edition of his first book, and he skillfully weaves together stories of the eccentricities of his characters and the technical wonders of their work to create a riveting narrative about what scientists do and why they do it. The telescope itself is the main character. It is huge, seven stories tall, with a mirror that is two hundred inches wide and took fourteen years to cast and polish. Although there are now larger telescopes and telescopes in space, the Hale telescope is still used by astronomers on almost every clear night. Preston's rendering of their obsessions and adventures is a witty and illuminating portrait of scientists in action and a luminous story of what modern astronomy is all about.

_____ a. *First Light* is the title of a book.

_____ b. This paragraph was written by the author of *First Light*.

_____ c. The purpose of *First Light* is to detail the eccentricities of scientists.

_____ d. *First Light* tells the story of the astronomers who use the Hale Telescope.

_____ e. The author of the paragraph likes *First Light*.

Passage 2

The Incas had never acquired the art of writing, but they had developed a complicated system of knotted cords called *quipus*. These were made of the wool of the alpaca or llama, dyed in various colors, the significance of which was known to the officials. The cords were knotted in such a way as to represent the decimal system. Thus an important message relating to the progress of crops, the amount of taxes collected, or the advance of an enemy could be speedily sent by trained runners along the post roads.

_____ a. Because they could not write, the Incas are considered a simplistic, poorly developed society.

_____ b. Through a system of knotted cords, the Incas sent important messages from one community to another.

_____ c. Because runners were sent with cords, we can safely assume that the Incas did not have domesticated animals.

_____ **d.** Both the color of the cords and the way they were knotted formed part of the message of the *quipus*.

_____ **e.** The *quipus* were used for important messages.

Passage 3

There was a time when scholars held that early humans lived in a kind of beneficent anarchy, in which people were granted their rights by their peers and there was no governing or being governed. Various early writers looked back to this Golden Age but the point of view that humans were originally *children of nature* is best known to us in the writings of Rousseau, Locke, and Hobbes. These men described the concept of *social contract*, which they said had put an end to the *state of nature* in which the earliest humans were supposed to have lived.

_____ **a.** For Rousseau, Locke, and Hobbes, the concept of *social contract* put an end to the time of beneficent anarchy in which early humans lived.

_____ **b.** According to the author, scholars today do not hold that early humans lived in a state of anarchy.

_____ **c.** Only Rousseau, Locke, and Hobbes wrote about early humans as *children of nature*.

_____ **d.** The early writers referred to in this passage lived through the Golden Age of early humans.

_____ **e.** We can infer that the author of this passage feels that concepts of government have always been present in human history.

Passage 4

History has been all wrong about the painter Pierre Bonnard (1867–1947). He is not one of the late Impressionist painters after all. He is a Modernist, a man looking forward, not back. That, at least, is the viewpoint that was expressed in a recent exhibition of his work at the Metropolitan Museum of Art in New York. The exhibition, the first to show only Bonnard's later paintings, challenged viewers to rethink their ideas about this painter.

_____ **a.** The author believes history has been mistaken about Bonnard.

_____ **b.** A recent exhibition presented a new view of Bonnard's work.

_____ **c.** The Metropolitan Museum of Art held its first exhibition of Bonnard's work.

_____ **d.** People may have had incorrect ideas about the work of Bonnard.

_____ **e.** Bonnard is in some ways an Impressionist and in some ways a Modernist painter.

_____ **f.** People may change their ideas about Bonnard after seeing the exhibition.

_____ **g.** Pierre Bonnard thought it was wrong that people called him an Impressionist.

Discourse Focus
Prediction

Reading is an active process. Meaning does not exist only on the page or in the mind of the reader. It is created by an active interaction between reader and text. Based on their general knowledge and the information in a text, good readers develop predictions about what they will read next; then they read to see if their expectations will be confirmed. If they are not confirmed, readers reread, creating new predictions. Most often, however, readers are not greatly surprised; readers continue reading. This exercise is designed to give you practice in the process of consciously developing and confirming expectation. You will read the beginning of an article, stopping at several points to consider what you expect to read about next. Readers cannot always predict precisely what an author will talk about next, but you can practice using clues from the text and your general knowledge to more efficiently predict content.

Math Fears Subtract From Memory, Learning

Example

1. Above is the title of an article about feelings toward mathematics. Based on the title, do you think the article reports on people who have positive or negative feelings toward math? What words make you think so?

   _____

2. Based on the title, what effects can these feelings have on people? Can you list two?

   _____

   _____

Explanation

1. The article is about negative feelings. The phrase *math fears* refers to fear of mathematics.

2. The title refers to two effects of these fears. The first is that they decrease (*subtract from*) memory. The second is that they decrease learning.

3. Before you continue reading the article, decide how you expect it to begin. Remember, you cannot always predict exactly what an author will do, but you can use knowledge of the text and your general knowledge to make good guesses. Which one of the following seems the most likely beginning?

   _____ a. A description of how memory works

   _____ b. A description of learning theory

   _____ c. A description of math fears in students

   _____ d. A description of math fears in older adults

Now read to see if your expectations were correct.

> By about age 12, students who are afraid of mathematics start to avoid math courses, do poorly in the few math classes they do take, and earn low scores on math tests. Some scientists have thought that kids having little ability in math in the first place are understandably afraid of working with numbers.

4. The article begins with a discussion of students' math fears. Is that what you expected?

5. What do you expect to read about next? What words or phrases give you this idea?

_____

_____

Now read to see if your expectations are correct.

> That conclusion doesn't add up, at least for college students, according to a study in the *June Journal of Experimental Psychology: General*. On the contrary, people's worries about math decrease, for a short time, the mental functioning needed for doing arithmetic and decrease the ability to do math, report Mark H. Ashcraft and Elizabeth P. Kirk, both psychologists at Cleveland (Ohio) State University. Math anxiety has this effect by making it difficult to hold new information in mind while, at the same time, using it, the researchers believe. Psychologists consider this ability, known as working memory, to be necessary for dealing with numbers.

6. The first paragraph talks about what *some* scientists *have thought* was the explanation for math anxiety, suggesting that other scientists may have recently developed a different explanation. Instead of thinking that people are afraid of math because they are not good at it, the newer explanation is that people's fears about math affect their brain's ability to do math.

   Did you expect the paragraph to give a new explanation? If not, why not? Even if you didn't guess exactly what the author was going to do, do you think your expectations were good ones anyway?

7. Now that the author has indicated that there is a different explanation, what do you think he will discuss next? What aspects of the text and/or your general knowledge help you to make this prediction?

_____

_____

Discuss your predictions with your classmates. Then read to see if your expectations are confirmed.

> Ashcraft and Kirk ran three experiments, each with 50 to 60 college students. Experiments included approximately equal numbers of male and female students who reported low, moderate, or high levels of math anxiety on a questionnaire.

8. Were your expectations confirmed in this section of the text?

_____

9.   What other topics do you think will be discussed in the rest of this article? Check (✓) all those issues below that *might* be discussed. Be prepared to defend your choices.*

_____ a. Descriptions of the Aschcraft and Kirk experiments

_____ b. Descriptions of previous experiments

_____ c. Reactions of other scientists to these experiments

_____ d. Definitions of math anxiety

_____ e. Differences in the way math is taught in different countries

_____ f. Ways to overcome/succeed despite math anxiety

_____ g. Reasons not to worry about math anxiety

---

*The entire article can be read at https://www.sciencenews.org/article/math-fears-subtract-memory-learning.

UNIT 6

Reading Selections 1A–1B
Genetic Engineering

The following selections address genetically engineered (GE) crops, also called genetically modified (GM) crops. These are agricultural plants that have been "improved" by scientists. Their genes have been changed in order to create plants with desirable characteristics, for example, plants that are resistant to insect pests or that can grow with very little rainfall.

Selection 1A Graphics

Genetic engineering can be controversial. Before looking at the debates that surround it, it is important to have some basic information about its uses and regulation (that is, the rules or controls on its use).

Global Use of GM Crops

ISAAA (The International Service for the Acquisition of Agri-biotech Applications) is a not-for-profit international organization that closely follows the global use and regulation of GM crops (biotech crops). It has published an annual report summarizing this information since 1996, the first year that there were large-scale plantings of biotech crops.

On pages 146–148 there are three infographics from ISAAA reports. Skim* the infographics to get a general idea of the type of information each provides and how it is organized. Then skim and scan* to answer the Comprehension questions below.

---

*For an introduction to skimming and scanning, see Unit 1.

Answer the following questions according to the information in the figures. For statements preceded by T / F / N, circle T if the statement is true, F if the statement is false, and N if there is not enough information given in the infographics to tell whether the statement is true or false.

1. In 2016, how many countries grew GM crops? _____ Had that changed by 2019? _____

2. **T / F / N**   Most Biotech crops are grown in industrial countries like the USA.

3. What GM crop is planted most (in terms of area/hectares)? _____

4. What GM crop has received most regulatory approvals? _____

5. **T / F / N**   Forty countries have approved GM crops for one or more uses.

6. Figure 1 reports the number of "approved events" (legal approvals) for GM crops for three different purposes: "food use," "feed use," and "cultivation." What is the difference between food use and feed use?

   _____

7. **T / F / N**   It appears that countries are more worried about growing GM crops than eating them.

8. In Figure 2, why are some country names printed in orange? _____

9. **T / F / N**   Most countries in the world use GM crops.

10. Has your country been growing GM crops? Has it been using GM crops? _____

11. **T / F / N**   These infographics present both positive and negative points about GM crops.

12. What are five positive effects of using GM crops? _____

    _____

13. **T / F / N**   There are no negative effects of using GM crops.

FIGURE 1. Global Status of Commercialized Biotech/GM Crops in 2016

GLOBAL STATUS OF COMMERCIALIZED BIOTECH/GM CROPS IN 2016

185.1 MILLION HECTARES BIOTECH CROPS

IN **26** COUNTRIES PLANTED BY **18** MILLION FARMERS

FASTEST ADOPTED CROP TECHNOLOGY IN RECENT TIMES

DEVELOPING COUNTRIES GREW MORE BIOTECH CROPS IN 2016

19 DEVELOPING COUNTRIES — 99.6 MILLION HECTARES

7 INDUSTRIAL COUNTRIES — 85.5 MILLION HECTARES

— 185.1 MILLION HECTARES —

3 OF THE TOP 5 COUNTRIES GROWING BIOTECH CROPS ARE DEVELOPING COUNTRIES

TOP 5 COUNTRIES GROWING BIOTECH CROPS:
USA (72.9 Million Hectares)
Brazil (49.1)
Argentina (23.8)
Canada (11.6)
India (10.8)

BIOTECH CROPS INCREASED ~110-FOLD FROM 1996-2016; ACCUMULATED AREA IS 2.1 BILLION HECTARES

MAJOR BIOTECH CROPS

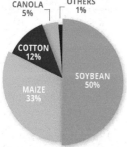

CANOLA 5%
OTHERS 1%
COTTON 12%
SOYBEAN 50%
MAIZE 33%

BIOTECH SOYBEAN
REACHED 50% OF GLOBAL BIOTECH CROP AREA IN 2016

OTHER BIOTECH CROPS IN THE MARKET:

SUGAR BEET PAPAYA SQUASH EGGPLANT POTATO

3,768 APPROVED EVENTS FOR BIOTECH CROPS IN 40 COUNTRIES (1994-2016)

FOOD USE (1,777)
FEED USE (1,238)
CULTIVATION (753)

MAIZE
HAS LARGEST NUMBER OF APPROVED EVENTS SINCE 1994
218 APPROVALS IN 29 COUNTRIES

BENEFITS OF BIOTECH CROPS

INCREASE CROP PRODUCTIVITY

US$167.8 BILLION GLOBAL FARM INCOME GAINS (1996-2015) GENERATED BY **BIOTECH CROPS**

CONSERVE BIODIVERSITY

PRODUCTIVITY GAINED THROUGH BIOTECHNOLOGY (1996-2016) HELPED SAVE

174 MILLION HECTARES OF LAND FROM PLOUGHING & CULTIVATION

PROVIDE A BETTER ENVIRONMENT

REDUCED PESTICIDE APPLICATIONS
DECREASED ENVIRONMENTAL IMPACT FROM HERBICIDE & INSECTICIDE USE BY **19%**

REDUCE CO2 EMISSIONS

REDUCED GREENHOUSE GASES & HELPED MITIGATE CLIMATE CHANGE. IN 2015, 26.7 BILLION KGS CO2 WAS SAVED EQUIVALENT TO REMOVING

~12 MILLION CARS OFF THE ROAD FOR 1 YEAR

HELP ALLEVIATE POVERTY & HUNGER

BIOTECH CROPS BENEFITED **18 MILLION SMALL FARMERS** AND THEIR FAMILIES TOTALING **>65 MILLION PEOPLE**

ISAAA

For more information, visit ISAAA website:
www.isaaa.org

Source: ISAAA. 2016. Global Status of Commercialized Biotech/GM Crops: 2016. *ISAAA Brief* No. 52.

 isaaa.org   @isaaa_org   isaaavideos

#GMCrops2016
#ISAAAReport2016

FIGURE 2. Global Map of Biotech Crop Countries and Mega-Countries in 2019

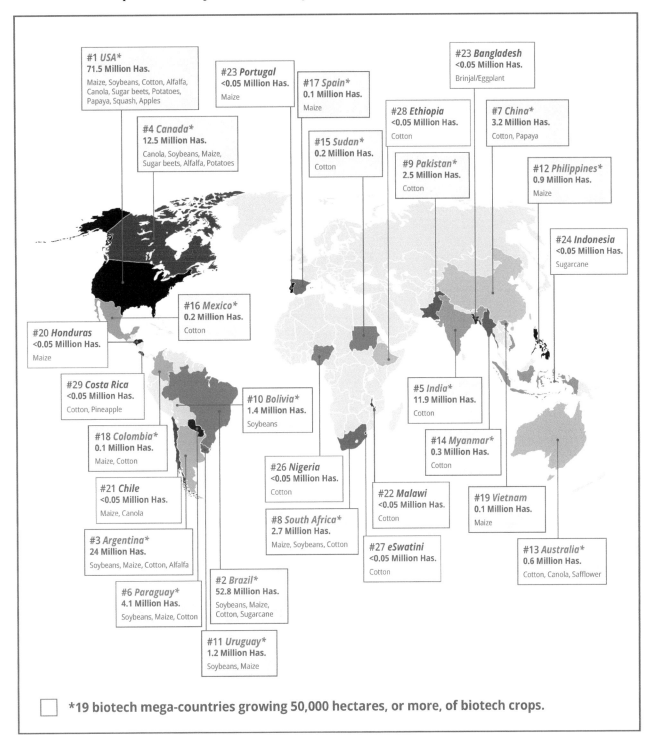

#1 *USA**
71.5 Million Has.
Maize, Soybeans, Cotton, Alfalfa, Canola, Sugar beets, Potatoes, Papaya, Squash, Apples

#4 *Canada**
12.5 Million Has.
Canola, Soybeans, Maize, Sugar beets, Alfalfa, Potatoes

#23 *Portugal*
<0.05 Million Has.
Maize

#17 *Spain**
0.1 Million Has.
Maize

#15 *Sudan**
0.2 Million Has.
Cotton

#23 *Bangladesh*
<0.05 Million Has.
Brinjal/Eggplant

#28 *Ethiopia*
<0.05 Million Has.
Cotton

#7 *China**
3.2 Million Has.
Cotton, Papaya

#9 *Pakistan**
2.5 Million Has.
Cotton

#12 *Philippines**
0.9 Million Has.
Maize

#24 *Indonesia*
<0.05 Million Has.
Sugarcane

#16 *Mexico**
0.2 Million Has.
Cotton

#20 *Honduras*
<0.05 Million Has.
Maize

#29 *Costa Rica*
<0.05 Million Has.
Cotton, Pineapple

#10 *Bolivia**
1.4 Million Has.
Soybeans

#5 *India**
11.9 Million Has.
Cotton

#18 *Colombia**
0.1 Million Has.
Maize, Cotton

#14 *Myanmar**
0.3 Million Has.
Cotton

#21 *Chile*
<0.05 Million Has.
Maize, Canola

#26 *Nigeria*
<0.05 Million Has.
Cotton

#22 *Malawi*
<0.05 Million Has.
Cotton

#19 *Vietnam*
0.1 Million Has.
Maize

#3 *Argentina**
24 Million Has.
Soybeans, Maize, Cotton, Alfalfa

#8 *South Africa**
2.7 Million Has.
Maize, Soybeans, Cotton

#27 *eSwatini*
<0.05 Million Has.
Cotton

#13 *Australia**
0.6 Million Has.
Cotton, Canola, Safflower

#6 *Paraguay**
4.1 Million Has.
Soybeans, Maize, Cotton

#2 *Brazil**
52.8 Million Has.
Soybeans, Maize, Cotton, Sugarcane

#11 *Uruguay**
1.2 Million Has.
Soybeans, Maize

*19 biotech mega-countries growing 50,000 hectares, or more, of biotech crops.

FIGURE 3. Regulations on GM Products by Country

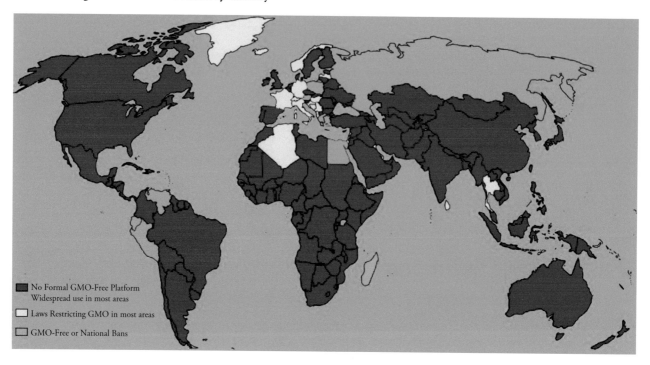

No Formal GMO-Free Platform
Widespread use in most areas

Laws Restricting GMO in most areas

GMO-Free or National Bans

1. What do you already know about GM crops? Is your impression positive or negative?

2. GM crops are very controversial. Why do you think some people think that these crops might save the world? Why do you think some people oppose them just as strongly?

3. Have you ever eaten any GM food? How do you know?

The Debate on Genetic Modification

It is widely expected that the world population will reach 9 billion people within a few generations. This raises the frightening possibility of widespread famine. To meet the challenge of feeding the world of the future, experts agree that global food production will need to double by 2050.

How can this challenge be met? One approach to increasing global food production is the use of genetically modified (GM) crops. However, widespread adoption of GM crops is complicated by questions concerning the immediate and long-term effects of these engineered plants.

GM crops were first introduced commercially in the 1990s. Since that time, the majority of scientists and health providers—including the American Medical Association, the National Academy of Sciences, the American Association for the Advancement of Science and the World Health Organization—have come to the conclusion that GMOs (genetically modified organisms) do not pose a risk to consumers.

Despite this, some groups and individuals are critical of the technology. Some are worried about possible negative effects on human health and the environment. Others have ethical concerns about genetic modification. Many critics do not trust the information about GMOs; they believe that corporations have influenced the research in order to increase their profits.

On the other hand, supporters of genetic engineering are concerned that the technology is not contributing all that it could to society. They are frustrated by the slow pace with which governments develop policies supporting research and applications to farming. They see strict regulations and a lack of public funding as limiting what GM crops could be doing to improve human health and the environment. They believe that genetic engineering can contribute much more to the quality and quantity of healthy foods, and to farming methods that reduce the dangers of pesticides and chemical fertilizers.

While the debate about these and other questions related to genetic engineering goes on, emerging genetic-engineering technologies are adding complexities to the conversation. New discoveries are changing the way we think about the production and consumption of food in a highly globalized world.

Technology will almost certainly be part of the solution to the problem of feeding the planet's expanding population, but the details of how GM crops fit in the global food supply are not yet clear.

Critical Reading / Critical Thinking: Evaluating Sources

Assume that you are writing a report on benefits and dangers of genetically modified foods. You understand that the average citizen cannot be expected to comprehend all of the science and technology behind these new products. However, if people are to participate in public debate, vote for or against politicians and policy on this issue, it is important to read critically and arrive at one's own conclusions.

Your report will attempt to present a balanced picture of the current situation and future prospects. However, as you read possible sources of material for your report, you discover that it is difficult to separate fact from fiction and to identify trustworthy sources of information. You need to be careful and critical in your reading of the research.

The following excerpts from articles and editorials present a wide variety of opinions on the topic of genetic engineering. For each excerpt, answer the questions that follow it and decide if it would be a useful source for your report. For statements preceded by T / F / N, circle T if the statement is true, F if the statement is false, and N if there is not enough information given to tell whether the statement is true or false. Be prepared to defend your choices. As you read, consider the following guidelines. Your teacher may want you to work individually, in pairs, or in small groups as you decide what to believe and what you might do as a result of your conclusions.

Guidelines for Evaluating Sources

1. What is the author(s)' opinion concerning the value of GMO foods?

2. What evidence do they provide to support the position taken? How well documented are the claims? Do they support assertions with reference to research by independent scholars, or do they merely ask you to believe what they say?

3. How would you characterize the author(s)' language and tone of argument? Is it appealing more to reason or to emotion?

4. What are the credentials of the author(s)?

5. Have the author(s) provided enough information? Do you need additional sources?

Source 1

Genetically Engineered Crops: Experiences and Prospects is now available from the National Academies Press. This volume builds on previous reports published between 1987 and 2010 by examining the possible positive and negative effects of GE crops. It is an effort to predict what GE technologies hold for the future. This report indicates where there are uncertainties about the economic, agricultural, health, safety, and other impacts of GE crops. It recommends filling gaps in current safety assessments, making clearer regulations about GE crops, and improving explanations of GE technology. This report attempts to clarify the situation for the general public.

1. **T / F / N**   *Genetically Engineered Crops: Experiences and Prospects* is a recently published report.

2. **T / F/ N**   The authors of the report believe that GMOs are beneficial.

3. **T / F/ N**   The authors of *Genetically Engineered Crops: Experiences and Prospects* conducted research experiments to test the conclusions of previous reports.

4. According to the text, who is the intended audience for the report? _____

5. Do you think you will use this source in your report? Why or why not? _____

_____

Source 2

Genetically modified crops and foods are neither safe nor necessary to feed the world, a new report by genetic engineers shows. The second edition of *GMO Myths and Truths,* co-authored by genetic engineers Dr. John Fagan and Dr. Michael Antoniou and researcher Claire Robinson, has been released as a free online download by Earth Open Source. The second edition follows the publication two years ago of the first edition. That report was downloaded 120,000 times just a few weeks after publication and was read online by several times that many visitors. At 330 pages, the new edition is nearly three times the length of the original and summarizes many new studies.

1. **T / F / N** The authors of *GMO Myths and Truths* believe that GMOs are harmful.

2. **T / F / N** The authors of this paragraph believe the value of the report can be gauged by its size (330 pages) and the number of people who have downloaded it (120,000).

3. **T / F / N** The authors of this paragraph conducted the research that is summarized in the report.

4. Do you think you will use this source in your report? Why or why not? _____

_____

Source 3

Writing in the *New York Times,* Jane E. Brody provides a cautious "yes" in response to the question about the safety of GMO foods: "In the decades since the first genetically modified foods reached the market, no adverse health effects among consumers have been found, and the majority of experts – including the American Medical Association, the National Academy of Sciences, the American Association for the Advancement of Science and the World Health Organization—believe that GMOs pose no immediate threat. This is not to say there are none, but as hard as opponents of the technology have looked, none have yet been definitely identified."

1. Which of the following sentences best expresses the meaning of the paragraph?

_____ **a.** GMO foods have caused no adverse health effects.

_____ **b.** For the past 10 years, no problems have been attributed to GMO foods.

_____ **c.** Opponents of the GMO technology have worked hard to find adverse health effects.

_____ **d.** At this time GMO foods may be safe, but it is too soon to know for sure.

2. Do you think Jane Brody's argument appeals to emotions or reason? Underline portions of text that support your answer.

_____

3. Do you think you will use this source in your report? Why or why not? _____

_____

Source 4

According to Dr. Edward Group of the Global Healing Center, "GMOs pose a danger to all of us and the evidence cannot be ignored. Environmentally, they have created super weeds that destroy farmland, and they have eliminated some organisms from ecosystems, leading to new superbugs that replaced them. Research has shown a dramatically higher risk of health problems from eating GMOs; toxic DNA from these plants may survive digestion. It's even been found in the blood of pregnant women and their unborn children!"

1. **T / F / N** Dr. Group is an opponent of GMOs.

2. What are "super weeds" and "super bugs?" What dangers to they represent? _____

    _____

3. **T / F / N** Dr. Group provides the sources for his opinions.

    _____

4. What kind of organization do you think The Global Healing Center is? _____

    _____

5. Do you think Dr. Group's argument appeals to emotions or reason? Underline portions of text that support your answer. _____

    _____

6. Do you think you will use this source in your report? Why or why not? _____

    _____

Source 5

There has been a rapid increase of studies on genetically engineered (GE) crops in recent years. As a result, the public is demanding a clear picture of the potential dangers and advantages of GMOs. Our committee was given the task of examining the evidence and summarizing our results for scientifically literate consumers. We recognized that some members of the public are skeptical of the literature on GE crops; they are concerned that many experiments and results have been conducted or influenced by the industries that are profiting from these crops. Therefore, when we referred to articles in the three major chapters of the report regarding current GE crops, we identified the affiliations of their primary authors when possible. We also provided the specific sources of funding. That information is available on our study's website.

1. **T / F / N** The authors of this paragraph examined studies concerned with the safety of genetically engineered crops.

2. Where do you think this paragraph appeared?

    _____ **a.** In a local newspaper.   _____ **c.** In an advertisement.

    _____ **b.** In a government research report. _____ **d.** In a college textbook

3. **T / F / N** The authors of this paragraph provide information about the research they studied in the text of the report and on their website.

4. Do you think you will use this source in your report? Why or why not? _____

_____

Source 6

As journalists, not scientists, we know that we do not understand all the technical issues involved, but we believe that consumers have a right to know about the food they purchase. The regulations governing genetically engineered (GE) crops vary greatly from country to country because of differences in the political, legal, and cultural characteristics of countries. There is no reason to expect these differences to change in the immediate future, so trade difficulties will continue to be significant. The technology of genetic engineering is changing rapidly. This makes the development of regulations very difficult. We recommend testing of all new varieties of plants—whether genetically engineered or conventionally bred. It is important to know if they have new characteristics with potential risks for the consumer. We propose an approach to regulation that is based in part on new technologies that will be able to compare the genetic profiles of new and existing plants. In addition, we believe that GE crop governance should be transparent and participatory; that is, regulators should make clear how decisions are being made, and the public should be involved in the process.

1. **T / F / N** According to the authors it is difficult for nations to agree on processes for regulating GE crops.

2. **T / F / N** The authors of this paragraph believe that genetically engineered crops are safe.

3. Where do you think the authors of this paragraph work?

_____ **a.** A research institute   _____ **c.** A university

_____ **b.** A newspaper   _____ **d.** A government

4. What are the factors that the authors believe account for the variation in regulatory processes for genetically engineered crops? _____

5. How would the authors of this paragraph improve the regulatory process? _____

_____

6. Do you think you will use this source in your report? Why or why not? _____

_____

Source 7

The European Union regulation of agricultural biotechnology is hopelessly confused because the definition of "Genetically Modified Organisms" has not been agreed upon; neither policy makers nor scientists have been able to come to a consensus about the phrase. The result is that the cultivation of "GMOs" is prohibited in much of Europe. At the same time, genetically engineered foods are imported from other countries. This is understandable because decisions are being made on the basis of politics rather than science. The EU should conduct a careful examination of the pros and cons, the costs and benefits of each new agricultural product —"GMO" or otherwise. All crops, whether cultivated or imported, should be assessed on a case-by-case basis.

1. **T / F / N** According to the paragraph, the definition of GMO used by scientists is better than that used by policy makers.

2. **T / F / N** In the EU, genetically modified foods are not available for purchase and consumption.

3. (Check all items that are true.) The author believes that…

   _____ **a.** the regulation of food production and importation is hopelessly confused.

   _____ **b.** GMO production should be prohibited in the EU.

   _____ **c.** decisions about GMOs should be made by popular vote.

   _____ **d.** biotechnology is the only solution to the problem of regulation.

   _____ **e.** science is more reliable than politics in determining the risks of GMOs.

4. Do you think you will use this source in your report? Why or why not? _____

   _____

Discussion/Composition

What have you learned about GMOs? List three points you could write about.

1. _____

2. _____

3. _____

Reading Selection 2
Psychology

BEFORE YOU BEGIN

1. The following is the first line of a radio show about *multitasking*.

   Multitasking is a way of life for kids—chatting online or on the cell phone, studying, surfing the web, quickly bouncing back and forth from one activity to the next.

   Use the context and your knowledge of stems and affixes to define *multitasking*.

2. Are you a good multitasker? How do you know? Give examples.

3. Is multitasking important in today's world? Why or why not?

4. Do you believe that younger people are better or worse at multitasking than their parents?

Increasingly scientists are asked to describe technical research for a general audience. Below is an interview with a professor of neuroscience describing his research on multitasking. It was posted in the United States on the website for National Public Radio. Your teacher may want you to do the Vocabulary from Context exercise on page 159 before you begin.

How Multitasking Affects Human Learning
National Public Radio, Weekend Edition*

LYNN NEARY, host

1 Multitasking is a way of life for kids—chatting online or on the cell phone, studying, surfing the Internet, quickly bouncing back and forth from one activity to the next.

2 UCLA psychology professor Russell Poldrack wanted to find out how this type of functioning affects the brain. Does a kid who's instant messaging his friends with a TV in the background learn as much from the history textbook as the kid who's at the desk in a quiet room?

3 NEARY: Russell Poldrack has published a study on multitasking. He joins us now from NPR West. Good to have you with us.

4 Professor RUSSELL POLDRACK (UCLA): Thank you. It's a pleasure to be here.

5 NEARY: Maybe you could explain exactly what you looked at in your study first.

6 Prof. POLDRACK: We used a technique to image the brain called functional magnetic resonance imaging, or FMRI, and this technique lets us look at what the brain is doing while a person is engaged in a task. The question we asked was, do the brain systems that are involved in learning differ in their activity depending on whether the person is focused on learning or whether they're distracted at the same time?

---

*Students can listen to the program by going to https://www.npr.org/2007/03/03/7700581/how-multitasking-affects-human-learning

7 So we compared people under some condition of learning a very simple task, basically learning to categorize some simple shapes into different categories, and they learned under different conditions. Some of the time they learned while they were focused on the task and other times they learned while they were also doing something else at the same time, while they were distracted.

8 NEARY: And what did you discover?

9 Prof. POLDRACK: That learning while you are distracted fundamentally changes the brain systems that are involved in learning. When you learn while you're focused on a task, you engage a set of brain systems called the hippocampus, which are responsible for generating and storing sort of rich, complex, conscious memories of the past.

10 Whereas, when people learned under a dual task condition, while they were distracted, they were more likely to engage a different set of brain regions called the basal ganglia, which are more involved in building habits and much less flexible types of knowledge.

11 NEARY: But there are benefits to multitasking, aren't there?

12 Prof. POLDRACK: There certainly are. In today's society we can't get by without multitasking, but what psychologists have discovered, whenever we multitask, we perform worse than we do if we focus on a task. And the idea is that we can't really do two things at a time, and there's a cost to that switching back and forth.

13 NEARY: Does your research indicate that there really are certain kinds of tasks that we need to have our undivided attention focused on, that there are certain things that we do that we really shouldn't be trying to multitask at the same time?

14 Prof. POLDRACK: Well, our research suggested that that's the case when you're trying to learn new information, because it's clear that learning is badly impaired when you're doing it while you're also doing other things. So it suggests, for example, that if a kid is trying to learn a history lesson, for example, the one thing they really don't want to be doing is, at the same time, you know, being on the web or being on their cell phone texting friends, because that's going to be really detrimental to learning.

15 NEARY: On the other hand, in today's world it's almost impossible, even for an adult, to go someplace in a quiet room and just concentrate on one thing at one time. Our workplace demands multitasking.

16 Prof. POLDRACK: That's true. And I think the point that we have to take from the research is that we have to be aware that there is a cost to the way that our society is changing, that humans are not built to work this way. We're really built to focus. And when we sort of force ourselves to multitask we're driving ourselves to perhaps be less efficient in the long run even, though it sometimes feels like we're being more efficient. There's a sort of myth of multitasking, I think that when people are juggling lots of things, they feel like they're doing more and it becomes kind of a self-fulfilling prophecy, that they keep juggling more things because they feel like they're doing it well, when in the end we may be actually hurting ourselves.

17 NEARY: So is this generation going to be really substantially different from their parents because of the way they work?

18 Prof. POLDRACK: That is the million-dollar question. I think we just simply don't know the answer to that. You know, once kids who are growing up today start becoming adults, then we'll be able to see, as adults, do they really differ from what adults look like who didn't grow up in such a fast-paced multi-tasking society. What we know about the brain is that it's very adaptable but at the same time there are built-in fundamental limits to the kinds of information the brain can process, and it may be that the ability to really do multiple things at once might be one of those built-in limits.

19 Now, one thing I should add is, the research doesn't necessarily extend to cases where the information is just in the background; so for example sending text messages compared to things like listening to music or having television on in the background, because the research is really focused on kind of active multitasking.

20 NEARY: Russell Poldrack is a professor of behavioral neuroscience at the University of California, Los Angeles. Thank you very much, Professor.

21 Prof. POLDRACK: Sure. It's a pleasure.

{NPR transcripts are created on a rush deadline by a contractor for NPR, and accuracy and availability may vary. This text may not be in its final form and may be updated or revised in the future. Please be aware that the authoritative record of NPR's programming is the audio.}

Comprehension

Indicate whether each of the statements below is true (T) or false (F) according to the interview.

1. **T / F** The tasks that were studied by Professor Poldrack were very difficult.

2. **T / F** Different parts of the brain are involved in learning when a person is focused on a task as compared to when a person is distracted.

3. **T / F** People always perform worse when they multitask.

4. **T / F** If a student is studying for a history test, there shouldn't be music playing in the background.

5. **T / F** We should never multitask.

6. **T / F** Professor Poldrack probably talks on the phone while he is driving.

Discussion/Composition

Exercise 1

1. In what sense does Professor Podrack say that multitasking is a myth? Does this affect how you feel about it? Will you do anything different in your life?

2. Do you agree with this saying, "Slicing your attention is like slicing a plum—you lose some of the juice"? Does this mean that you shouldn't slice your plum or your time? Are there some times when multitasking is necessary and/or a good thing?

3. Many people believe that technology is a problem, that it is the main cause of today's multitasking lives. Is technology the problem or is it how humans adapt to technology?

4. We know that the human brain is adaptable. But how adaptable? If people grow up spending a lot of time multitasking, when they need to concentrate on just one thing, will they be better or worse at it?

Researchers don't agree. Some think this is like cross training. You get good at having lots of information, and when you want to concentrate on one of them, it's easy for the brain. Other people say, no, you only get good at what you practice. What do you think the future will bring, the best of both worlds, or people who can't concentrate? Why?

Exercise 2: Judging Effectiveness

What do you think makes a good beginning for a report on scientific research for the general public?

Below are the opening sections from two reports in the popular media on research about teens and multitasking. Quickly skim* each one. *Do not worry about unfamiliar vocabulary.* Decide which one you like best and why. After you decide, your teacher may want you to discuss your opinion in pairs or small groups. There is no single correct answer; be prepared to defend your choices.

Passage 1

(From a National Public Radio broadcast and website transcript)

Multitasking is a way of life for kids—chatting online or on the cell phone, studying, surfing the Internet, quickly bouncing back and forth from one activity to the next.

UCLA psychology professor Russell Poldrack wanted to find out how this type of functioning affects the brain. Does a kid who's instant messaging his friends with a TV in the background learn as much from the history textbook as the kid who's at the desk in a quiet room?

Passage 2

(From the *Washington Post* newspaper and website)

It's homework time and 17-year-old Megan Casady of Silver Spring is ready to study.

She heads down to the basement, turns on MTV, and boots up her computer. Over the next half hour, Megan will send about a dozen instant messages discussing the potential for a midweek snow day. She'll take at least one cellphone call, fire off a couple of text messages, scan* Weather.com, volunteer to help with a campus cleanup day at James Hubert Blake High School where she is a senior, post some comments on social media, and check out the new pom squad pictures another friend has posted on hers.

In between, she'll define "descent with modification" and explain how "the tree analogy represents the evolutionary relationship of creatures" on a worksheet for her AP biology class.

Call it multitasking homework, Generation Net style.

The students who do it say multitasking makes them feel more productive and less stressed. Researchers aren't sure what the long-term impact will be because no studies have probed its effect on teenage development. But some fear that the penchant for flitting from task to task could have serious consequences on young people's ability to focus and develop analytical skills.

---

*For an introduction to skimming and scanning, see Unit 1.

Exercise 3: Summarizing Research

In academic contexts, you often need to summarize information you read. For example, you summarize when you are taking notes, you write research summaries, and some test questions involve summarizing.

Below are two descriptions of research on multitasking. In one or two sentences summarize each study.

Passage 1

(From an NPR description of a University of Michigan study)

The scientists asked several dozen student volunteers to switch back and forth between different types of arithmetic problems. If they had to switch rapidly from multiplication to division, it took them quite a bit longer to finish. For instance, it might take a minute to finish 10 multiplication problems, but a mix of 10 multiplication and division problems might take 15 or 20 seconds longer.

_____

_____

Passage 2

(From a science and technology website)

One study by researchers at the University of California at Irvine looked at interruptions among office workers. They found that workers took an average of twenty-five minutes to recover from interruptions such as phone calls or answering e-mail and return to their original task. Discussing multitasking with the *New York Times*, Jonathan B. Spira, an analyst at the business research firm Basex, estimated that extreme multitasking— information overload—costs the US economy $650 billion a year in lost productivity.

_____

_____

Vocabulary from Context

Both the ideas and the vocabulary from the exercise below are taken from "How Multitasking affects Human Learning". Use the context provided to determine the meanings of the italicized words. Write a definition, synonym, or description in the space provided.

1. _____

2. _____

3. _____

4. _____

5. _____

6. _____

Scientists have begun to study multitasking in teenagers. In one study, they used a way to take a picture of the brain. This *technique* (1), which creates *images* (2) of the brain, is called functional magnetic resonance imaging (FMRI). The scientists first imaged the brain when people were *focused* (3) on doing only one thing. They wanted to know whether people who were *concentrating on* (4) learning performed the same as people who were doing something else at the same time. The *task* (5) they studied was putting simple shapes into groups. People who did this *categorizing*

7. _____

8. _____

9.

10. _____

11. _____

12. _____

13. _____

14. _____

15. _____

16. _____

17. _____

18. _____

19. _____

(6) task under different conditions performed differently. Scientists discovered that people who were working under the *condition* (7) of focusing on one thing, giving it their *undivided attention* (8), used a different part of the brain than people who were doing two things and therefore were *distracted* (9).

The people who were concentrating used a *region* (10) of the brain that people use *consciously* (11), when they are aware of and trying to store complex memories of the past. The distracted people (those learning under the *dual* (12) task condition) used a different region—an area that builds *habits* (13), things that we do without thinking.

Multitasking does not seem to work well when people are trying to learn things that require undivided attention. When people are trying to learn new information, multitasking *impairs* (14) learning. For example, texting friends will be *detrimental* (15) to studying for a test. This is the cost of multitasking: people perform worse on a task if they do not focus on it. We may think that we are using time in the best possible way, but we are not being *efficient* (16). In fact, research suggests that the common belief that we can multitask when we are doing difficult tasks is a *myth* (17), that it may not be possible at all. But there are still *benefits* (18) to some multitasking. Most people in today's society need to multitask sometimes, for some kinds of tasks. And what we don't know is whether kids will be better at multitasking than their parents. After all, people and brains are *adaptable* (19) and humans may be able to change to meet a new world.

Figurative Language and Idioms

This exercise gives you additional clues to understand the meanings of unfamiliar vocabulary in context, in this case figurative language and idioms. In the paragraph of "How Multitasking Affects Human Learning" indicated by the number in parentheses, find the word or phrase that best fits the meaning given. Your teacher may want to read these aloud as you quickly scan* the paragraph to find the answer.

1. (6) What phrase means *doing some work?* _____

2. (10) What word means *use?* _____

3. (16) What phrase means *a prediction or expectation that causes itself to come true?* _____

4. (18) What phrase means *the most important or difficult question which people do not know the answer to?*

   _____

5. (19) What phrase means *not in the front of the mind, doesn't require attention?* _____

_____

*For an introduction to scanning, see Unit 1.

Dictionary Study

Many words have more than one meaning. When you use a dictionary to discover the meaning of an unfamiliar word, you need to use the context to determine which definition is appropriate. Use the dictionary entries provided to select the best definition for each of the italicized words in the following sentences. Write the number of the definition in the space provided.

_____ **1a.** Multitaskers *bounce* back and forth from one activity to the next,

_____ **1b.** *juggling* lots of things.

_____ **2.** Whenever we multitask, we *perform* worse than we do if we focus on a task.

_____ **3.** People who completed a task while they were distracted, engaged a different set of brain *regions*.

_____ **4.** When you multitask, there is a *cost* to switching back and forth.

_____ **5.** To be efficient, a brain needs to be able to *store* complex memories.

1a. bounce /ˈbaʊns/ verb
bounc·es; bounced; bounc·ing

1 a [+ obj]: to cause (a ball, rock, etc.) to hit against a surface and quickly move in a different and usually opposite direction ▪ He was bouncing a tennis ball against/off the garage door. ▪ bouncing the ball back and forth b [no obj]: to move in one direction, hit a surface (such as a wall or the floor), and then quickly move in a different and usually opposite direction—usually + off ▪ The ball bounced off the wall. ▪ A rock bounced off the road and hit our car's windshield. ▪ The light will bounce off the mirror and shine into the next room.

2 a [no obj]: to move with a lot of energy and excitement ▪ He bounced [=bounded] into the room to welcome his guests. ▪ The kids are bouncing off the walls. [=the kids are very/too excited and have a lot of energy] b: to move or jump up and down [no obj] ▪ The children love to bounce on the bed/trampoline. ▪ The winner bounced up and down with delight. ▪ Her curls bounced as she jumped. [+ obj] ▪ He bounced the baby on his knee.

3 a [no obj] of a check: to be returned by a bank because there is not enough money in the bank account to pay the amount that is on the check ▪ She gave me a check for 20 dollars, but the check bounced, and I never got the money. b [+ obj]: to write (a check) that is returned without payment by the bank ▪ He bounced a 100-dollar check at the grocery store. ▪ The store charges a $15 fee for a bounced check.

4 [no obj]: to go quickly and repeatedly from one job, place, etc., to another ▪ He bounces back and forth between Miami and Houston.—often + from ▪ bouncing from place to place ▪ She bounces from one job to another. ▪ Our teacher's always bouncing from one subject to another.

5 to return (an e-mail) to the sender instead of delivering it [+ obj] ▪ I tried to send you an e-mail, but it got bounced back to me. [=the e-mail or computer system was not able to deliver it] [no obj] ▪ I tried to send you an e-mail but it bounced.

1b. jug·gle /ˈʤʌgəl/ verb

jug·gles; jug·gled; jug·gling

  1 to keep several objects in motion in the air at the same time by repeatedly throwing and catching them [no obj] ▪ He is learning to juggle. [+ obj] ▪ He juggled four balls at once.

  2 [+ obj]: to do (several things) at the same time ▪ She somehow manages to juggle a dozen tasks at once. ▪ It can be hard to juggle family responsibilities and/with the demands of a full-time job. — see also juggling act at 1act

  3 [+ obj]: to make changes to (something) in order to achieve a desired result ▪ I'll have to juggle my schedule a bit to get this all to work out.

    — jug·gler /ˈʤʌglɚ/ noun, plural jug·glers [count] ▪ a juggler at the circus

---

2. per·form /pɚˈfoɚm/ verb

per·forms; per·formed; per·form·ing

  1 [+ obj]: to do an action or activity that usually requires training or skill ▪ The doctor had to perform surgery immediately. ▪ A team of six scientists performed [=carried out] the experiment. ▪ He has been unable to perform [=complete, fulfill] his duties since the accident. ▪ The magician performed some amazing tricks. ▪ The gymnasts performed their routines perfectly. ▪ You are required to perform 50 hours of community service. ▪ The wedding (ceremony) was performed by a justice of the peace. = A justice of the peace performed the wedding (ceremony). ▪ You can't expect me to perform miracles. [=to do something that is impossible]

  2 to entertain an audience by singing, acting, etc. [no obj] ▪ The band will be performing on the main stage. ▪ She's a wonderful singer who loves to perform in front of a live audience. [+ obj] ▪ The band will perform songs from their new album. ▪ The class performed the play for the school. ▪ He performed [=acted] the part/role of Othello. [=he played Othello; he said the words and did the actions of the character Othello]

  3 [no obj] — used to describe how effective or successful someone or something is ▪ The stock market is performing well/badly. ▪ The engine/computer was performing poorly. ▪ I perform best under pressure.

---

3. re·gion /ˈriːʤən/ noun

plural re·gions

  1 [count]: a part of a country, of the world, etc., that is different or separate from other parts in some way ▪ The bird returns to this region every year. ▪ The plant grows in tropical regions. [=areas] ▪ He's the company sales manager for the entire Southwest region. — often + of ▪ the agricultural/coastal/mountainous regions of the country ▪ the Amazon region of South America ▪ the desert regions of the world ▪ the winemaking regions of France ▪ the unknown regions of outer space

  2 [count] : a place on your body : an area that is near a specified part of your body ▪ She has a pain in the lower back region. — often + of ▪ He felt a pain in the region [=vicinity] of his heart.

  3 the regions Brit : the parts of a country that are not close to the capital city ▪ attempts to go outside of London and stimulate cultural life in the regions

---

4. ¹cost /ˈkɑːst/ noun

plural **costs**

  1   the price of something: the amount of money that is needed to pay for or buy something [count] ▪ The original cost [=price] of the house was $200,000. ▪ She attends college at a cost of $15,000 a year. ▪ The average cost of raising a family has increased dramatically. ▪ We offer services at a fraction of the cost of other companies. ▪ bringing/driving down the cost of computers = lowering/reducing the cost of computers ▪ The person at fault in the accident is expected to bear the cost of repairs. [=is expected to pay for the repairs] [noncount] ▪ What's the difference in cost? ▪ We were able to update the room for very little cost. [=money, expense] ▪ They believe that everyone should have access to adequate medical care, regardless of cost. **synonyms** ¹price

  2   [count]: an amount of money that must be spent regularly to pay for something (such as running a business or raising a family) ▪ The cost of doing business in this area is high. ▪ We need better cost control. ▪ The company needs to do some cost cutting. [=needs to find ways to save money] — usually plural ▪ production/manufacturing/operating costs ▪ By keeping costs down, the company will make larger profits from its products. ▪ the firm's efforts to control costs ▪ Those are just some of the hidden costs [=expenses] of owning a house. ▪ The government covers most of the costs of the program. [=pays for most of the program] ▪ The family's medical costs have increased in the past year. ▪ The company has tried to cut costs [=spend less money] in several areas. — see also **cost of living**

  3   something that is lost, damaged, or given up in order to achieve or get something [noncount] ▪ Winning the war, he believes, was worth the cost in lives. — often used after *at* ▪ They had won the battle, but at what cost? Far too many people had died. ▪ He had achieved fame, but at a cost; he'd lost many friends and no longer talked to anyone in his family. ▪ She completed the project on time but at the cost of her health. [=the work she did to complete the project on time damaged her health] ▪ He always says what he thinks, even at the cost of hurting someone's feelings. [count] ▪ What are the costs and benefits of the new law? ▪ To do something **at all costs** or (less commonly) **at any cost** is to do it even if you have to suffer, work very hard, lose everything you have, etc. ▪ She was determined to win at all costs. [=no matter what] ▪ Obscene language should be avoided at all costs. [=never use obscene words] ▪ He is determined to preserve his reputation at any cost.

  4   **costs** [plural]: the money used to pay for a court case ▪ She was fined 50 dollars and ordered to pay court costs.

---

5. ¹store /ˈstoɚ/ verb

stores; stored; stor·ing

  [+ obj] 1 a: to put (something that is not being used) in a place where it is available, where it can be kept safely, etc. ▪ I stored my furniture until I found a new apartment. ▪ She stores her jewels in a safe. ▪ The wine should be stored at room temperature. — often + *away* ▪ The grain was stored away for the winter. ▪ We stored away her old toys in the attic. **b:** to collect and put (something) into one location for future use ▪ The body stores fat. ▪ The solar panels store energy. — often + *up* ▪ The squirrels are storing up nuts for the winter. ▪ Plants store up the sun's energy. ▪ (Brit) If you get yourself into debt, you're only storing up trouble/problems for the future.

  2   to place (information) in a person's memory or a computer's memory ▪ They're studying how our brains store memories. — often + *away* ▪ He stored away his childhood memories. ▪ The file is stored away on the backup drive.

Vocabulary Review

Are these pairs of words and phrases similar in meaning or opposite in meaning? Circle S if similar; circle O if opposite.

1. **S / O**   substantially   fundamentally basically

2. **S / O**   texting   instant messaging

3. **S / O**   concentrate   distracted

4. **S / O**   undivided   dual

5. **S / O**   impaired   distracted

6. **S / O**   benefits   costs

7. **S / O**   conscious   aware

8. **S / O**   focus   concentrate

9. **S / O**   bouncing   switching

Reading Selection 3
Short Story

BEFORE YOU BEGIN

1. What is a lottery?

2. Why do you think lotteries have become popular throughout the world?

When "The Lottery" first appeared in the *New Yorker* magazine in 1948, letters flooded the magazine expressing admiration, anger, and confusion at the story. For a long time, Shirley Jackson refused to discuss the story, apparently believing that people had to make their own evaluation of it and come to a personal understanding of its meaning. Whatever people may think of it, they all agree that it is unusual.

Read "The Lottery" carefully and make your own judgment. Your teacher may want you to do Vocabulary from Context Exercise 1 on page 173 before you begin reading.

The Lottery
By Shirley Jackson

1   The morning of June 27th was clear and sunny, with the fresh warmth of a full-summer day; the flowers were blossoming profusely, and the grass was richly green. The people of the village began to gather in the square, between the post office and the bank, around ten o'clock; in some towns there were so many people that the lottery took two days and had to be started on June 26th, but in this village, where there were only about three hundred people, the whole lottery took only about two hours, so it could begin at ten o'clock in the morning and still be through in time to allow the villagers to get home for noon dinner.

2   The children assembled first, of course. School was recently over for the summer, and the feeling of liberty sat uneasily on most of them; they tended to gather together quietly for a while before they broke into boisterous play, and their talk was still of the classroom and the teacher, of books and reprimands. Bobby Martin had already stuffed his pockets full of stones, and the other boys soon followed his example, selecting the smoothest and roundest stones; Bobby and Harry Jones and Dickie Delacroix—the villagers pronounced the name "Dellacroy"—eventually made a great pile of stones in one corner of the square and guarded it against the raids of the other boys. The girls stood aside, talking among themselves, looking over their shoulders at the boys, and the very small children rolled in the dust or clung to the hands of their older brothers or sisters.

3   Soon the men began to gather, surveying their own children, speaking of planting and rain, tractors and taxes. They stood together, away from the pile of stones in the corner, and their jokes were quiet, and they smiled rather than laughed. The women, wearing faded house dresses and sweaters, came shortly after their menfolk. They greeted one another and exchanged bits of gossip as they went to join their husbands. Soon the women, standing by their husbands, began to call to their children, and the children

came reluctantly, having to be called four or five times. Bobby Martin ducked under his mother's grasping hand and ran, laughing, back to the pile of stones. His father spoke up sharply, and Bobby came quickly and took his place between his father and his oldest brother.

4   The lottery was conducted—as were the square dances, the teen-age club, the Halloween program—by Mr. Summers, who had time and energy to devote to civic activities. He was a round-faced, jovial man, and he ran the coal business; and people were sorry for him, because he had no children and his wife was a scold. When he arrived in the square, carrying the black wooden box, there was a murmur of conversation among the villagers, and he waved and called, "Little late today, folks." The postmaster, Mr. Graves, followed him, carrying a three-legged stool; and the stool was put in the center of the square, and Mr. Summers set the box down on it. The villagers kept their distance, leaving a space between themselves and the stool, and when Mr. Summers said, "Some of you fellows want to give me hand?" there was a hesitation before two men, Mr. Martin and his oldest son, Baxter, came forward to hold the box steady on the stool while Mr. Summers stirred up the papers inside it.

5   The original paraphernalia for the lottery had been lost long ago, and the black box now resting on the stool had been put into use even before Old Man Warner, the oldest man in town, was born. Mr. Summers spoke frequently to the villagers about making a new box, but no one liked to upset even as much tradition as was represented by the black box. There was a story that the present box had been made with some pieces of the box that had preceded it, the one that had been constructed when the first people settled down to make a village here. Every year, after the lottery, Mr. Summers began talking again about a new box, but every year the subject was allowed to fade off without anything's being done. The black box grew shabbier each year; by now it was

no longer completely black but splintered badly along one side to show the original wood color, and in some places faded or stained.

6   Mr. Martin and his oldest son, Baxter, held the black box securely on the stool until Mr. Summers had stirred the papers thoroughly with his hand. Because so much of the ritual had been forgotten or discarded, Mr. Summers had been successful in having slips of paper substituted for the chips of wood that had been used for generations. Chips of wood, Mr. Summers had argued, had been all very well when the village was tiny, but now that the population was more than three hundred and likely to keep on growing, it was necessary to use something that would fit more easily into the black box. The night before the lottery, Mr. Summers and Mr. Graves made up the slips of paper and put them into the box, and it was then taken to the safe of Mr. Summers's coal company and locked up until Mr. Summers was ready to take it to the square next morning. The rest of the year, the box was put away, sometimes one place, sometimes another; it had spent one year in Mr. Graves's barn and another year underfoot in the post office, and sometimes it was set on a shelf in the Martin grocery and left there.

7   There was a great deal of fussing to be done before Mr. Summers declared the lottery open. There were the lists to make up—of heads of families, heads of households in each family, members of each household in each family. There was the proper swearing-in of Mr. Summers by the postmaster, as the official of the lottery; at one time, some people remembered, there had been a recital of some sort, performed by the official of the lottery, a perfunctory, tuneless chant that had been rattled off duly each year; some people believed that the official of the lottery used to stand just so when he said or sang it; others believed that he was supposed to walk among the people; but years and years ago this part of the ritual had been allowed to lapse. There had been also a ritual salute, which the official of the

lottery had had to use in addressing each person who came up to draw from the box, but this also had changed with time, until now it was felt necessary only for the official to speak to each person approaching. Mr. Summers was very good at all this; in his clean white shirt and blue jeans, with one hand resting carelessly on the black box, he seemed very proper and important as he talked interminably to Mr. Graves and the Martins.

8 Just as Mr. Summers finally left off talking and turned to the assembled villagers, Mrs. Hutchinson came hurriedly along the path to the square, her sweater thrown over her shoulders, and slid into place in the back of the crowd. "Clean forgot what day it was," she said to Mrs. Delacroix, who stood next to her, and they both laughed softly. "Thought my old man was out back stacking wood," Mrs. Hutchinson went on, "and then I looked out the window and the kids was gone, and then I remembered it was the twenty-seventh and came a-running." She dried her hands on her apron, and Mrs. Delacroix said, "You're in time, though. They're still talking away up there."

9 Mrs. Hutchinson craned her neck to see through the crowd and found her husband and children standing near the front. She tapped Mrs. Delacroix on the arm as a farewell and began to make her way through the crowd. The people separated good-humoredly to let her through; two or three people said, in voices just loud enough to be heard across the crowd, "Here comes your Mrs., Hutchinson," and "Bill, she made it after all." Mrs. Hutchinson reached her husband, and Mr. Summers, who had been waiting, said cheerfully, "Thought we were going to have to get on without you, Tessie." Mrs. Hutchinson said, grinning, "Wouldn't have me leave m'dishes in the sink, now, would you Joe?" and soft laughter ran through the crowd as the people stirred back into position after Mrs. Hutchinson's arrival.

10 "Well, now," Mr. Summers said soberly, "guess we better get started, get this over with, so's we can go back to work. Anybody ain't here?"

"Dunbar," several people said. "Dunbar, Dunbar."

Mr. Summers consulted his list. "Clyde Dunbar," he said. "That's right. He's broke his leg, hasn't he? Who's drawing for him?"

11 "Me, I guess," a woman said, and Mr. Summers turned to look at her. "Wife draws for her husband," Mr. Summers said. "Don't you have a grown boy to do it for you, Janey?" Although Mr. Summers and everyone else in the village knew the answer perfectly well, it was the business of the official of the lottery to ask such questions formally. Mr. Summers waited with an expression of polite interest while Mrs. Dunbar answered.

"Horace's not but sixteen yet," Mrs. Dunbar said regretfully. "Guess I gotta fill in for the old man this year."

"Right," Mr. Summers said. He made a note on the list he was holding. Then he asked, "Watson boy drawing this year?"

12 A tall boy in the crowd raised his hand, "Here," he said. "I'm drawing for m'mother and me." He blinked his eyes nervously and ducked his head as several voices in the crowd said things like "Good fellow, Jack," and "Glad to see your mother's got a man to do it."

"Well," Mr. Summers said, "guess that's everyone. Old Man Warner make it?"

"Here," a voice said, and Mr. Summers nodded.

13 A sudden hush fell on the crowd as Mr. Summers cleared his throat and looked at the list. "All ready?" he called. "Now, I'll read the names— heads of families first—and the men come up and take a paper out of the box. Keep the paper folded in your hand without looking at it until everyone has had a turn. Everything clear?"

14 The people had done it so many times that they only half listened to the directions; most of them were quiet, wetting their lips, not looking around. Then Mr. Summers raised one hand high and

said, "Adams." A man disengaged himself from the crowd and came forward. "Hi, Steve," Mr. Summers said, and Mr. Adams said, "Hi, Joe." They grinned at one another humorlessly and nervously. Then Mr. Adams reached into the black box and took out a folded paper. He held it firmly by one corner as he turned and went hastily back to his place in the crowd, where he stood a little apart from his family, not looking down at his hand.

"Allen," Mr. Summers said. "Anderson… Bentham."

15 "Seems like there's no time at all between lotteries any more," Mrs. Delacroix said to Mrs. Graves in the back row. "Seems like we got through with the last one only last week."

"Time sure goes fast," Mrs. Graves said.

"Clark… Delacroix." …

"There goes my old man," Mrs. Delacroix said. She held her breath while her husband went forward.

"Dunbar," Mr. Summers said, and Mrs. Dunbar went steadily to the box while one of the women said, "Go on, Janey," and another said, "There she goes."

16 "We're next," Mrs. Graves said. She watched while Mr. Graves came around from the side of the box, greeted Mr. Summers gravely, and selected a slip of paper from the box. By now, all through the crowd there were men holding the small folded papers in their large hands, turning them over and over nervously. Mrs. Dunbar and her two sons stood together, Mrs. Dunbar holding the slip of paper.

"Harburt… Hutchinson."

"Get up there, Bill," Mrs. Hutchinson said, and the people near her laughed.

"Jones."

17 "They do say," Mr. Adams said to Old Man Warner, who stood next to him, "that over in the north village they're talking of giving up the lottery."

Old Man Warner snorted. "Pack of crazy fools," he said. "Listening to the young folks, nothing's good enough for them. Next thing you know, they'll be wanting to go back to living in caves, nobody work any more, live *that* way for a while. Used to be a saying about 'Lottery in June, corn be heavy soon.' First thing you know, we'd all be eating stewed chickweed and acorns. There's always been a lottery," he added petulantly. "Bad enough to see young Joe Summers up there joking with everybody."

18 "Some places have already quit lotteries," Mrs. Adams said.

"Nothing but trouble in that," Old Man Warner said stoutly. "Pack of young fools."

"Martin." And Bobby Martin watched his father go forward. "Overdyke… Percy."

"I wish they'd hurry," Mrs. Dunbar said to her older son. "I wish they'd hurry."

"They're almost through," her son said.

"You get ready to run tell Dad," Mrs. Dunbar said.

19 Mr. Summers called his own name and then stepped forward precisely and selected a slip from the box. Then he called, "Warner."

"Seventy-seventh year I been in the lottery," Old Man Warner said as he went through the crowd. "Seventy-seventh time."

"Watson." The tall boy came awkwardly through the crowd. Someone said, "Don't be nervous, Jack," and Mr. Summers said, "Take your time, son."

"Zanini."

20 After that, there was a long pause, a breathless pause, until Mr. Summers, holding his slip of paper in the air, said, "All right, fellows." For a minute, no one moved, and then all the slips of paper were opened. Suddenly, all the women began to speak at once, saying, "Who is it?" "Who's got it?" "Is it the Dunbars?" "Is it the Watsons?" Then the voices began to say, "It's Hutchinson. It's Bill. Bill Hutchinson's got it."

"Go tell your father," Mrs. Dunbar said to her older son.

21 People began to look around to see the Hutchinsons. Bill Hutchinson was standing quiet, staring down at the paper in his hand. Suddenly, Tessie Hutchinson shouted to Mr. Summers, "You didn't give him time enough to take any paper he wanted. I saw you. It wasn't fair!"

"Be a good sport, Tessie," Mrs. Delacroix called, and Mrs. Graves said, "All of us took the same chance."

"Shut up, Tessie," Bill Hutchinson said.

22 "Well, everyone," Mr. Summers said, "that was done pretty fast, and now we've got to be hurrying a little more to get done in time." He consulted his next list. "Bill," he said, "you draw for the Hutchinson family. You got any other households in the Hutchinsons?"

"There's Don and Eva," Mrs. Hutchinson yelled. "Make *them* take their chance!"

"Daughters draw with their husbands' families, Tessie," Mr. Summers said gently. "You know that as well as anyone else."

"It wasn't fair!" Tessie said.

23 "I guess not, Joe," Bill Hutchinson said regretfully. "My daughter draws with her husband's family. That's only fair. And I've got no other family except the kids."

"Then, as far as drawing for families is concerned, it's you," Mr. Summers said in explanation, "and as far as drawing for households is concerned, that's you, too. Right?"

"Right," Bill Hutchinson said.

"How many kids, Bill?" Mr. Summers asked formally.

"Three," Bill Hutchinson said. "There's Bill, Jr., and Nancy, and little Dave. And Tessie and me."

"All right, then," Mr. Summers said. "Harry, you got their tickets back?"

24 Mr. Graves nodded and held up the slips of paper. "Put them in the box, then," Mr. Summers directed. "Take Bill's and put it in."

"I think we ought to start over," Mrs. Hutchinson said, as quietly as she could. "I tell you it wasn't *fair*. You didn't give him time enough to choose. *Everybody* saw that."

Mr. Graves had selected the five slips and put them in the box, and he dropped all the papers but those onto the ground, where the breeze caught them and lifted them off.

"Listen, everybody," Mrs. Hutchinson was saying to the people around her.

"Ready, Bill?" Mr. Summers asked, and Bill Hutchinson, with one quick glance around at his wife and children, nodded.

25 "Remember," Mr. Summers said, "take the slips and keep them folded until each person has taken one. Harry, you help little Dave." Mr. Graves took the hand of the little boy, who came willingly with him up to the box. "Take a paper out of the box, Davy," Mr. Summers said. Davy put his hand into the box and laughed. "Take just one paper," Mr. Summers said. "Harry, you hold it for him." Mr. Graves took the child's hand and removed the folded paper from the right fist and held it while little Dave stood next to him and looked up at him wonderingly.

26 "Nancy next," Mr. Summers said. Nancy was twelve, and her school friends breathed heavily as she went forward, switching her skirt, and took a slip daintily from the box. "Bill, Jr.," Mr. Summers said, and Billy, his face red and his feet overlarge, nearly knocked the box over as he got a paper out. "Tessie," Mr. Summers said. She hesitated for a minute, looking around defiantly, and then set her lips and went up to the box. She snatched a paper out and held it behind her.

27 "Bill," Mr. Summers said, and Bill Hutchinson reached into the box and felt around, bringing his hand out at last with the slip of paper in it.

The crowd was quiet. A girl whispered, "I hope it's not Nancy," and the sound of the whisper reached the edges of the crowd.

"It's not the way it used to be," Old Man Warner said clearly. "People ain't the way they used to be."

"All right," Mr. Summers said. "Open the papers. Harry, you open little Dave's."

28 Mr. Graves opened the slip of paper, and there was a general sigh through the crowd as he held it up and everyone could see that it was blank. Nancy and Bill, Jr., opened theirs at the same time, and both beamed and laughed, turning around to the crowd and holding their slips above their heads.

"Tessie," Mr. Summers said. There was a pause, and then Mr. Summers looked at Bill Hutchinson, and Bill unfolded his paper and showed it. It was blank.

"It's Tessie," Mr. Summers said, and his voice was hushed. "Show us her paper, Bill."

29 Bill Hutchinson went over to his wife and forced the slip of paper out of her hand. It had a black spot on it, the black spot Mr. Summers had made the night before with the heavy pencil in the coal-company office. Bill Hutchinson held it up, and there was a stir in the crowd.

"All right, folks," Mr. Summers said, "Let's finish quickly."

30 Although the villagers had forgotten the ritual and lost the original black box, they still remembered to use stones. The pile of stones the boys had made earlier was ready; there were stones on the ground with the blowing scraps of paper that had come out of the box. Mrs. Delacroix selected a stone so large she had to pick it up with both hands and turned to Mrs. Dunbar. "Come on," she said. "Hurry up."

Mrs. Dunbar had small stones in both hands, and she said, gasping for breath, "I can't run at all. You'll have to go ahead and I'll catch up with you."

31 The children had stones already, and someone gave little Davy Hutchinson a few pebbles.

Tessie Hutchinson was in the center of a cleared space by now, and she held her hands out desperately as the villagers moved in on her. "It isn't fair," she said. A stone hit her on the side of the head.

Old Man Warner was saying, "Come on, come on, everyone." Steve Adams was in the front of the crowd of villagers, with Mrs. Graves beside him.

"It isn't fair, it isn't right," Mrs. Hutchinson screamed, and then they were upon her.

Exercise 1

Without referring to the story, indicate if each statement below is True (T) or False (F).

1. _____ The lottery was always held in summer.

2. _____ The lottery had not changed for many generations.

3. _____ The villagers were angry at Mrs. Hutchinson for being late.

4. _____ In the first drawing, only one person from each family drew a paper from the black box.

5. _____ The lottery was a custom only in this small village.

6. _____ Bill Hutchinson thought the first drawing was unfair.

7. _____ Tessie Hutchinson drew the paper with the black dot in the final drawing.

8. _____ The people wanted to finish in a hurry because they didn't like Tessie.

9. _____ The lottery was a form of human sacrifice.

Exercise 2

The following exercise requires a careful reading of "The Lottery." Indicate if each statement below is True (T) or False (F) according to your understanding of the story. Use information in the passage and inferences that can be drawn from the passage to make your decisions. You may refer to the story if necessary.

1. _____ Old Man Warner believed that the lottery assured the prosperity of the village.

2. _____ The date of the lottery was not rigidly fixed but occurred any time in summer when all of the villagers could be present.

3. _____ Mr. Summers never managed to make a new box for the lottery because people were unwilling to change the traditions that remained from the past.

4. _____ A family might contain several households.

5. _____ Mr. Warner felt that stopping the lottery would be equal to returning to prehistoric times.

6. _____ Only Mr. Warner remembered when the lottery was started.

7. _____ The villagers were hesitant to take part in the final step in the lottery.

Drawing Inferences

1. When did you first realize that this was a strange lottery? That winning the lottery was not desirable?

2. What details did the author add to make the lottery seem like a "normal" lottery? What details indicate that the lottery was strange? What details have double meanings?

3. Why do you think everyone had to take part in the final step of the lottery?

4. What was Mr. Warner's attitude toward the lottery? In what way and why did his attitude differ from those of other members of the community? What group in every society does Mr. Warner represent?

5. Why did Tessie want to include Don and Eva in the final drawing?

6. Which aspects of the lottery have changed? Which have not changed?

Discussion

1. How do you think the lottery began? Why was it started? Why does it take place at that time of year?

2. Why do you think the community continues the lottery?

3. Would you take part in the lottery if you were a member of the community?

4. This story is about a physical sacrifice in which a person is killed. Sacrifice is characterized by the suffering of one member of a group for the benefit of the group as a whole and by a sense of relief when one realizes that he or she has not been selected. This relief is so great that it leads to unconcern toward the fate of the person(s) to be sacrificed. Using this definition, can you think of specific institutions in modern societies in which sacrifices take place? Aside from physical sacrifice, what other types of sacrifice are possible?

 To read more about obedience to authority, see Unit 9.

Discussion/Composition

Was the lottery fair?

Exercise 1

Use the context provided to determine the meanings of the italicized words. Write a definition, synonym, or description of each of the italicized vocabulary items in the space provided.

1. _____

2. _____

3. _____

4. _____

5. _____

6. _____

7. _____

8. _____

I like any game of chance, but I most enjoy taking part in a lottery. The lottery is like an unchanging religious ceremony, and it is perhaps this *ritual* (1) quality of the lottery that people enjoy. Unlike other games of chance, a lottery does not require a great deal of *paraphernalia* (2). The only equipment needed is a bowl filled with slips of paper. I enjoy the excitement of watching the official pick the winning number. The moment before the *drawing* (3) is very serious. The judge *gravely* (4) approaches the bowl and looks at the crowd *soberly* (5). The crowd is quiet except for the low *murmur* (6) of excitement. Suddenly the winner is selected. After the lottery is over, everyone but the winner throws away his or her piece of paper, and the *discarded* (7) slips are soon blown away by the wind. People begin to *disengage* (8) themselves from the crowd and the lottery is over.

Exercise 2

This exercise is designed to give you additional clues to determine the meanings of unfamiliar vocabulary items in context. In the paragraph of "The Lottery" indicated by the number in parentheses, find the word that best fits the meaning given. Your teacher may want to read these aloud as you quickly scan* the paragraph to find the answer.

1. (2) Which word means *noisy* and *excited?* _____

2. (2) Which word means *criticisms; severe or formal scoldings?* _____

3. (3) Which word means *information, usually about other people, not always factual?* _____

4. (7) Which word at the beginning of the paragraph means *taking care of details?* _____

5. (7) Which word at the bottom of the paragraph means *endlessly?* _____

_____

*For an introduction to scanning, see Unit 1.

Exercise 3

This exercise should be done after you have finished reading "The Lottery." The exercise is designed to give you practice using context clues to guess the meaning of unfamiliar vocabulary. Give a definition, synonym, or description of each of the words and phrases below. The number in parentheses indicates the paragraph in which the word can be found. Your teacher may want you to do these orally or in writing.

1. (4) devote _____

2. (4) stirred up _____

3. (5) fade off _____

4. (5) shabbier _____

5. (7) lapse _____

6. (9) craned _____

7. (9) tapped _____

8. (10) consulted _____

UNIT 7

Nonprose Reading
Charts and Graphs

One of the most important kinds of nonprose reading in both the academic and business worlds involves understanding charts, graphs, and diagrams, and their relationship to the prose that accompanies them. This exercise contains information about what is sometimes called "global warming," the climate change that scientists believe is having serious consequences on weather worldwide.

> **BEFORE YOU BEGIN**

1. What do you know about global warming? Your teacher may want you to discuss this first in pairs or groups.

2. Why do you think scientists are concerned about an increase in the average temperature worldwide?

3. What do you know about the causes of global warming?

On page 177 is a description of the basic science of global warming from former United States Vice President Al Gore's book, *An Inconvenient Truth*, written for a general audience. After you read it, answer the questions that follow.

The Basic Science of Global Warming

The Sun's energy enters the atmosphere in the form of light waves and heats up the Earth. Some of that energy warms the Earth and then is re-radiated back into space in the form of infrared waves.

Under normal conditions, a portion of the outgoing infrared radiation is naturally trapped by the atmosphere—and that is a good thing, because it keeps the temperature on Earth within comfortable bounds. The greenhouse gases on Venus are so thick that its temperature is far too hot for humans. The greenhouse gases surrounding Mars are almost nonexistent, so the temperature there is far too cold. That's why the Earth is sometimes referred to as the "Goldilocks planet"—the temperatures here have been just right.

The problem we now face is that this thin layer of atmosphere is being thickened by huge quantities of human-caused carbon dioxide and other greenhouse gases. And as it thickens, it traps a lot of the infrared radiation that would otherwise escape the atmosphere and continue out to the universe. As a result, the temperature of the Earth's surface—including oceans—is getting dangerously warmer.

That's what the climate crisis is all about.

FIGURE 1

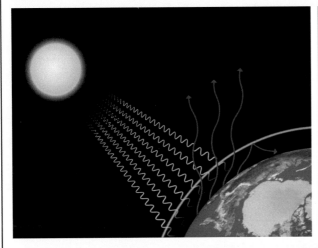 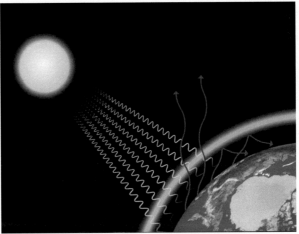

Comprehension

1. **T / F**   The Sun's rays that warm the Earth are all absorbed by the Earth.

2. **T / F**   The fact that some infrared radiation is trapped by the Earth's atmosphere is a good thing.

3. A greenhouse is a glass building in which plants are grown that need protection from the cold. Why do you think carbon dioxide is called a greenhouse gas? _____

4. In your own words, briefly explain why the temperature of the Earth's atmosphere is rising.

   _____

5. What do you think the Gore is referring to when he talks about "human-caused carbon dioxide?"

   _____

Following are more charts and graphs about climate change. This section is adapted from a university website that answered commonly asked questions about global warming. Each question is followed by an answer and then supporting data. Information is also provided from other research sites. Look at these questions and data. Don't be concerned about unfamiliar vocabulary as long as you are able to understand the overall message. Then answer the questions that follow. True/False items are indicated by a T / F preceding a statement.

Question: Is global warming happening?
Answer: Yes.

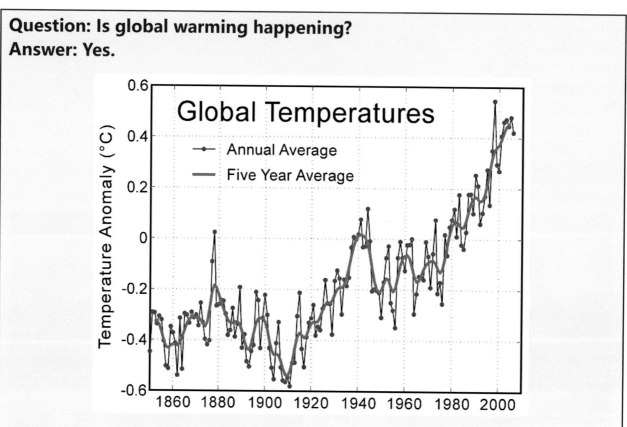

FIGURE 2. Line plot of global mean land-ocean temperature index, 1880 to present. Zero on this figure is mean temperature for the base period 1951-1980. The black line is the annual mean and the solid red line is the five-year mean. The blue bars show uncertainty estimates, due to incomplete sampling.

Comprehension

1. **T / F** The chart reports data for the most populous areas around the world.

2. What does the zero in the middle of the chart represent? _____

3. This graph reports what it calls "temperature anomalies" over time. What are these?

_____

4. Some presentations of this data also show the actual value for the zero in the middle of the chart. Do you think this is unnecessary, or would you have found it useful or interesting?

_____

5. Why do you think the chart shows data for both yearly and five-year average temperatures? _____

6. **T / F** According to this graph, the mean temperature began rising for the first time in 1880.

7. **T / F** The rate of temperature increase in the period 1980–2010 was greater than the period 1900–1980.

8. Summarize the data reported in a single sentence. _____

_____

Question: Are there observable effects that may be tied to global warming?

Answer: Yes

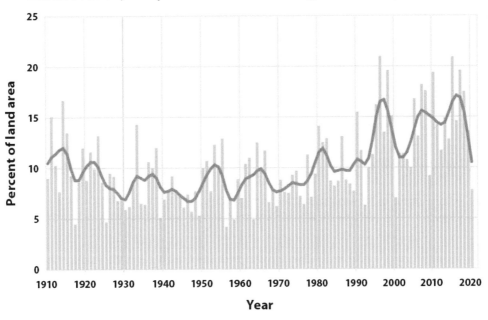

Extreme One-Day Precipitation Events in the Contiguous 48 States, 1910–2020

For more information, visit U.S. EPA's "Climate Change Indicators in the United States" at www.epa.gov/climate-indicators.

FIGURE 3. As one example, this figure shows the percentage of US area (excluding Alaska and Hawaii) where a much greater than normal portion of total annual precipitation has come from extreme single-day precipitation events. The bars represent individual years, while the line is a nine-year weighted average.

Comprehension

1. What years does the graph cover? _____

2. **T / F** This graph shows total amount of precipitation over those years.

3. **T / F** The orange line represents the data averaged over periods of 10 years.

4. **T / F** According to the graph, only the United States experienced extreme precipitation events during this period.

5. Scientists explain that extreme precipitation is a result of global warming. What do you think the connection is? Discuss this with your classmates. If you don't know, look at Figure 4.

Sometimes data is reported with both prose and graphic representations. Here is a presentation of data that is similar to what you saw in Figure 3. Use information in the prose and graph to answer the questions that follow.

Because evaporation increases with water temperature, warmer water increases the moisture content of storms. When storm conditions trigger a downpour, more moisture falls in the form of big, one-time rainfalls and snowfalls. Partly as a result, the number of large flood events has increased decade by decade, on every continent. In many areas of the world, global warming also increases the percentage of annual precipitation that falls as rain instead of snow, which has led to more flooding in spring and early summer.

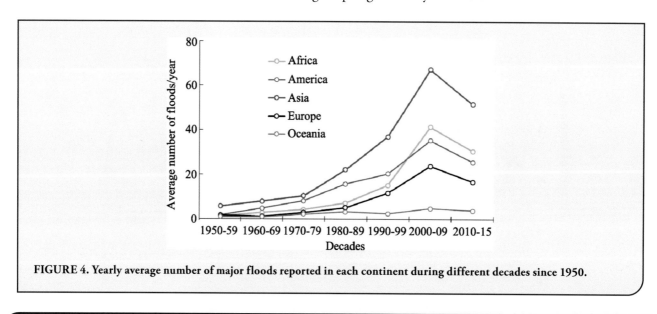

FIGURE 4. Yearly average number of major floods reported in each continent during different decades since 1950.

Comprehension

1. According to the description above the graph, why does global warming contribute to flooding?

   _____

2. What are the differences in the information provided in this passage (prose and graph) and in Figure 3?

   _____

   _____

   _____

3. If you want to show effects of global warming, do you prefer one presentation to the other?

   • Is one easier for you to understand? _____

   • Do you find one more persuasive? Why? _____

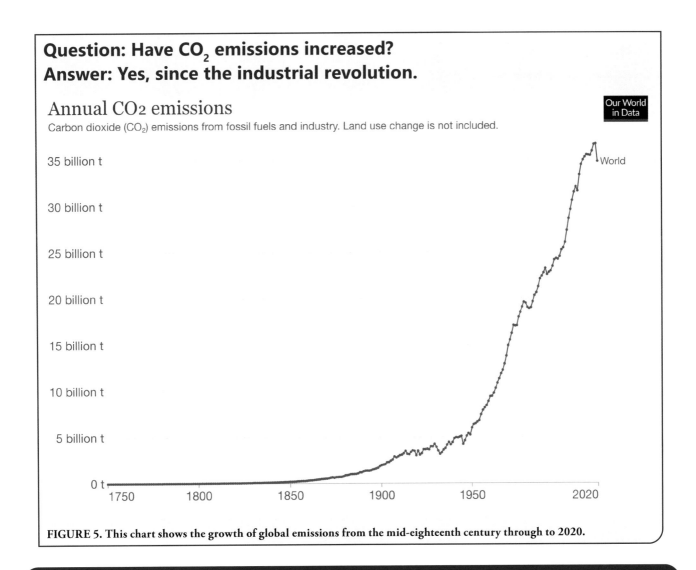

Question: Have CO₂ emissions increased?
Answer: Yes, since the industrial revolution.

Annual CO₂ emissions

Carbon dioxide (CO_2) emissions from fossil fuels and industry. Land use change is not included.

Our World in Data

FIGURE 5. This chart shows the growth of global emissions from the mid-eighteenth century through to 2020.

Comprehension

1. Describe the change in CO_2 emissions shown in this graph in one sentence. _____

_____

Question: How about CO$_2$ emissions prior to the industrial revolution?
Answer: See below.

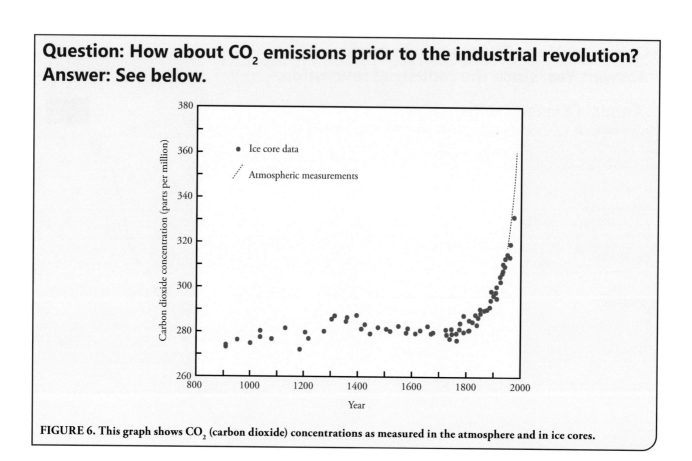

FIGURE 6. This graph shows CO$_2$ (carbon dioxide) concentrations as measured in the atmosphere and in ice cores.

1. In a single sentence, describe the findings reported in this chart.

    _____

    _____

2. Some sources reporting this figure also include a prose description. Here is a description originally published by the United Nations.

    > Ice buried below the surface of the Greenland and Antarctic ice caps contains bubbles of air trapped when the ice originally formed. These samples of fossil air, some of them over 200,000 years old, have been retrieved by drilling deep into the ice. Measurements from the youngest and most shallow segments of the ice cores, which contain air from only a few decades ago, produce carbon dioxide concentrations nearly identical to those that were measured directly in the atmosphere at the time the ice formed. But the older parts of the cores show that carbon dioxide amounts were about 25% lower than today for the ten thousand years previous to the onset of industrialization, and over that period changed little.

a. Underline the single sentence that describes the findings reported in Figure 6.

b. Can you think of circumstances when it might be best to present the figure alone? When would it be best to include the prose?

_____

_____

Question: Who are the biggest contributors to global CO2 emissions?
Answer: Top contributors are China, US, India, Russia.

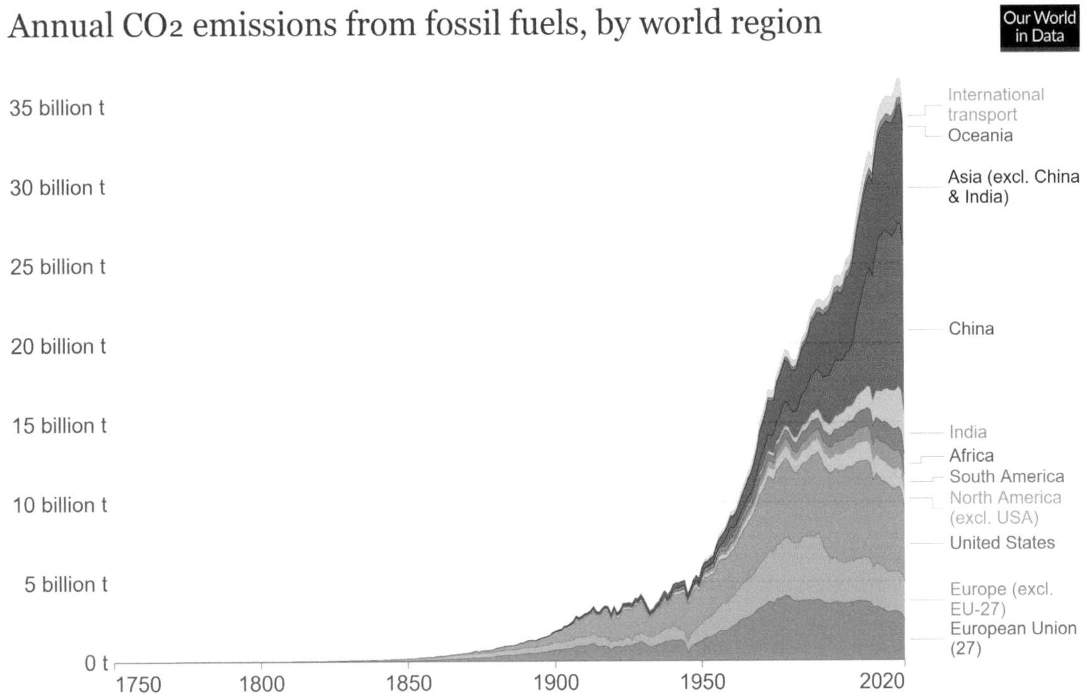

Annual CO₂ emissions from fossil fuels, by world region

FIGURE 7

Comprehension

1 a. According to this graph, which regions are the four biggest contributors to global CO2 emissions in 2020?

_____

b. Why doesn't the graph show the same results as listed under "Answer," above?

_____

2. Where does your country appear on this graph? _____

Question: Will today's emissions patterns continue?
Answer: See below.

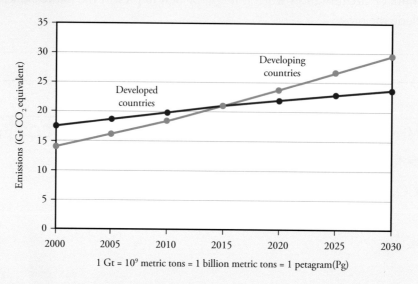

1 Gt = 10^9 metric tons = 1 billion metric tons = 1 petagram(Pg)

Figure 8 provides a projection of future greenhouse gas emissions of developed and developing countries. According to the graph, total emissions from the developing world have exceeded those from the developed world.

Comprehension

1. What are "developed countries"? Give an example.

   _____

2. What are "developing countries"? Give an example.

   _____

3. According to this projection, when did developing countries surpass developed countries in producing harmful emissions? _____

4. Why do you think this occurred?

   _____

   _____

   _____

Exercise 1

The questions below are based on Figures 1–8 (pages 177–184).

1. Following is a list of predicted consequences of global warming. Why do you think that increased temperatures worldwide might cause these? Use information from this unit and your own knowledge.

   a. Increased wildfires _____

   b. More and stronger hurricanes and typhoons _____

   c. Danger to food production and water supplies _____

   d. Increases in infectious diseases _____

2. If you don't live in an area that has hurricanes, wildfires, or flooding, should you be concerned about these things? Why do you think scientists are so concerned?

   _____

   _____

3. Based on your background knowledge and what you have read here, do you believe that global warming is a serious danger? Why or why not?

   _____

   _____

Exercise 2

Below is a summary of postings from other educational websites. It argues that global warming is not only a scientific issue, but also an ethical one. Read this argument and respond to the questions below.

Ethics and Global Climate Change

Increasingly, scholars have noted that climate change poses significant moral challenges. Professors Stephen Gardiner and Lauren Hartzell-Nichols of the University of Washington work in the areas of environmental studies and social values. They argue that climate change creates major interrelated ethical challenges.

The first challenge comes from the fact that "climate change is a truly global phenomenon. Once emitted, greenhouse gas emissions can have climate effects anywhere on the planet, regardless of their source." This is supported by a World Health Organization (WHO) report that has shown that the growing health effects of climate change affect different regions in very different ways. The places that have contributed the least to warming the Earth are the most vulnerable to the death and disease higher temperatures can bring. The lead author of the WHO report, Professor Jonathan Patz, explains, "Those least able to cope and least responsible for the greenhouse gases that cause global warming are most affected… Herein lies an enormous global ethical challenge."

Gardiner and Hartzell-Nichols' second challenge is that "current emissions have profoundly intergenerational effects." Greenhouse gas emissions typically remain in the atmosphere for a long time, "contributing to negative climate impacts for centuries, or even millennia." This is unfair to future generations.

Finally, Gardiner and Hartzell-Nichols argue that people today don't have a way to deal with climate change in areas such as international justice, intergenerational ethics, scientific uncertainty, and what Gardiner and Hartzell-Nichols term "the appropriate relationship between humans and the rest of nature." For example, what responsibilities do humans have to protect animal life?

The way we meet these challenges will determine the future of our planet and those who live on it.

1. Gardiner and Hartzell-Nichols say that their three ethical dilemmas are "mutually reinforcing," that is, the difficulties of each challenge work to make the others more challenging. What are the three challenges, and how might they work together? _____

2. Figure 9 shows World Health Organization data on the health effects of global warming by region. In what way does the figure illustrate the challenge of unequal/unfair effects described in the passage above?

_____

FIGURE 9. The health effects of global warming by subregion. The map shows the estimated deaths per million attributable to global climate change between the years 2000 and 2050.

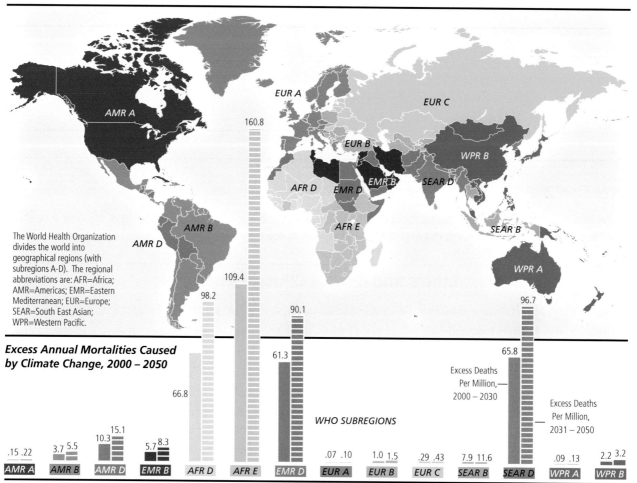

The World Health Organization divides the world into geographical regions (with subregions A-D). The regional abbreviations are: AFR=Africa; AMR=Americas; EMR=Eastern Mediterranean; EUR=Europe; SEAR=South East Asian; WPR=Western Pacific.

Excess Annual Mortalities Caused by Climate Change, 2000 – 2050

SOURCE: WORLD HEALTH ORGANIZATION

LUCIDITY INFORMATION DESIGN, LLC

3. The challenge of unequal/unfair effects mentioned in this article largely describes the relationship between wealthy and poor nations. Does the future situation projected in Figure 8, focusing on the relationship between developed and developing countries, support this analysis, or does it present a contrasting picture?

4. It can take a number of years to collect worldwide data on these issues; data collected at one time may not be published for a number of years. International sites published data collected in 2000 in 2021. Why do you think this is the case? Do you think these overall global health effects change quickly? Why or why not?

Discussion/Composition

1. Is there a solution to global warming?

   • Can it be solved by a single country? A single region? An individual?

   • What do you think world leaders should do? National leaders? Individuals?

2. A person's or group's "carbon footprint" is the amount of carbon dioxide (and other carbon compounds) emitted as a result of using fossil fuels. Why do individuals and/or governments resist efforts to reduce carbon dioxide emissions? List four arguments you could use to persuade a friend or a government official to reduce their carbon footprint. Your teacher may want you to write a letter of persuasion after you have identified arguments you could use.

   _____

   _____

   _____

   _____

3. Below is a list of things that people can do to reduce their carbon footprint. Which if any of these actions are you most likely to take? Least likely? Why?

   • Drive less and/or use more efficient cars.

   • Use energy efficient lighting, including LED light bulbs.

   • Lower your thermostats in winter time, raise them in summer time to reduce heating and air conditioning usage.

   • Insulate buildings. This can save a lot of energy and money.

   • In areas where available, use an energy provider that uses renewable energy resources, such as wind, water, or solar power.

Word Study
Context Clues

Exercise 1

In the following exercise, do *not* try to learn the italicized words. Concentrate on developing your ability to guess the meanings of unfamiliar words using context clues.* Read each sentence carefully and write a definition, synonym, or description of the italicized word on the line provided.

1. _____ As he reached for the rock above him, his rope broke, and he hung *precariously* (1) by one hand as the rescuers ran toward him.

2. _____ The tired soldiers *trudged* (2) through knee-deep mud for hours before they found a dry place to sleep.

3. _____ In the past, the world seemed to run in an orderly way. Now, however, everything seems to be in a state of *turmoil* (3).

4. _____ Monkeys are well known for their *grooming* (4) habits; they spend hours carefully cleaning bits of dirt and straw from their coats.

5. _____ *Matrimony* (5) doesn't seem to agree with Liz—she's been unhappy ever since she got married.

6. _____ Using a long, slender instrument called a *probe* (6), doctors are able to locate and remove pieces of metal from a patient's wounds.

7. _____ The following Monday, when the president *convened* (7) the second meeting of the committee, we all sat down quietly and waited for the meeting to begin.

8. _____ We think of plants in general as absorbing food; we think of animals as *ingesting* (8) or "eating" it.

9. _____ Vladimir is considered an *autocratic* (9) leader because he makes decisions without seeking the opinions of others.

10. _____ There is an element of word magic here: entomology and *limnology* (10) sound more important than merely insect biology and freshwater biology.

---

*For an introduction to using context clues, see Unit 1.

Exercise 2

This exercise is designed to give you practice using context clues from a passage. Use your general knowledge along with information from the entire text below to write a definition, synonym, or description of the italicized word on the line provided. Read through the entire passage before making a decision. Note that some of the words appear more than once; by the end of the passage you should have a good idea of their meaning. Do not worry if your definition is not exact; a general idea of the meaning will often allow you to understand the meaning of a written text.

Major Personality Study Finds that Traits Are Mostly Inherited
Daniel Goleman

The *genetic* makeup of a child is a stronger influence on personality than child *rearing*, according to the first study to examine identical twins *reared* in different families. The *findings shatter* a widespread belief... in the *primacy* of family influence and are sure to lead to engender fierce debate.

The *findings* were the first major results to emerge from a long-term project at the University of Minnesota in which... more than 350 pairs of twins have gone through six days of extensive testing that has included analysis of blood, brain waves, intelligence, and allergies.

For most of the traits measured, more than half the variation was found to be due to *heredity*, leaving less than half determined by the influence of parents, home environment, and other experiences in life.

The Minnesota *findings* stand in sharp contradiction to standard wisdom on nature versus *nurture* in forming adult personality. Virtually all major theories since Freud have given far more importance to environment, or *nurture*, than to *genes*, or nature.

genetic/genes: _____

rearing/reared: _____

findings: _____

shattered: _____

primacy: _____

heredity: _____

nurture: _____

Word Study
Stems and Affixes

Below is a list of some commonly occurring stems and affixes.* Study their meanings, and then do the exercises that follow. Your teacher may ask you to give examples of other words you know that are derived from these stems and affixes.

Prefixes		
multi-	many	*multiply, multiple*
peri-	around	*periscope, perimeter*
semi-	half, partly	*semisweet, semicircle*
tri-	three	*triangle*
ultra-	beyond, excessive, extreme	*ultramodern*
uni-	one	*unicycle, unify, universe*
Stems		
-aster-, -astro-, -stellar-	star	*astronomy, stellar*
-auto-	self	*automobile, automatic*
-bio-	life	*biology*
-cycle-	circle	*bicycle, cycle*
-mega-	great, large	*megaton, megalopolis*
-mort-	death	*mortal, immortality*
-phil-	love	*philosophy*
-polis-	city	*metropolis*
-psych-	mind	*psychology*
-soph-	wise	*philosophy, sophomore*
Suffixes		
-ity	condition, quality, state of being	*unity, ability*
-ness	condition, quality, state of being	*sadness, happiness*

Exercise 1

For each item, select the best definition of the italicized word or phrase, or answer the question.

1. To apply to some universities, you must fill out the application form and include a short *autobiography*.

   _____ **a.** sample of your writing   _____ **c.** list of courses you have taken

   _____ **b.** account of your life written by you   _____ **d.** list of schools you have attended

---

*For a list of all stems and affixes that appear in *Reader's Choice*, see Appendix B.

2. The police officer used a *megaphone.*

   _____ **a.** a portable radio
   _____ **c.** an instrument to make one's voice louder

   _____ **b.** a long stick
   _____ **d.** a telephone in the car

3. Dr. Swanson has written articles about *interstellar* travel.

   _____ **a.** underwater
   _____ **c.** high-speed

   _____ **b.** long-distance
   _____ **d.** outer space

4. Janet is interested in *autographs* of famous people.

   _____ **a.** pictures
   _____ **c.** families

   _____ **b.** personalities
   _____ **d.** signatures

5. An *asterisk* is a written symbol that looks like…

   _____ **a.** /.   _____ **b.** *.   _____ **c.** %.   _____ **d.** @.

6. The government is financing a study of the effects on humans of living in a *megalopolis.*

   _____ **a.** an apartment in a large building
   _____ **c.** a dangerous part of a city

   _____ **b.** an extremely large city
   _____ **d.** a city with a large police force

7. Children learning to ride bicycles probably already know how to ride a…

   _____ **a.** unicycle.
   _____ **c.** tricycle.

   _____ **b.** megacycle.
   _____ **d.** motorcycle.

8. What is the perimeter of this rectangle?

   _____ **a.** 14

   _____ **b.** 4

   _____ **c.** 2

   _____ **d.** 5

9. *Nautical* means "pertaining to sailors, ships, or navigation." Explain how the word *astronaut* is formed.

   _____

10. Why are the clothes that nurses, police officers, and soldiers wear called *uniforms*?

    _____

11. People who study population often speak of the world *mortality rate.* What is the opposite of mortality rate?

    _____

Exercise 2

Word analysis can help you to guess the meanings of unfamiliar words. Using context clues and what you know about word parts, write a synonym, description, or definition of the italicized word or phrase.

1. _____ I enjoy reading *biographies* (1) of jazz performers.

2. _____ The O'Neills hired a full-time nanny to help them care for their newborn *triplets* (2).

3. _____ The new art museum will be named for the *multimillionaire* (3) who donated the money to build it.

4. _____ About 4.4 million people live in the Detroit *metropolitan* (4) area.

5. _____ All the hospital's private rooms were occupied, so Michelle had to stay in a *semiprivate* (5) one.

6. _____ Winston Churchill wrote a *multivolume* (6) history of World War II.

7. _____ Race car drivers need to have good *peripheral* (7) vision so they can see another car driving alongside them without turning their heads.

8. _____ That jeweler doesn't cut diamonds; he works mainly with *semiprecious* (8) stones such as opals.

9. _____ He was shot during the robbery, but it is not a mortal *wound* (9).

10. _____ My teeth are falling out; my dentist wants me to make an appointment with a *periodontist* (10).

11. _____ The president's *popularity* (11) with the voters has never been greater than it is today.

Exercise 3

Following is a list of words containing some of the stems and affixes* introduced in this unit and the previous ones. Definitions of these words appear on the right. Put the letter of the appropriate definition next to each word.

1. _____ *psychologist*   a. worldly wise; knowing; finely experienced

2. _____ *philanthropist*   b. a substance capable of killing microorganisms

3. _____ *sophisticated*   c. the science of life or living matter

4. _____ *biochemist*   d. one who studies the chemistry of living things

5. _____ *biology*   e. one who shows love for humanity by doing good works for society

6. _____ *antibiotic*   f. one who studies mental processes and behavior

---

*For a list of all the stems and affixes that appear in *Reader's Choice*, see Appendix B.

7. _____ *multicolored*	**a.**	starlike; shaped like a star
8. _____ *asteroid*	**b.**	affecting two sides or parties
9. _____ *periscope*	**c.**	having many colors
10. _____ *astronomer*	**d.**	pertaining to, involving, or affecting only one side
11. _____ *unilateral*	**e.**	a scientific observer of the planets, stars, and outer space
12. _____ *bilateral*	**f.**	an optical instrument that allows a submarine to observe the surface from below the water

13. _____ *cycle*	**a.**	a recurring period of time in which certain events repeat themselves in the same order and at the same intervals
14. _____ *semicircle*	**b.**	the study of the influence of the stars on human affairs
15. _____ *trilogy*	**c.**	excessive devotion to national interests as opposed to international considerations
16. _____ *astrology*	**d.**	a series or group of three related dramas, operas, novels, etc.
17. _____ *ultraviolet*	**e.**	invisible rays of the spectrum lying beyond the violet end of the visible spectrum
18. _____ *ultranationalism*	**f.**	a half circle

Paragraph Reading
Restatement and Inference

This exercise is similar to the one found in Unit 5. Each passage below is followed by five statements. The statements are of four types.

1. Some of the statements are restatements of ideas in the original paragraph. They give the same information in a different way.

2. Some of the statements are inferences (conclusions) that can be drawn from the information given in the paragraph.

3. Some of the statements are false based on the information given.

4. Some of the statements cannot be judged true or false based on information given in the original paragraph.

Put a check (✓) next to all restatements and inferences (types 1 and 2). Note: Do not check a statement that is true of itself but cannot be inferred from the paragraph.

Passage 1

It was the weekend before the exam. We were at the Walkers' house and it was pouring rain. Jack came in late, drenched to the skin. He explained that a car had broken down on the road and he had stopped to help push it onto the shoulder and out of the traffic. I remember thinking then how typical that was of Jack. So helpful, so accommodating.

_____a. Jack came in late because it was raining.

_____b. Jack came in late because his car had broken down.

_____c. The narrator thinks Jack is typical.

_____d. The narrator bases his opinion of Jack on this one experience.

_____e. Jack often helps other people.

Passage 2

The illustrations in books make it easier for us to believe in the people and events described. The more senses satisfied, the easier is belief. Visual observation tends to be the most convincing evidence. Children, being less capable of translating abstractions into actualities, need illustration more than adults. Most of us, when we read, tend to create only vague and ghostlike forms in response to the words. Illustrators, when they read, must see. Great illustrators see accurately.

_____a. Illustrations help us to believe events described in words.

_____b. When most people read, they do not picture events as accurately as can a great illustrator.

_____c. Children are less able than adults to visualize events described in books.

_____d. The author believes illustrators are especially able to imagine visual details described with words.

_____e. The author believes all illustrators see accurately.

Passage 3

The gourd plant has been described as one of nature's greatest gifts to humankind. Of all the known plants, the gourd is the only one experts believe spanned the entire globe in prehistoric times. It appears as one of the first cultivated plants in regions throughout the world and was used by every known culture in the Temperate and Tropical Zones. Gourds played an important role in the changes that took place as humans became tool users and masters of their environment. Evidence from Florida and the Ocampo Caves in Mexico indicates that gourds were used as containers long before baskets or pottery served that purpose. Samples of the oldest known pottery imitate the familiar shapes of bottle gourds, suggesting that the bottle gourd was familiar to, and most likely used by, the earliest cultures not only in Africa and North America, but in Asia, too.

_____a. It appears that gourds were used around the globe in every human culture.

_____b. While used in Africa and North America, bottle gourds were probably not familiar to early cultures in Asia.

_____c. Gourds were the only prehistoric plant used around the globe in the Temperate and Tropical Zones.

_____d. Finding baskets in the shape of bottle gourds suggests that basket makers were familiar with gourds.

_____e. Making gourd containers was the first use of tools.

Passage 4

The dusty book room whose windows never opened, through whose panes the summer sun sent a dim light where gold specks danced and shimmered, opened magic windows for me through which I looked out on other worlds and times than those in which I lived. The narrow shelves rose halfway up the walls, their tops piled with untidy layers that almost touched the ceiling. The piles on the floor had to be climbed over, columns of books flanked the window, falling at a touch.

_____**a.** The room is dusty and shadowy, filled with books from floor to ceiling.

_____**b.** The sun never enters the room.

_____**c.** The author spent time in this room as a child.

_____**d.** The author did not like the room.

_____**e.** Through the windows in the room, the author saw worlds other than those in which he lived.

Passage 5

By voting against mass transportation, voters have chosen to continue on a road to ruin. Our interstate highways, those much praised golden avenues built to whisk suburban travelers in and out of downtown, have turned into the world's most expensive parking lots. That expense is not only economic—it is social. These highways have created great walls separating neighborhood from neighborhood, disrupting the complex social connections that help make a city livable.

_____**a.** Interstate highways have created social problems.

_____**b.** Highways create complex social connections.

_____**c.** By separating neighborhoods, highways have made cities more livable.

_____**d.** The author supports the idea of mass transportation.

_____**e.** The author agrees with a recent vote by the citizens.

Paragraph Analysis
Reading for Full Understanding

This exercise is similar to the one found in Unit 3. Read each passage carefully. Try to determine the author's main idea while attempting to remember important details. For each of the questions below, select the *best* answer. True/False items are indicated by a T / F preceding a statement. You may refer to the passage to answer the questions.

Passage 1

1 By about age 12, students who feel threatened by mathematics start to avoid math courses,
2 do poorly in the few math classes they do take, and earn low scores on math-achievement
3 tests. Some scientists have theorized that kids having little math aptitude in the first place
4 justifiably dread grappling with numbers. However, it is not that simple, at least for college
5 students, according to a study in the June *Journal of Experimental Psychology: General*.
6 According to the study, people's intrusive worries about math temporarily disrupt mental
7 processes needed for doing arithmetic and drag down math competence, report Mark H.
8 Ashcraft and Elizabeth P. Kirk, both psychologists at Cleveland (Ohio) State University.
9 Math anxiety exerts this effect by making it difficult to hold new information in mind while
10 simultaneously manipulating it, the researchers hold. Psychologists regard this capacity,
11 known as working memory, as crucial for dealing with numbers. "Math anxiety soaks up
12 working memory resources and makes it harder to learn mathematics, probably beginning
13 in middle school," Ashcraft says.

---

1. What did psychologists Ashcraft and Kirk find?

    _____ a. Doing poorly in math causes math anxiety.

    _____ b. College students learn math differently than 12-year-olds do.

    _____ c. Worrying about math makes it harder to do math.

    _____ d. Students should take harder math classes starting in middle school.

2. What term is used to mean *remembering new information at the same time as you are working with it*?

    _____ a. math anxiety   _____ c. disruptive mental process

    _____ b. math aptitude   _____ d. working memory

3. What theory does the Ashcraft and Kirk study challenge?

    _____ a. Math anxiety improves math performance.

    _____ b. Math anxiety is a result of low math aptitude.

    _____ c. Starting to study math at a young age improves math performance.

    _____ d. The more math aptitude one has, the less working memory is needed.

4. What does *crucial for* mean (in the next-to-the-last sentence)?

_____ a. required for   _____ c. identical to

_____ b. harmful to   _____ d. ordinary in

5. The purpose of this passage is to...

_____ a. report a study about math anxiety.   _____ c. criticize the way math is taught.

_____ b. describe how to teach math better.   _____ d. praise the work of Ashcraft and Kirk.

6. Which of the following is a reasonable inference to draw from this passage?

_____ a. Students who have math anxiety should not be forced to take math classes after middle school.

_____ b. Math aptitude cannot accurately be determined until middle school.

_____ c. Teachers should try to help students avoid worrying when they do math problems.

_____ d. Taking more difficult math classes will improve a student's working memory.

Passage 2

1 The cicada exemplifies an insect species which
2 uses a combinatorial communication system.
3 In their life cycle, communication is very
4 important, for only through the exchange of
5 sounds do cicadas know where to meet and
6 when to mate. Three different calls are employed
7 for this purpose. Because of their limited sound
8 producing mechanisms, cicadas can make only
9 ticks and buzzes. The only way they can distinguish between congregation and courtship
10 calls is by varying the rate with which they make ticks and buzzes. The congregation call
11 consists of 12 to 40 ticks, delivered rapidly, followed by a two-second buzz. It is given by
12 males but attracts cicadas of both sexes. Once they are all together, the males use courtship
13 calls. The preliminary call, a prolonged, slow ticking, is given when the male notices a female
14 near him. The advanced call, a prolonged series of short buzzes at the same slow rate, is given
15 when a female is almost within grasp. The preliminary call almost invariably occurs before
16 the advanced call, although the latter is given without the preliminary call occurring first
17 if a female is suddenly discovered very nearby. During typical courtship, though, the two
18 calls together result in ticking followed by a buzzing—the same pattern which comprises the
19 congregation call but delivered at a slower rate. In this way, cicadas show efficient use of their
20 minimal sound-producing ability, organizing two sounds delivered at a high rate as one call
21 and the same sounds delivered at a slow rate as two or more calls.

1. The cicada congregation call...

_____ a. attracts only males.   _____ c. is given only by males.

_____ b. is given by both sexes.   _____ d. attracts only females.

2. During typical courtship, when a male first notices a female near him, he gives...

_____ **a.** the two courtship calls together.　　　_____ **c.** 12 to 40 rapid ticks.

_____ **b.** a series of slow ticks.　　　_____ **d.** a two-second buzz.

3. How does the congregation call differ from the two courtship calls together?

_____ **a.** It is delivered at a slower rate.　　　_____ **c.** The ticks precede the buzzes.

_____ **b.** It is delivered at a faster rate.　　　_____ **d.** The buzzes precede the ticks.

4. According to this passage, why is communication so important for cicadas?

_____ **a.** It helps them defend themselves against other insect species.

_____ **b.** It warns them of approaching danger.

_____ **c.** It separates the males from the females.

_____ **d.** It is necessary for the continuation of the species.

Passage 3

1　Robert Spring, a nineteenth century forger, was so good at his profession that he was able to
2　make his living for 15 years by selling false signatures of famous Americans. Spring was born in
3　England in 1813 and arrived in Philadelphia in 1858 to open a bookstore. At first he prospered
4　by selling his small but genuine collection of early US autographs. Discovering his ability at
5　copying handwriting, he began imitating signatures of George Washington and Ben Franklin
6　and writing them on the title pages of old books. To lessen the chance of detection, he sent his
7　forgeries to England and Canada for sale and circulation.

8　Forgers have a hard time selling their products. A forger can't approach a respectable buyer
9　but must deal with people who don't have much knowledge in the field. Forgers have many ways
10　to make their work look real. For example, they buy old books to use the aged paper of the title
11　page, and they can treat paper and ink with chemicals.

12　In Spring's time, right after the Civil War, Britain was still fond of the Southern states, so
13　Spring invented a respectable maiden lady known as Miss Fanny Jackson, the only daughter
14　of the famous Southern General "Stonewall" Jackson. For several years Miss Fanny's financial
15　problems forced her to sell a great number of letters and manuscripts belonging to her famous
16　father. Spring had to work very hard to satisfy the demand. All this activity did not prevent
17　Spring from dying in poverty, leaving sharp-eyed experts the difficult task of separating his
18　forgeries from the originals.

1. Why did Spring sell his false autographs in England and Canada?

_____ **a.** There was a greater demand there than in America.

_____ **b.** There was less chance of being detected there.

_____ **c.** Britain was Spring's birthplace.

_____ **d.** The prices were higher in England and Canada.

2. After the Civil War, there was a great demand in Britain for...

_____ **a.** Southern money.

_____ **b.** signatures of George Washington and Ben Franklin.

_____ **c.** Southern manuscripts and letters.

_____ **d.** Civil War battle plans.

3. Robert Spring spent 15 years...

_____ **a.** running a bookstore in Philadelphia.

_____ **b.** corresponding with Miss Fanny Jackson.

_____ **c.** as a forger.

_____ **d.** as a respectable dealer.

4. According to the passage, forgeries are usually sold to...

_____ **a.** sharp-eyed experts.   _____ **c.** book dealers.

_____ **b.** persons who aren't experts.   _____ **d.** owners of old books.

5. Who was Miss Fanny Jackson?

_____ **a.** the only daughter of General "Stonewall" Jackson

_____ **b.** a little-known girl who sold her father's papers to Robert Spring

_____ **c.** Robert Spring's daughter

_____ **d.** an imaginary person created by Spring

Passage 4

1 A brain freeze is a brief, stabbing headache that can happen when you eat, drink or inhale something
2 cold. Because a common trigger for brain freeze is biting into ice cream, a brain freeze is also called
3 an ice cream headache. Technically known as cold stimulus headaches, these can occur when you
4 suddenly expose your unprotected head to cold temperatures, such as by diving into cold water, or, more
5 commonly, when a cold substance passes across the roof of your mouth and the back of your throat.

6 Scientists are unsure about the exact mechanism that causes this pain. One theory is that the cold
7 temporarily causes a rapid change in blood flow in the vessels in the roof of the mouth. In reaction
8 to the cold, blood vessels suddenly narrow to prevent the loss of body heat and then widen again,
9 which might result in a message sent to the brain that is perceived as pain behind the eyes and nose
10 and in the forehead. The pain lasts only a few minutes and, though sudden and severe, is harmless
11 and not indicative of any disease.

12 There is some evidence that people who suffer from migraine headaches are more susceptible to
13 ice cream headaches than are others. However, about 40% of people who don't usually get headaches
14 can experience brain freezes, making them quite common. There is no single prescription for how
15 to stop them. Most people have their own methods, such as curling the tongue and pressing the
16 underside against the roof of the mouth. But there is clear agreement on how best to prevent them:
17 eat very cold foods slowly.

1. **T / F**   A brain freeze and an ice cream headache are the same thing.

2. In the second sentence, what does *trigger* mean?

    _____ **a.** synonym   _____ **b.** cure   _____ **c.** result   _____ **d.** cause

3. **T / F**   You can get an ice cream headache from diving into cold water.

4. What is one theory about what causes a brain freeze?

    _____ **a.** Body temperature changes rapidly.   _____ **c.** A migraine headache starts.

    _____ **b.** Blood vessels change size rapidly.   _____ **d.** Messages to the brain are interrupted.

5. **T / F**   The author believes that the most effective way to stop a brain freeze is to press the bottom of the
    tongue against the roof of the mouth.

6. **T / F**   We can infer that if you get brain freezes, you should make an appointment with a doctor.

7. The purpose of this passage is…

    _____ **a.** to explain.   _____ **c.** to criticize.

    _____ **b.** to convince.   _____ **d.** to give advice.

Discourse Focus
Prediction

This exercise is similar to one found in Unit 5. It is designed to give you practice in consciously developing and confirming expectations. You will read the first few sections of an article, stopping to respond to the questions that appear at several points throughout. Remember you cannot always predict precisely what an author will do, but you can use clues from the text and your general knowledge to make good guesses. Work with your classmates on these items, defending your predictions with parts of the text. Do not worry about unfamiliar vocabulary.

> **The Troubled State of Calculus**
>
> *A Push to Revitalize College Calculus Teaching Has Begun*
>
> Calculus: a large lecture hall, 200 or so bored students, a lecturer talking to a blackboard filled with Greek symbols, a thick, heavy textbook with answers to even-numbered problems, a seemingly endless chain of formulas, theorems and proofs.

Example

1. Above are the title, the subtitle, and an inset from an article on calculus. On the basis of these, what aspect of calculus do you think the article might be about? List two possibilities.

    _____

    _____

2. Does the author seem to think that calculus instruction is successful or unsuccessful at the present time? _____ What words give you this impression? _____

    _____

Explanation

1. The main title indicates that calculus instruction is *troubled*. The subtitle tells us that there is a movement to improve calculus teaching. The inset describes a "typical," boring calculus class, suggesting what is troubled and what needs to be improved. Based on this information in the text you might have decided that the article would be about such things as current problems with calculus instruction and about proposals for improving instruction. If you have personal knowledge of calculus instruction, you may have some more specific ideas about the kinds of problems and solutions that might be mentioned.

2. Obviously the author has a negative opinion of calculus instruction. He refers to it as *troubled* in the main title and indicates a need to *revitalize* (to give new life to) it in the subtitle. The inset describes a *large* lecture hall, with *bored* students and *heavy* books: the opposite of a lively situation.

3. Before you continue reading the article, decide how you expect it to begin. Remember, you cannot always predict precisely what an author will do, but you can use knowledge of the text and your general knowledge to make good guesses. Which of the following seems the most likely beginning? Circle your choice.

a. The author will describe traditional ways of teaching calculus.

b. The author will describe math instruction in general.

c. The author will describe new ways to teach calculus.

d. The author will describe the general state of calculus instruction.

Now read to see if your expectations are confirmed.

> **By Ivar Peterson**
> More than half a million students take an introductory calculus course in any given year, and the number is growing. A large proportion have no choice. Calculus is a barrier that must be overcome on the way to a professional career in medicine or engineering. Even disciplines like history now sometimes require some college mathematics. But for many people in the last few years who have passed through such a course, the word *calculus* brings back painful memories.

4. The article appears to be critical of current teaching practices. Is this what you expected?

_____

5. Did you expect the article to begin with a general description of calculus instruction?

_____

6. What do you expect to read about next? What words or phrases point in this direction? What do you know about calculus and schools in general that would lead you to predict this?

_____

_____

Now read to see if your expectations are confirmed.

> In many universities about half of the students who take introductory calculus fail the course. A surprisingly large number must take the course several times to get through. At the same time, engineering and physical sciences professors complain that even the students who pass don't know very much about calculus and don't know how to use it.
>
> "The teaching of calculus is a national disgrace," says Lynn A. Steen, president of the Mathematical Association of America, based in Washington, DC, and a professor at St. Olaf College in Northfield, Minn. "Too often calculus is taught by inexperienced instructors to ill-prepared students in an environment with insufficient feedback," he says. "The result is a serious decline in the number of students pursuing advanced mathematics, and a majority of college graduates who have learned to hate mathematics."

7. Were your expectations confirmed? If not, why not? Did you misunderstand something in the previous section? Do you think your expectations were valid? Would they provide a better outline for the author than the one he used?

_____

_____

8. At this point, the author has summarized his criticisms of the teaching of calculus. What do you think he will say next?

_____

_____

Discuss your choices with your classmates. Then read to see if your expectations are confirmed.

Now a small group of educators has started a movement to change what is taught in an introductory calculus course, to improve the way it is taught and to bring the teaching of calculus into the computer age. Earlier this year, 25 faculty members, administrators, scientists, and others representing diverse interests met at Tulane University in New Orleans to see what could be done.

One big surprise was a general agreement that there is room for change. When participants came to the meeting, says mathematician Peter L. Renz of Bard College in Annandale-on-Hudson, NY, although they recognized the problem, "we all believed that there was nothing we could do about calculus." Yet despite this pessimism, many of the participants brought worthwhile suggestions.

9. Were your expectations confirmed in these two paragraphs?

_____

10. What do you think the author will do next? What aspects of the text and your general knowledge help you to create this prediction?

_____

_____

Read to see if your expectations are confirmed.

A key question is the role of handheld calculators and computers. For the price of a calculus textbook, students can buy a scientific calculator. "The first thing that one can do on that basis is to eliminate an awful lot of the routine problems," says mathematician Ronald G. Douglas, dean of the physical sciences school at the State University of New York at Stony Brook. The ideas are still important, and instructors may need some traditional techniques to illustrate what is going on, he says, but drilling students in something that any calculator or computer can now do becomes much less important.

The conference participants agreed that the routine use of calculators would help shift the focus of calculus back to its fundamental ideas and away from students mechanically plugging numbers into formulas to get "nice" answers. Until now, says Douglas, "all we've been teaching people in some sense has been a kind of pattern recognition."

11. Were your predictions confirmed?

_____

12. What other kinds of problems and solutions do you predict are discussed in the final sections of this article (which are not reprinted here)? Be prepared to defend your predictions.

_____

_____

UNIT 8

Reading Selection 1
Business

> **BEFORE YOU BEGIN**
>
> 1. What do you do with clothing that you no longer wear?
>
> 2. Do you know where old clothing goes after you dispose of it?
>
> 3. Have you ever wondered how it is that clothing that comes from North America (for example with logos from US schools or sports teams) is often worn by people around the world in very poor countries? Do you have any idea how that happens?
>
> 4. Do you know what free-trade agreements are?

Read "New Life for Used Clothes" to learn about the global trade in used clothing. Your teacher may want you to do Vocabulary from Context Exercise 1 on page 211 before you begin reading.

New Life for Used Clothes

By Bob Fernandez, Jonathan Wilson / Knight Ridder Newspapers

1 SCARBOROUGH, Ontario—Amid a worldwide glut of US used clothes, Toronto businessmen like Farokh Gahadali have carved out a profitable niche. He and dozens of other immigrant entrepreneurs buy tens of millions of pounds of used clothing from the United States for less than 20 cents a pound, sort the garments in industrial parks around Toronto, then ship the items for resale in Africa, Asia and Latin America.

2 The clothes are sorted into as many as 400 categories—by garment type, fiber and quality—to reap the most profit. Polyester dresses are shipped to Pakistan, baby clothes and cotton trousers to the Congo, winter coats to Albania and jeans to Japan. "You could write a book about the used clothing industry" in Toronto, said Gahadali, an executive with H. Salb International. "There's a whole infrastructure living off this business," from sorters to truckers to accountants to used-clothing brokers.

A collector of funky hats, Goodwill worker Melvin Brown inspects baled clothes waiting to be uploaded and taken to Ontario. Brown rescued his smiley-faced hat from a bin of used clothes destined for baling.

3 In one of the widening ripples of the new global economy in clothing, Toronto has come to dominate the North American sorting industry. At the same time, it has driven out of business up to 40 percent of the US firms that once did the same thing. Thousands of American jobs have been lost. The last major Philadelphia clothing sorter, Dumont Export, ceased its processing operations in 2000, eliminating about 120 jobs. The business, said owner Jerry Usatch, "has shifted to where the companies have advantages in labor." Today that's Canada; tomorrow it could be somewhere else.

4 How Toronto became the North American center of the used-clothing industry is partly a story of how this dynamic Canadian city has transformed itself in the past two decades. Of the Toronto area's 5 million people, about 45 percent are immigrants—one of the highest percentages of any major city in the world, according to Canadian officials. Canadian authorities began to loosen immigration laws in the 1970s as birth rates among native Canadians declined and fears arose of an eventual labor shortage, said Larry Bourne, an immigration expert at the University of Toronto.

Laws changed

5 Millions from Asia, Africa and the Caribbean poured into Canada's cities, providing the entrepreneurial energy, the abundant low-wage labor and, maybe most important, the contacts in the developing world to run clothing-sorting businesses, experts say. "Toronto is now the multicultural center of North America," said Bourne, calling the changes "one of the most dramatic social transformations anywhere." Parts of the city are filled with ethnic restaurants, movie theaters playing Indian "Bollywood" hits, foreign-language newspapers, Asian supermarkets and cultural centers.

6 Owners of the more than 15 sorting companies that have sprung up in the immigrant working-class suburb of Scarborough, east of Toronto, were reluctant to discuss details of their operations... The companies, with names such as Global Textile Exporters, Fripes Export, Alysco International and Cantex, operate in old factories or warehouses. They are among 50 such businesses in the Toronto area with an estimated 5,000 to 10,000 workers, say US and Canadian experts.

7 According to US government trade figures, used-clothing exports to Canada soared more than 613 percent over the past decade to 190 million pounds…. as Americans—enjoying plummeting prices on new imported clothes—bought ever more quantities. That's about 25 percent of the nation's clothing exports—more than 4,000 tractor-trailer loads a year.

8 But growth of the clothes-sorting business also has brought concerns to the Toronto area. The industry is highly competitive and deals mostly in cash transactions…. A year ago, Canadian authorities at Toronto's airport confiscated almost $200,000 in cash found in the carry-on bags of a Sri Lankan businessman traveling from London. While law-enforcement officials suspected that the man was laundering the money, he said he operated a clothing-sorting company in Toronto. The money, exchanged in a London pub, was payment for a shipment of clothing to Kenya. After a trial, the Canadian government returned his money.

9 Then last spring, an immigrant workers-rights group staged a protest outside Northstar Trading, a used-clothing sorter in the Toronto suburb of Etobicoke for failing to pay about 20 immigrant laborers their wages.

Labor practices faulted

10 The episode brought the used-clothing industry to the attention of authorities. The Ontario Ministry of Labour has ordered Northstar, which has closed, to pay the back wages and the order has been appealed, said government spokeswoman Belinda Sutton.

11 US clothing sorters have suffered from foreign competition. "A lot of the business has shifted north of the border," said Bernard Brill, executive vice president of the Secondary Materials and Recycled Textiles association in Bethesda, Md. He notes that an Environmental Protection Agency official told him a truckload of used clothing destined for a recycler ultimately supports 22 jobs.

12 In recent years Brill has seen his US membership dwindle as Toronto companies took a larger share of the sorting business. Where the annual convention once brought 50 to 60 clothing-processing companies, Brill said, only 10 to 12 companies showed up at this year's convention....

13 The organization is pushing US trade officials to negotiate with other countries that have erected trade barriers against the rising tide of used clothing from North America. Countries such as Mexico, Venezuela and Nigeria say dirt-cheap used clothing wrecks their apparel-manufacturing industries, weakening domestic economies. But advocates of open trade say used garments benefit poor people who can't afford new ones. "At a time when the nation is negotiating all these new free-trade agreements, the status of used clothing is left off the table because officials say the matter is too sensitive to discuss," Brill said. "We're opening our doors and we're putting thousands of our people out of work in apparel plants in North Carolina and places like that, but other countries are not open to our products," he said.

14 Ed Stubin, president of TransAmericas Trading in New York, one of the last big clothing graders in the Northeast, criticizes nonprofit organizations for selling excess used clothing directly to Canada or other countries for sorting instead of creating jobs in the US, Goodwill and Salvation Army officials say they sell where they can get the best price.

Comprehension

Answer the following questions. True/False questions are indicated by a T / F preceding a statement.

1. **T / F**   Toronto has become the North American center of the used-clothing industry.

2. **T / F**   Most of the clothes sorted in Toronto are Canadian.

3. **T / F**   Sorted clothes earn a higher profit than unsorted clothing.

4. **T / F**   Thousands of new jobs have been created in the US by selling clothing to Canada.

5.   According to the article, which areas of the world do many of Canada's new immigrants come from?

_____

6.   What three characteristics of its new immigrant community helped a Canadian city become a center of the global used-clothing industry? _____

_____

7. **T / F**   According to the article, immigrant worker-rights groups are particularly happy about the success of the Canadian used-clothing industry.

8. **T / F**   Countries such as Mexico, Venezuela, and Nigeria say used garments benefit poor people who can't afford new clothes.

9. What business advantages do sorters in Houston, Texas, have?

_____

_____

Critical Reading

1. Why do sorted clothes reap the most profit?

2. Looking at Paragraph 7, how does global trade create used clothes in the United States?

3. Why do Canadian law enforcement officials care if a businessman carries large amounts of cash into Canada?

4. Why have some countries created trade barriers against used clothing from North America?

5. Why do nonprofit agencies such as Goodwill or the Salvation Army have "excess used clothing" (Paragraph 14)?

Discussion/Composition

1. **Simulation.** The global used-clothing industry creates opportunities for some people and problems for others. The author says that in the negotiations of free-trade agreements, "the status of used clothing is left off the table because officials say the matter is too sensitive to discuss" (Paragraph 13). However, you and your classmates will be negotiating a trade agreement with respect to the used-clothing industry.

    a. **Groups.** Break up into groups representing various groups who will be affected by any such agreement.

        • New immigrants to Canada working in the used-clothing industry
            ° This group is grateful to have jobs but worries about the lack of regulation of their working conditions.

        • New immigrants to Canada who own used-clothing businesses
            ° This group is very successful and doesn't want any regulation.

        • Workers in the used-clothing business in the United States
            ° This group is very concerned about losing their jobs. They want some regulations that don't allow all of the clothing collected in the US to be sorted in Canada.

        • Nonprofit organization in the United States that collects used clothes
            ° This group is interested in helping poor people in the United States by collecting used clothing and selling it for as much as they can get. They are not interested in regulation.

- Shoppers in a developing country
  - This group is glad to have cheap clothing from North America.
- A clothing manufacturer in a developing country
  - This group is worried that the competition of used clothing from North America is destroying the local clothing industry and weakening the local economy.

b. **Statements.** In groups, prepare statements that will begin your negotiation. First brainstorm additional concerns and desires of your group. What do you want to avoid happening? What do you want any formal agreement to accomplish? Now work on preparing a two-to three-minute presentation to the members of the other groups, arguing for a specific policy. Remember that in order to persuade people in a negotiation, you have to make your needs clear while, at the same time, responding to their concerns. You may use your time however you wish; you may have one speaker or more. The following are examples of issues you might want to address.

- What are the negative or positive effects on your group of the current situation (no policy)?

- What are the needs and concerns of your group?

- Why should others care about your concerns?

- What policy are you proposing?

- Why should others support it?

c. **Opening negotiations.** You will deliver your statements as the opening/public part of negotiations.

d. **Private negotiations.** Now enter into negotiations with your classmates to see if you can arrive at an agreement. These will be less formal conversations. Your teacher may want one representative from each group to sit around a table negotiating while other members pass notes to them, giving suggestions. As is the case in all negotiations, you may or may not be able to reach an agreement at this time.

e. **Written statements**. Your teacher may ask each group for a written statement arguing your position.

2. How are you personally affected by the globalization of trade?

- Are the effects mostly positive or negative? Does this change whether you think long term or short term?

- Do you believe that the effects on most people worldwide are largely positive or negative?

- Do you ever take actions (like buying locally) to counteract some negative effects?

Exercise 1

Both the ideas and the vocabulary in the following paragraphs are taken from "New Life for Used Clothes." Use the context provided to determine the meanings of the italicized words and phrases. Write a definition, synonym, or description in the space provided.

1. _____

2. _____

3. _____

4. _____

5. _____

6. _____

7. _____

8. _____

9. _____

Americans buy and get rid of a lot of clothing. As a result, worldwide there is a *glut* (1) of US used clothes on the market. This oversupply makes it difficult to earn money selling used clothes. It takes clever and creative business people, willing to take risks, to be successful in such a market. In North America the most successful of such *entrepreneurs* (2) have been immigrants to Canada. They often come from Asia, Africa, and Latin America. Because of this, they have contacts in the *developing world* (3) to whom they can sell clothing. These business people are so good at what they do that companies in the United States have had a hard time winning in the worldwide *competition* (4) to find markets.

Not everyone thinks the global market is a good thing. Some countries set up rules and regulations that don't allow goods that would compete with local industries to be imported into their countries. These *trade barriers* (5) are intended to protect the local economy. But it is difficult to protect *domestic* (6) industries against global trade. And there has been a stronger trend toward *free-trade agreements* (7). Opening borders to allow trade without restrictions or fees can help send goods around the world. But it can take long discussions to reach an agreement, and results of these *negotiations* (8) will not please everyone. For workers and local industries, there are long- and short-term benefits and dangers to free trade. Sometimes people trying to help others are criticized. In the United States, *nonprofit agencies* (9) that collect and sell used clothing in order to raise money to help poor people are sometimes criticized for using non-US companies to sell the clothes. This is a complicated issue.

Exercise 2

This exercise gives you additional clues to determine the meaning of unfamiliar vocabulary in context. In the paragraph in "New Life for Used Clothes" indicated by the number in parentheses, find the word or phrase that best fits the meaning given. Your teacher may want to read these aloud as you quickly scan* the paragraph to find the answer.

1. (2) Which word means *an underlying framework or structure that supports an industry or system?*
    _____

2. (2) Which word means *people who buy or sell for other people; intermediaries?* _____

3. (4) Which word means *energetic, powerful?* _____

4. (7) Which compound word means *a huge two-part truck?* _____

5. (8) Which word means *taken away by a government official?* _____

Exercise 3

This exercise gives you additional practice using context to determine the meaning of unfamiliar vocabulary. Give a definition, synonym, or description of each of the words below. The description or number in parentheses indicates the paragraph of "New Life for Used Clothes" in which the word or phrase can be found. Your teacher may want you to do these orally or in writing.

1. (photo caption) funky _____

2. (2) sorted _____

3. (2) reap _____

4. (3) shifted _____

5. (7) soared _____

6. (7) plummeting _____

7. (12) dwindle _____

8. (13) wrecks _____.

Figurative Language and Idioms

Like the previous exercises, this one is designed to give you practice using context clues to guess the meaning of unfamiliar vocabulary, in this case, figurative language and idioms. Give a definition, synonym, or description of each of the phrases below. The number in parentheses of "New Lives for Used Clothes" indicates the paragraph in which the phrase can be found. Your teacher may want you to do these orally or in writing.

1. (1) carved out a profitable niche _____

2. (3) widening ripples _____

3. (6) sprung up _____

---

*For an introduction to scanning, see Unit 1.

4. (11) north of the border _____

5. (13) rising tide _____

6. (13) dirt-cheap _____

7. (13) left off the table _____

8. (13) opening our doors _____

Vocabulary Review

Are these pairs of words similar in meaning or opposite in meaning? Circle S if similar; circle O if opposite.

1. S / O   soared   plummeted

2. S / O   plummet   dwindle

3. S / O   apparel   garment

4. S / O   revenue   profit

Dictionary Study

Many words have more than one meaning. When you use a dictionary to discover the meaning of an unfamiliar word, you need to use the context to determine which definition is appropriate. Use the dictionary entries provided to select the best definition for each of the italicized words in the following sentences. Write the number of the definition in the space provided.

_____ **1.** When Canadian authorities discovered a man bringing large amounts of cash into the country that he said was payment for used clothing, they suspected he was *laundering* the money.

_____ **2.** Some countries *erect* strong trade barriers against certain kinds of goods from other countries.

_____ **3.** Thousands of people have been put out of work in apparel *plants* in North Carolina.

_____ **4.** Because of competition from Canada, one of the last *graders* in the northeast of the United States is going out of business. (Note: You won't find this noun form in the dictionary; find the closest meaning.)

laun·der [lôn'd′r]

–noun

a water trough, esp. one used in mining for washing dirt from the ore

[Etymology: ME, contr. < *lavender,* washerwoman < OFr *lavandier* < ML *lavandarius* < LL *lavandaria,* things to be washed < L *lavandus,* ger. of L *lavare,* to wash: see lave]

–transitive verb

1 to wash, or wash and iron (clothes, etc.)

2 to exchange or invest (money) in such a way as to conceal that it came from an illegal or improper source

3 to make (something improper or offensive) seem less so

–intransitive verb

1 to withstand washing a fabric that launders well

2 to do laundry

e·rect [i-**rekt**]

–adjective

1. upright in position or posture: to stand or sit erect.
2. raised or directed upward: a dog with ears erect.
3. Botany. vertical throughout; not spreading or declined: an erect stem; an erect leaf or ovule.
4. Heraldry.
   a (of a charge) represented palewise: a sword erect.
   b of an animal or part of an animal) represented upright: a boar's head erect.
5. Optics. (of an image) having the same position as the object; not inverted.

–verb (used with object)

6. to build; construct; raise: to erect a house.

7. to raise and set in an upright or vertical position: to erect a telegraph pole.
8. to set up or establish, as an institution; found.
9. to bring about; cause to come into existence: to erect barriers to progress.
10. Geometry. to draw or construct (a line or figure) upon a given line, base, or the like.
11. to form or create legally (usually fol. by *into*): to erect a territory into a state.
12. Optics. to change (an inverted image) to the normal position.
13. Machinery. to assemble; make ready for use. *–verb (used without object)*
14. to become erect; stand up or out.

[Origin: 1350–1400; ME < L *eréctus* raised up (ptp. of *érigere*), equiv. to é- E + *reg*- guide, direct (see ROYAL) + *-tus* ptp. suffix]

---

plant [plant, plänt]

–noun

1. any of a kingdom (Plantae) of eukaryotes generally characterized by the ability to carry on photosynthesis in its cells which contain chloroplasts and have cellulose in the cell wall, including all thallophytes and embryophytes
2. a young tree, shrub, or herb, ready to put into other soil for growth to maturity; a slip, cutting, or set
3. an herb, as distinguished from a tree or shrub
4. the tools, machinery, buildings, grounds, etc. of a factory or business
5. the equipment, buildings, etc. of any institution, as a hospital, school, etc.
6. the apparatus or equipment for some particular mechanical operation or process the power plant of a ship
7. SLANG a person placed, or thing planned or used, to trick, mislead, or trap

[Etymology: ME *plante* < OE < L *planta*, sprout, twig, prob. back-form. < *plantare*, to smooth the soil for planting < planta, sole of the foot < IE *plat-*, var. of base *pla-*, broad, flat > plain]

–transitive verb

1. **a** to put into soil, esp. into the ground, to grow
   b to set plants in (a piece of ground)
2. to set firmly as into the ground; fix in position
3. to fix in the mind; implant (an idea, etc.)
4. to settle (a colony, colonists, etc.); found; establish
5. to furnish or stock with animals
6. to put a stock of (oysters, young fish, etc.) in a body of water
7. SLANG to deliver (a punch, blow, etc.) with force
8. SLANG
   a to place (a person or thing) in such a way as to trick, trap, etc.
   b to place (an ostensible news item) in a newspaper, etc. with some ulterior motive, as in order to mold public opinion
9. SLANG
   a to hide or conceal
   b to place (something) surreptitiously where it is certain to be found or discovered

[Etymology: ME *planten* < OE *plantian* & OFr *planter*, both < L *plantare* < the n.]

---

grade [greyd] verb, **grad·ed, grad·ing.**

–verb (used with object)

1. to arrange in a series of grades; class; sort: a machine that grades two thousand eggs per hour.
2. to determine the grade of.
3. to assign a grade to (a student's work); mark: I graded forty tests last night.
4. to cause to pass by degrees, as from one color or shade to another.

5. to reduce to a level or to practicable degrees of inclination: to grade a road.
6. to cross (an ordinary or low-grade animal) with an animal of a pure or superior breed. *–verb (used without object)*
7. to incline; slant or slope: The road grades steeply for a mile.
8. to be of a particular grade.

Reading Selection 2
Sociology

BEFORE YOU BEGIN

Since the 1970s, the marriage rate has been declining in many countries around the world. In the United States, for example, more than half of adults live alone.

The following is taken from a chapter in a book called *Going Solo: The Extraordinary Rise and Surprising Appeal of Living Alone.* Written by a sociologist, the book argues that the past 50 years has seen what he calls a "social experiment." For the first time in human history, large numbers of people of all ages and in all places are living as what he calls *singletons:* people who live alone.

1. Is this a trend that you are seeing in your community?

2. Do you think this is happening more in some parts of the world than others? What makes you think so?

3. To answer the following True/False questions, use your experience and knowledge to guess what you will find when you read this article.

   a. **T / F** The United States has the largest percentage of people living alone.

   b. **T / F** Communal societies with strong government support like Sweden and Denmark have fewer people living alone than the US.

   c. **T / F** China is one of the nations with the fastest growth in single-person households.

4. What do you think are reasons why many people around the world are living alone?

Read the passage below from *Going Solo* to find out how a sociologist analyzes these issues. The article begins by describing the situation in the United States, then looks at the issue worldwide. Read first for the main ideas of the article, then do Comprehension Exercise 1. The questions in Comprehension Exercise 2 may require you to return to the text. Your teacher may want you to do Vocabulary from Context Exercise 1 on page 220 before you begin.

Excerpt from *Going Solo*
By Eric Klinenberg

1   For the first time in human history, great numbers of people—of all ages, in all places—have begun to live as singletons.* Until recently, most of us married young and parted only at death. If death came early, we remarried quickly; if late, we moved in with family, or they with us. Now we marry later. (The Pew Research Center reports that the average age of first marriage for men and women in the US is the highest ever recorded.) We divorce, and stay single for years or decades. If we live longer than our spouses, we do whatever we can to avoid moving in with others—even, perhaps especially, our children. We cycle in and out of different living arrangements: alone, together, together, alone.

2   Not long ago, it might have made sense to think of living on our own as a transitional stage between more long-lasting living situations, whether coupling up with a partner or moving into an institutional home. But today, for the first time in centuries, the majority of all American adults are single. The typical American will spend more of his or her adult life unmarried than married, and for much of this time he or she will live alone. Naturally, we are adapting. We are learning to go solo, and crafting new ways of living.

Going Solo by the Numbers

3   Numbers never tell the whole story, but in this case the statistics are startling. In 1950, 22 percent of American adults were single. Four million lived alone, and they accounted for 9 percent of all households. Living alone was usually a short-lived stage on the road to marriage.

4   Today, more than 50 percent of American adults are single, and 31 million—roughly one out of every seven adults—live alone. (This figure excludes 8 million Americans who live in voluntary and non-voluntary group residences, such as assisted living facilities, nursing homes, and prisons.) People who live alone make up 28 percent of all US households, which means that they are now tied with childless couples as the most prominent residential type—more common than the nuclear family, the multigenerational family, and the roommate or group home. Surprisingly, living alone is also one of the most stable household arrangements. Over a five-year period, people who live alone are more likely to stay that way than everyone except married couples with children.

5   Contemporary solo dwellers are primarily women: about 17 million, compared to 14 million men. The majority, more than 15 million, are middle-aged adults between the ages of thirty-five and sixty-four. The elderly account for about 10 million of the total.** Young adults between eighteen and thirty-four number more than 5 million, compared to 500,000 in 1950, making them the fastest-growing segment of the solo-dwelling population.

---

*In this book I use the term "singletons" for people who live alone. "Singles" may or may not live alone (some live with a romantic partner, or roommates, or children), and so not all singles are singletons.

**In this book, I use the terms "old people" and "the elderly" to refer to those age sixty-five and above. The reasons for this have more to do with the statistics on aging, which typically classify people as elderly once they reach age sixty-five, than on an argument about the age when one becomes old.

6   Unlike their predecessors, people who live alone today cluster together in metropolitan areas and inhabit all regions of the country. The cities in the US with the highest proportion of people living alone include Washington, DC, Seattle, Denver, San Francisco, Minneapolis, Chicago, Dallas, New York City, and Miami. One million people live alone in New York City, and in New York's borough of Manhattan, more than half of all residences are one-person dwellings....

Going Solo Around the Globe

7   The rise of living alone has been a transformative social experience. It changes the way we understand ourselves and our closest relationships. It shapes the way we build our cities and develop our economies. It alters the way we become adults, as well as how we age and the way we die. It touches every social group and nearly every family, no matter who we are or whether we live with others today.

8   Consider another piece of evidence: Today Americans are actually less likely to live alone than are residents of many other nations, including those we generally regard as more communal. The four countries with the highest rates of living alone are Sweden, Norway, Finland, and Denmark, where roughly 40 to 45 percent of all households have just one person. By investing in each other's social welfare and providing mutual support, the Scandinavians have freed themselves to be on their own.

9   In Japan, where social life has historically been organized around the family, about 30 percent of all households now have a single dweller, and the rate is far higher in urban areas. Germany, France, and the United Kingdom have different cultural traditions, but they share a greater proportion of one-person households than the United States. Same for Australia and Canada. And the nations with the fastest growth in one-person households? China, India, and Brazil. At the global level the number of people living alone has skyrocketed, having risen from about 153 million in 1996 to 202 million in 2006—a 33 percent increase in a single decade.

Why do People Live Alone?

10   So what is driving the widespread rise in living alone? Unquestionably, both the wealth generated by economic development and the social security provided by modern welfare states have enabled the spike. Put simply, one reason that more people live alone than ever before is that today more people can afford to do so. Yet there are a great many things that we can afford to do but choose not to, which means the economic explanation is just part of the explanation.

11   Four large-scale social changes made it possible for large numbers of people to live well while living alone: the rising status of women, the communications revolution, mass urbanization, and the longevity revolution. In the case of the first change, the position of women, today the level of men's and women's participation in higher education and the paid workforce is more balanced than ever before. Economically, many more women can now afford to live alone.

12   The second change is the communications revolution, which has allowed people throughout the world to experience the pleasures of social life even when they're home alone. Between the phone, the television, and the internet, individuals can communicate with the outside world at all hours of the day and night. What matters is not whether we live alone, but whether we feel alone.

13   Mass urbanization is the third condition supporting the rise of the singleton society. In the modern world, most people who live alone also have another way to connect with each other: simply leaving their home and participating in their city's social life. Mass urbanization has led to a booming subculture of singles who share similar values and ways of life.

14 The fourth change is that people are living longer than ever before. More specifically, because women often outlive their spouses by decades, rather than years, aging alone has become an increasingly common experience. In 1900, about 10 percent of the widowed elderly in the United States lived alone; by 2000, 62 percent did. Today it's not unusual for women to spend a quarter or a third of their lives in a place of their own, and men are spending a greater share of their adult years living alone, too.

15 Aging alone is not easy. But according to a recent review of the literature on aging, studies of the entire elderly population have found that "those living alone are healthier than those living with adults other than a spouse, or even, in some cases, than those living with a spouse."*** Indeed, in recent decades, old people have demonstrated a clear preference for living alone rather than moving in with family or friends or to an institutional home. This, again, is not only an American phenomenon. From Japan to Germany, Italy to Australia, aging alone has become common, even among ethnic groups that have long exhibited a clear preference for keeping multigenerational homes.

16 Since any one of us could live alone someday, it is good for everyone to make it a healthier, happier, more social experience. And that's a challenge we can only overcome together.

***Grundy, E., & Murphy, M (2007). Marital status and family support for the oldest-old. In J-M Robine, E.M. Crimmins, S. Horiuchi, Y. Zeng (Eds.), *Human longevity, individual life duration, and the growth of the oldest-old*, p. 432.

Comprehension

Exercise 1: Main Ideas

Indicate if each statement below is true (T) or false (F) according to your understanding of the passage.

1. **T / F**   The author would consider all unmarried people *singletons*.

2. **T / F**   For the first time in history large numbers of people are living alone.

3. **T / F**   Living as a singleton should be thought of as a transitional stage.

4. **T / F**   The majority of American adults are single.

5. **T / F**   Americans are less likely to live alone than people in many other countries.

Exercise 2: Supporting Details

To answer the following questions, you will probably need to scan* the article for specific pieces of information. Indicate if each statement below is true (T) or false (F) according to your understanding of the passage.

1. **T / F**   The age at which people marry in the US has been going down.

2. **T / F**   The percentage of male and female singletons in the US is about equal.

3. **T / F**   Middle-aged Americans are the fastest-growing singleton population.

*For an introduction to scanning, see Unit 1.

4. **T / F** In the Manhattan borough of New York City, more than half the households have people living alone.

5. **T / F** Urban areas of Japan have 30 percent single-dweller households.

Look at the questions that you guessed about before you began reading. How well did you do?

6. **T / F** The United States has the largest percentage of people living alone.

7. **T / F** Communal societies like Sweden and Denmark have fewer people living alone than the US.

8. **T / F** China is one of the nations with the fastest growth in single-person households.

Critical Reading

1. Below is a statement that the author makes later in the book *Going Solo:*

> Living alone may not be the social problem that it's generally said to be, but it creates all kinds of challenges for those who do it, and for those who care for them.

What challenges do you think the author goes on to discuss? What do you see as the challenges of living alone?

2. Below is another statement from later in the book *Going Solo.* The author argues that having no partner is better than having the wrong one. What kind of evidence does the author give? Do you agree with him?

> What is important is not whether we live alone, but whether we feel alone... As divorced or separated people often say, there's nothing lonelier than living with the wrong person... There is good evidence that people who never marry are just about as happy as people who are currently married, but also much happier and less lonely than people who are widowed or divorced. We also have good evidence that bad marriages produce stress and sickness for those who live through them; one recent study reports that "individuals in low-quality marriages have worse health than do divorced individuals."

Discussion/Composition

1. What are the four large-scale social changes that the author believes make possible the rise in the number of singletons?

   • How does each one make it possible for large numbers of people to live alone?

   • Do you agree that these are the best explanations for why more people are living alone? Can you think of other reasons?

2. What do you think makes living alone attractive for the young, the middle-aged, and the old? Do you think that the reasons differ according to age? Use information from the passage and your own experience to make your argument.

3. Do you believe it is a good thing or a bad thing to grow old living alone? Use information from the passage and your own experience to make your argument.

Vocabulary from Context

Exercise 1

The vocabulary in the exercise below is taken from "Going Solo." But the ideas certainly are not! Use the context provided to determine the meanings of the italicized words. Write a definition, synonym, or description in the space provided.

1. _____
2. _____
3. _____
4. _____
5. _____
6. _____
7. _____
8. _____
9. _____
10. _____
11. _____
12. _____
13. _____
14. _____
15. _____
16. _____
17. _____
18. _____
19. _____
20. _____

After John and Mary died, their adult children were shocked to discover the truth: Their parents were not married! They had gotten a *divorce* (1) 20 years before, but never told anyone! The children couldn't believe that their parents had been divorced for two decades and they didn't know. They were completely surprised and didn't want to tell other people, this *startling* (2) news. They didn't want to talk about it, and they wanted to *avoid* (3) all the questions they would be asked. It took them a while to get used to this new information. They had to *adapt* (4) to a new way to think about their parents. The children had always thought they had a traditional *nuclear family* (5): father, mother, children. There was a *transition* (6) period while they got used to this new information. But after a while they decided it was exciting, and they decided to try to find out why their parents had gotten a divorce but never told anyone.

They wondered if perhaps there was some financial reason not to be legally married any more. Perhaps their parents didn't have enough money to pay for something together, so they could no longer *afford* (7) to be married. The children had another idea. Their parents had paid money to the government every month when they worked so that they would receive *social security* (8) when they were older. Perhaps they received more money being divorced.

They wondered if this was just a *stage* (9) their parents had gone through, a period that they thought they would pass through. But this was a long stage. And this didn't explain why their parents still *dwelled* (10) together. Their parents still lived in the same *residence* (11), neither one had moved out. So the children decided that the decision was *mutual* (12); John and Mary had clearly made the decision together. And they put a lot of time and effort into being together; they each *invested* (13) a lot in the relationship. They did everything *communally* (14), working on everything together, and were always careful of each other's *welfare* (15). The health and happiness of the other person was the most important thing to them.

All of the *evidence* (16) that they had, all of these facts and information, suggested that their parents really liked each other and liked being together. The divorce did not *alter* (17) how their parents felt about each other. The children decided to stop worrying. After all, culture and communities *shape* (18) our ideas, and at the present time, ideas are changing. Lots of *contemporary* (19) people are divorced. Not everyone has a *spouse* (20), a husband or a wife. They realized this would have to remain something they could never explain or understand. This would just have to remain a great family mystery.

Exercise 2: Quantitative Vocabulary

"Going Solo" includes vocabulary that is commonly used in texts that describe numerical data. Both the ideas and quantitative vocabulary below are taken from "Going Solo." Use the context provided to determine the meanings of the italicized words and phrases. Write a definition, synonym, or description in the space provided.

1. _____

2. _____

3. _____

4. _____

5. _____

6. _____

7. _____

8. _____

9. _____

10. _____

11. _____

12. _____

Since 1950, it has become more and more common for adults in the United States to live alone. The numbers are not exact, but *roughly* (1) 31 million adults now live alone. Less than 50 percent of adults live with other people; the *majority* (2) lives alone.

What can explain this large *segment* (3) of the population living alone? Part of the *rise* (4) in the number of singletons can be *accounted for* (5) by the fact that now, a smaller part of the population is getting married. The *proportion* (6) of adults who are married dropped from 70% in 1950 to 50% in 2012. The marriage *rate* (7) is much lower now than right after World War II, when there was a *boom* (8) in the proportion of the population marrying as thousands of soldiers returned home. This *spike* (9) in the number of married couples led to a baby boom.

Things have changed a lot since the time when most people lived in households of married adults with young children. In the years after World War II, households in the US were *primarily* (10) made up of two-parent families. Today the picture is different. No longer are two parent families the *most prominent* (11) household type. The percentage of all singleton households in the US is now *tied* (12) with the percentage of households made up of couples with no children. Each makes up 28% of the household types in the country. And they are both now more common than any other type of living arrangement in the US.

Exercise 3

This exercise gives you additional practice using context to determine the meaning of vocabulary. Give a definition, synonym, or description of each of the words below. The numbers in parentheses indicate the paragraph in which the meaning of the word can be found. Your teacher may want you to do these orally or in writing.

1. (1) cycle _____

2. (1) arrangements _____

3. (4) multigenerational _____

4. (11, described in 14) longevity_____

Exercise 4

This exercise gives you additional clues to determine the meaning of vocabulary in context. In the paragraph of "Going Solo" indicated by the number in parentheses, find the word or phrase that best fits the meaning given. Your teacher may want to read these aloud as you quickly scan* the paragraph to find the answer.

1. (2) Which word means *creating, inventing, designing?* _____

2. (4) Which word means *unchanging; permanent?* _____

3. (6) Which word means *gather; collect; congregate; bunch; crowd?* _____

4. (9) Which word means *rose or increased very rapidly?* _____

Vocabulary Review

In each line, circle the word that is not similar in meaning.

1. skyrocket   boom   spike   cluster

2. alter   shape   segment   craft

3. dwelling   welfare   residence

---

*For an introduction to scanning, see Unit 1.

Reading Selection 3
Sociolinguistics

Amy Tan was born in 1952 to immigrant parents from China. Her parents wanted her to become a famous neurosurgeon and concert pianist. At one point she was a doctoral student in the UC–Berkeley Linguistics Department, and she is a member of a garage rock band, The Rockbottom Remainders. But at the age of 24, she experienced a difficult year of personal loss and self-discovery, and she became a writer. She is the author of *The Joy Luck Club, The Kitchen God's Wife, The Hundred Secret Senses, The Bonesetter's Daughter,* and *Saving Fish from Drowning,* all *New York Times* best sellers. She has received many literary awards, and she was the co-producer and co-screenwriter for the film adaptation of *The Joy Luck Club.* To learn more about her, go to www.amytan.net.

> **BEFORE YOU BEGIN**
>
> 1. Why are you learning English? What role do you expect it to play in your future?
>
> 2. How important is it to speak grammatically correct, unaccented English?
>
> 3. Do you believe people treat nonnative English speakers differently depending on their command of English? Have you ever been in situations where you believe you were treated disrespectfully or dismissed because of your use of English?
>
> 4. Do you think it is the same with other languages? Are people treated differently depending on their proficiency with other languages you speak?

In this essay Amy Tan examines her understanding of English as a tool of communication for her as a writer and for her mother as an immigrant. She raises important questions for teachers and learners of English to consider.

Read the essay to get a general understanding of Tan's analysis, and then do the exercises that follow. Your teacher may want you to do Vocabulary from Context Exercise 1 on page 229 before you begin.

Mother Tongue

By Amy Tan

1   I am not a scholar of English or literature. I cannot give you much more than personal opinions on the English language and its variations in this country or others.

2   I am a writer. And by that definition, I am someone who has always loved language. I am fascinated by language in daily life. I spend a great deal of my time thinking about the power of language—the way it can evoke an emotion, a visual image, a complex idea, or a simple truth. Language is the tool of my trade. And I use them all—all the Englishes I grew up with.

3   Recently, I was made keenly aware of the different Englishes I do use. I was giving a talk to a large group of people, the same talk I had already given to half a dozen other groups. The talk was about my writing, my life, and my book *The Joy Luck Club,* and it was going along well enough, until I remembered one major difference that made the whole talk sound wrong. My mother was in the room. And it was perhaps the first time she had heard me give a lengthy speech, using the kind of English I have never used with her. I was saying things like "the intersection of memory and imagination" and "There is an aspect of my fiction that relates to thus-and-thus"—a speech filled with carefully wrought grammatical phrases, burdened, it suddenly seemed to me, with nominalized forms, past perfect tenses, conditional phrases, forms of standard English that I had learned in school and through books, the forms of English I did not use at home with my mother.

4   Just last week, as I was walking down the street with her, I again found myself conscious of the English I was using, the English I do use with her. We were talking about the price of new and used furniture, and I heard myself saying this: "Not waste money that way." My husband was with us as well, and he didn't notice any such switch in English. And then I realized why. It's because over the twenty years we've been together I've often used the same kind of English with him, and sometimes he even uses it with me. It has become our language of intimacy, a different sort of English that relates to family talk, the language I grew up with.

5   So that you'll have some idea of what this family talk sounds like, I'll quote what my mother said during a conversation that I videotaped and then transcribed. During this conversation, she was talking about a political gangster in Shanghai who had the same last name as her family's, Du, and how in his early years the gangster wanted to be adopted by her family, who were rich by comparison. Later, the gangster became more powerful, far richer than my mother's family, and he showed up at my mother's wedding to pay his respects. Here's what she said in part:

6   "Du Yusong having business like fruit stand. Like off-the-street kind. He is Du like Du Zong—but not Tsung-ming Island people. The local people call *putong.* The river east side, he belong to that side local people. That man want to ask Du Zong father take him in like become own family. Du Zong father wasn't look down on him, but didn't take seriously, until that man big like become a mafia. Now important person, very hard to inviting him. Chinese way, came only to show respect, don't stay for dinner. Respect for making big celebration, he shows up. Mean gives lots of respect. Chinese custom. Chinese social life that way. If too important won't have to stay too long. He come to my wedding. I didn't see, I heard it. I gone to boy's side, they have YMCA dinner. Chinese age I was nineteen."

7 You should know that my mother's expressive command of English belies how much she actually understands. She reads the *Forbes* report, listens to *Wall Street Week,* converses daily with her stockbroker, reads Shirley MacLaine's books with ease—all kinds of things I can't begin to understand. Yet some of my friends tell me they understand fifty percent of what my mother says. Some say they understand eighty to ninety percent. Some say they understand none of it, as if she were speaking pure Chinese. But to me, my mother's English is perfectly clear, perfectly natural. It's my mother tongue. Her language, as I hear it, is vivid, direct, full of observation and imagery. That was the language that helped shape the way I saw things, expressed things, made sense of the world.

8 Lately I've been giving more thought to the kind of English my mother speaks. Like others, I have described it to people as "broken" or "fractured" English. But I wince when I say that. It has always bothered me that I can think of no way to describe it other than "broken," as if it were damaged and needed to be fixed, as if it lacked a certain wholeness and soundness. I've heard other terms used, "limited English," for example. But they seem just as bad, as if everything is limited, including people's perceptions of the limited-English speaker.

9 I know this for a fact, because when I was growing up, my mother's "limited" English limited my perception of her. I was ashamed of her English. I believed that her English reflected the quality of what she had to say. That is, because she expressed them imperfectly, her thoughts were imperfect. And I had plenty of empirical evidence to support me: the fact that people in department stores, at banks, and in restaurants did not take her seriously, did not give her good service, pretended not to understand her, or even acted as if they did not hear her.

10 My mother has long realized the limitations of her English as well. When I was a teenager, she used to have me call people on the phone and pretend I was she. In this guise, I was forced to ask for information or even to complain and yell at people who had been rude to her. One time it was to call her stockbroker in New York. She had cashed out her small portfolio, and it just so happened we were going to New York the next week, our first trip outside California. I had to get on the phone and say in an adolescent voice that was not very convincing, "This is Mrs. Tan."

11 My mother was standing in the back whispering loudly, "Why he don't send me check, already two weeks late. So mad he lie to me, losing me money."

12 And then I said in perfect English on the phone, "Yes, I'm getting rather concerned. You had agreed to send the check two weeks ago, but it hasn't arrived."

13 Then she began to talk more loudly. "What he want, I come to New York tell him front of his boss, you cheating me?" And I was trying to calm her down, make her be quiet, while telling the stockbroker, "I can't tolerate any more excuses. If I don't receive the check immediately, I am going to have to speak to your manager when I'm in New York next week." And sure enough, the following week, there we were in front of this astonished stockbroker, and I was sitting there red-faced and quiet, and my mother, the real Mrs. Tan, was shouting at his boss in her impeccable broken English.

14 We used a similar routine more recently, for a situation that was far less humorous. My mother had gone to the hospital for an appointment to find out about a CAT scan she had had a month earlier. She said she had spoken very good English, her best English, no mistakes. Still, she said, the hospital staff did not apologize when they informed her they had lost the CAT scan and she had come for nothing. She said they did not seem to have any sympathy when she told them she was anxious to know the exact diagnosis, since both her husband and her son had died of

brain tumors. She said they would not give her any more information until the next time and she would have to make another appointment for that. So she said she would not leave until the doctor called her daughter. She wouldn't budge. And when the doctor finally called her daughter, me, who spoke in perfect English—lo and behold—we had assurances the CAT scan would be found, promises that a conference call on Monday would be held, and apologies for any suffering my mother had gone through for a most regrettable mistake.

15 I think my mother's English almost had an effect on limiting my possibilities in life as well. Sociologists and linguists probably will tell you that a person's developing language skills are more influenced by peers than by family. But I do think that the language spoken in the family, especially in immigrant families which are more insular, plays a large role in shaping the language of the child. And I believe that it affected my results on achievement tests, IQ tests, and the SAT*. While my English skills were never judged poor, compared with math, English could not be considered my strong suit. In grade school I did moderately well, getting perhaps Bs, sometimes B-pluses, in English and scoring perhaps in the sixtieth or seventieth percentile on achievement tests. But those scores were not good enough to override the opinion that my true abilities lay in math and science, because in those areas I achieved As and scored in the ninetieth percentile or higher.

16 This was understandable. Math is precise; there is only one correct answer. Whereas, for me at least, the answers on English tests were always a judgment call, a matter of opinion and personal experience. Those tests were constructed around items like fill-in-the-blank sentence completion, such as "Even though Tom was_____ Mary thought he was

_____." And the correct answer always seemed to be the most bland combinations, for example, "Even though Tom was shy, Mary thought he was charming," with the grammatical structure "Even though" limiting the correct answer to some sort of semantic opposites, so you wouldn't get answers like "Even though Tom was foolish, Mary thought he was ridiculous." Well, according to my mother, there were very few limitations as to what Tom could have been and what Mary might have thought of him. So I never did well on tests like that.

17 The same was true with word analogies, pairs of words for which you were supposed to find some logical semantic relationship, for instance, "Sunset is to nightfall as _____ is to_____." And here you would be presented with a list of four possible pairs, one of which showed the same kind of relationship: *red* is to *stoplight, bus* is to *arrival, chills* is to *fever, yawn* is to *boring*. Well, I could never think that way. I knew what the tests were asking, but I could not block out of my mind the images already created by the first pair, *sunset* is to *nightfall*—and I would see a burst of colors against a darkening sky, the moon rising, the lowering of a curtain of stars. And all the other pairs of words—*red, bus, stoplight, boring*—just threw up a mass of confusing images, making it impossible for me to see that saying "A sunset precedes nightfall" was as logical as saying "A chill precedes a fever." The only way I would have gotten that answer right was to imagine an associative situation, such as my being disobedient and staying out past sunset, catching a chill at night, which turned into feverish pneumonia as punishment—which indeed did happen to me.

18 I have been thinking about all this lately, about my mother's English, about achievement tests. Because lately I've been asked, as a writer, why there are not more Asian-Americans represented

---

*IQ tests and the SAT: Two standardized tests taken by many children in the United States. The first tests general intelligence (*IQ* stands for Intelligence Quotient). The SAT is the Scholastic Aptitude Test, taken by students applying to US colleges and universities.

in American literature. Why are there few Asian-Americans enrolled in creative writing programs? Why do so many Chinese students go into engineering? Well, these are broad sociological questions I can't begin to answer. But I have noticed in surveys—in fact, just last week—that Asian-American students, as a whole, do significantly better on math achievement tests than on English tests. And this makes me think that there are other Asian-American students whose English spoken in the home might also be described as "broken" or "limited." And perhaps they also have teachers who are steering them away from writing and into math and science, which is what happened to me.

19 Fortunately, I happen to be rebellious and enjoy the challenge of disproving assumptions made about me. I became an English major my first year in college, after being enrolled as pre-med. I started writing nonfiction as a freelancer the week after I was told by my boss at the time that writing was my worst skill and I should hone my talents toward account management.

20 But it wasn't until 1985 that I began to write fiction. At first I wrote what I thought to be wittily crafted sentences, sentences that would finally prove I had mastery over the English language. Here's an example from the first draft of a story that later made its way into *The Joy Luck Club,* but without this line: "That was my mental quandary in its nascent state." A terrible line, which I can barely pronounce.

21 Fortunately, for reasons I won't get into here, I later decided I should envision a reader for the stories I would write. And the reader I decided on was my mother, because these were stories about mothers. So with this reader in mind—and in fact she did read my early drafts—I began to write stories using all the Englishes I grew up with: the English I spoke to my mother, which for lack of a better term might be described as "simple"; the English she used with me, which for lack of a better term might be described as "broken"; my translation of her Chinese, which could certainly be described as "watered down"; and what I imagined to be her translation of her Chinese if she could speak in perfect English, her internal language, and for that I sought to preserve the essence, but neither an English nor a Chinese structure. I wanted to capture what language ability tests could never reveal: her intent, her passion, her imagery, the rhythms of her speech and the nature of her thoughts.

22 Apart from what any critic had to say about my writing, I knew I had succeeded where it counted when my mother finished reading my book and gave me her verdict: "So easy to read."

Comprehension

Answer the following questions. Your teacher may want you to answer the questions orally, in writing, or by underlining appropriate portions of the text. True/False questions are indicated by a T / F preceding a statement. For some items, there is not a single correct answer. Be prepared to defend your choices.

1. What is the meaning of the title of the essay, "Mother Tongue"?

   _____

   _____

2. **T / F**   Tan speaks different kinds of English depending on her audience.

3. **T / F**   Tan often uses the same English with her husband as she does with her mother.

4. **T / F**   Tan tells the story of the Shanghai gangster to illustrate her mother's English.

5. Below are words and phrases that describe language. Check (✔) all those that characterize Tan's opinion of her mother's English.

   _____ **a.** perfectly clear   _____ **e.** broken

   _____ **b.** vivid   _____ **f.** fractured

   _____ **c.** direct   _____ **g.** limited

   _____ **d.** full of observation and imagery

6. **T / F**   Tan is embarrassed by her mother's English.

7. In which classes did Tan excel when she was in school? _____

8. **T / F**   Tan enjoyed taking English tests when she was in school.

9. **T / F**   Tan believes that children of immigrants should study math and science.

10. Who is Tan's primary audience when she writes? _____

11. **T / F**   Tan's mother enjoyed her daughter's stories.

Critical Reading

T / F   Tan's mother is limited by her imperfect English. Defend your answer with evidence from the text.

Tan decided to write using all the Englishes she grew up with, which she describes as:

a. Simple: the English she spoke to her mother

b. Broken: the English her mother spoke to her

c. Watered down: the English she used to translate her mother's Chinese

d. Her mother's internal language: the powerful language with which her mother understood the world

What experience do you have using different varieties of the same language? What factors make you decide which type of language to use?

Vocabulary from Context

Exercise 1

Both the ideas and the vocabulary in the exercise below are taken from "Mother Tongue." Use the context provided to determine the meanings of the italicized words. Write a definition, synonym, or description in the space provided.

1. _____
2. _____
3. _____
4. _____
5. _____
6. _____
7. _____
8. _____
9. _____

Many teenagers are *rebellious* (1), fighting against everything, especially what their parents want them to do. However, when Amy Tan was an *adolescent* (2), she was often cooperative and helpful to her mother. For example, once Tan's mother needed help talking to the man who sold her stocks and other financial investments. Tan phoned her mother's *stockbroker* (3), pretending to be her mother. Later when they went to see him in his New York office, they could see he was surprised when he met them. He was *astonished* (4) when he realized that the person he had been talking with on the phone was just a young girl. He thought he had been talking with a grown woman, but his *perception* (5) had been wrong. Tan's mature way of talking *belied* (6) her young age.

Tan also helped her mother talk with doctors. Once she went with her mother to hear her doctor's *diagnosis* (7) of a medical problem she had. When the doctor told her she had a brain tumor, she was frightened. However, the doctor said he could guarantee that the tumor was not cancerous but *benign* (8). He *assured* (9) her that she would be all right.

10. _____   As a nonnative speaker, Tan's mother spoke her own variety of English. Even though her grammar was not *impeccable* (10),

11. _____   her *intent* (11) was clear to most people. They could usually understand what she meant in spite of her grammatical mistakes.

12. _____   Her language was delightful to listen to. It was never *bland* (12); indeed, far from being ordinary and dull, it was a colorful version of English.

Exercise 2

This exercise is designed to give you practice using context clues to guess the meaning of unfamiliar vocabulary. Give a definition, synonym, or description of each of the italicized words or phrases below. The number in parentheses indicates the paragraph in which the word or phrase can be found. Your teacher may want you to do these orally or in writing.

1. (4) language of intimacy_____

2. (15) peers _____

3. (16) judgment call _____

4. (18) steering _____

Exercise 3

This exercise is designed to give you additional clues to determine the meaning of vocabulary items in context. In the paragraph of "Mother Tongue" indicated by the number in parentheses, find the word or phrase that best fits the meaning given. Your teacher may want to read these aloud as you quickly scan* the paragraph to find the answer.

1. (2) What phrase means *something considered necessary to carry out my occupation or profession?*

_____

2. (5) Which word means *member of a gang; someone who belongs to an organized group of criminals?*

_____

3. (8) Which word means *feel embarrassed, especially, to make a face showing embarrassment?*

_____

4. (9) Which two words mean *information or proof that is based on observation or practical experience?*

_____

5. (10) Which word means *identity; often a false identity or disguise?* _____

6. (10) What phrase means *sold her few financial investments for cash?* _____

7. (15) Which word means *isolated; separated from others as an island is from the mainland?*

_____

8. (21) Which word means *the most important or underlying meaning of something?*

_____

---

*For an introduction to scanning, see Unit 1.

Figurative Language and Idioms

Like the previous exercises, this one is designed to give you additional clues to understand the meaning of unfamiliar vocabulary in context, in this case, figurative language and idioms. Give a definition, synonym, or description of each of the words or phrases below. The number in parentheses indicates the paragraph of "Mother Tongue" in which the word or phrase can be found. Your teacher may want you to do these orally or in writing.

1. (3) Which word means *made difficult; weighted down; overloaded*? _____

2. (15) Which two words mean *greatest talent or skill*? _____

3. (17) What phrase means *ignore; forget*? _____

4. (19) What phrase means *shape or polish or improve my skills*? _____

5. (22) What phrase means *where it was important; when it mattered*? _____

Stems and Affixes

Both the ideas and the italicized words in the sentences below are taken from "Mother Tongue." Beneath the sentences is a list of synonyms and definitions. Use your knowledge of stems and affixes* and the context to match each italicized word with its definition by placing the appropriate letter on the line before each sentence.

_____ 1. Tan describes her mother's English as *vivid* and full of images.

_____ 2. Tan recorded and then *transcribed* her mother's speech so she could study her mother's language more closely.

_____ 3. Tan's telephone call to her mother's stockbroker *preceded* their visit to his office.

_____ 4. Tan's success as a writer *disproves* the claim that grades in school predict future performance.

_____ 5. When Tan writes a story, it helps her to *envision* her mother reading it.

a. shows to be not true; shows to be false or an error

b. came before; occurred earlier than

c. wrote down; made a written copy of

d. see a picture in her mind; imagine

e. lively; animated

---

*For a list of all stems and affixes that appear in *Reader's Choice*, see Appendix B.

Dictionary Study

Many words have more than one meaning. When you use a dictionary to discover the meaning of an unfamiliar word, you need to use the context to determine which definition is appropriate. Use the dictionary entries provided to select the best definition for each of the italicized words in the following sentences. Write the number of the definition in the space provided.

_____ 1. What was the *nature* of Tan's talk? It was an academic discussion of her writing, her life, and her book.

_____ 2. Tan speaks differently at home than when she is giving a professional talk, but she does not always notice the *switch* when she makes it.

_____ 3. Tan has a good *command* of many Englishes.

_____ 4. Tan believes her mother can give her *sound* advice about her writing.

_____ 5. After carefully reading Tan's work, her mother's *verdict* on it was positive.

---

na·ture [nā´chər]
—noun
  1   the essential character of a thing; quality or qualities that make something what it is; essence
  2   inborn character; innate disposition; inherent tendencies of a person
  3   the vital functions, forces, and activities of the organs: often used as a euphemism
  4   kind; sort; type; things of that nature
  5   any or all of the instincts, desires, appetites, drives, etc. of a person or animal
  6   what is regarded as normal or acceptable behavior
  7   the sum total of all things in time and space; the entire physical universe
  8   the power, force, principle, etc. that seems to regulate the physical universe: often personified, sometimes as Mother Nature
  9   the primitive state of man
  10 a simple way of life close to or in the outdoors
  11 natural scenery, including the plants and animals that are part of it

---

switch [swĭch]
—noun Abbr. **sw.**
  1   a thin flexible rod, stick, twig, used for whipping
  2   a shift or change from one (kind of) thing to another
  3   an abrupt, sharp, lashing movement
  4   a device that controls the flow of current in an electric circuit
  5   **a** a movable section of railroad track used to transfer a train from one track to another
      b siding (sense)
—transitive verb
switched, switching, switches.
  1   to whip with or as if with a switch
  2   To jerk or swish abruptly or sharply
  3   To shift, transfer, change, or divert
  4   **a** to operate the switch of (an electric circuit) so as to connect, disconnect, or divert
      b to turn (an electric light or appliance) on or off in this way
  5   to transfer (a railroad train or car) from one set of tracks to another by use of a switch
  6   to change or exchange

command [kuh-**mand**]

–verb (used with object)

1   to direct with specific authority or prerogative; order: *The captain commanded his men to attack.*
2   to require authoritatively; demand: *She commanded silence.*
3   to have or exercise authority or control over; be master of; have at one's bidding or disposal: *The Pharaoh commanded 10,000 slaves.*
4   to deserve and receive (respect, sympathy, attention, etc.): *He commands much respect for his attitude.*
5   to dominate by reason of location; overlook: *The hill commands the sea.*
6   to have authority over and responsibility for (a military or naval unit or installation); be in charge of.

–verb (used without object)

7   to issue an order or orders.
8   to be in charge; have authority.
9   to occupy a dominating position; look down upon or over a body of water, region, etc.

–noun

10   the act of commanding or ordering.
11   an order given by one in authority: *The colonel gave the command to attack.*
12   the possession or exercise of controlling authority: *a lieutenant in command of a platoon.*
13   expertise; mastery: *He has a command of French, Russian, and German.*

---

sound[1] [sound]

–noun

1   the sensation produced by stimulation of the organs of hearing by vibrations transmitted through the air or other medium.
2   mechanical vibrations transmitted through an elastic medium, traveling in air at a speed of approximately 1087 ft. (331 m) per second at sea level.
3   the particular auditory effect produced by a given cause: *the sound of music.*
4   any auditory effect; any audible vibrational disturbance: *all kinds of sounds.*
5   a noise, vocal utterance, musical tone, or the like: *the sounds from the next room.*
6   a distinctive, characteristic, or recognizable musical style, as from a particular performer, orchestra, or type of arrangement: *the big-band sound.*
7   *Phonetics.*
    a   SPEECH SOUND.
    b   the audible result of an utterance or portion of an utterance: *the s-sound in "slight;" the sound of m in "mere."*

sound[2] [sound]

–er, –est, adverb

–adjective

1   free from injury, damage, defect, disease, etc.; in good condition; healthy; robust: *a sound heart; a sound mind.*
2   financially strong, secure, or reliable: *a sound business; sound investments.*
3   competent, sensible, or valid: *sound judgment.*
4   having no defect as to truth, justice, wisdom, or reason: *sound advice.*
5   of substantial or enduring character: *sound moral values.*
6   following in a systematic pattern without any apparent defect in logic: *sound reasoning.*
7   uninterrupted and untroubled; deep: *sound sleep.*
8   vigorous, thorough, or severe: *a sound thrashing.*
9   free from moral defect or weakness; upright, honest, or good; honorable; loyal.
10   having no legal defect: *a sound title to property.*
11   theologically correct or orthodox, as doctrines or a theologian.

–adverb

12   deeply; thoroughly: *sound asleep.*

ver·dict [vûr′dĭkt]
—*noun*
1 **LAW** the formal finding of a judge or jury on a matter submitted to them in a trial
2 any decision or judgment

[Etymology: ME *verdit* < Anglo-Fr < ML *veredictum*, true saying, verdict < L *vere*, truly + *dictum*, a thing said.]

Vocabulary Review

Exercise 1

From the list below, select the word or phrase that correctly fits in each of the blanks in the paragraph that follows it. Some words will not be used.

sound	adolescents	block out	envision	steer
peers	astonish	strong suit	intent	rebellious

Being a teenager can be difficult. (1) _____ want to be accepted by their (2)_____ and sometimes these friends can (3)_____ them into troublesome or even dangerous situations. Sometimes parents worry too much. They can (4)_____ the worst possible things that could happen. They may forget how responsible their children really are. Worry may make parents (5) _____ of their minds all the ways in which their children have shown good judgment and made (6) _____ decisions. During these years, patience may not be the (7) _____ of either parents or teenagers.

Exercise 2

Are these pairs of words similar in meaning or opposite in meaning? Circle S if similar; circle O if opposite.

1. **S / O**   nature   essence

2. **S / O**   stockbroker   gangster

3. **S / O**   disproves   belies

4. **S / O**   vivid   bland

5. **S / O**   talent   strong suit

Reading Selection 4
Anthropology

> **BEFORE YOU BEGIN**

1. Following is an article from the field of anthropology. What is the task of an anthropologist?

2. If you wanted to describe customs of your country in order to help others understand an important aspect of your culture, what would you describe? Would it be your culture's religious practices? Would it be how people in your country handle their money? Would it be how the elderly are treated in your society? The way the culture treats visitors? Something else?

"The Sacred 'Rac'" is adapted from an introductory social anthropology textbook written for students in the United States. The article describes the customs of a tribe of people studied by the Indian anthropologist Chandra Thapar. Read the passage and answer the questions that follow. Your teacher may want you to do the Vocabulary from Context exercise on page 238 before you begin.

The Sacred "Rac"
By Patricia Hughes

1 An Indian anthropologist, Chandra Thapar, made a study of foreign cultures which had customs similar to those of his native land. One culture in particular fascinated him because it reveres one animal as sacred, much as the people in India revere the cow. The things he discovered might interest you since you will be studying India as part of this course.

2 The tribe Dr. Thapar studied is called the Asu and is found on the American continent north of the Tarahumara of Mexico. Though it seems to be a highly developed society of its type, it has an overwhelming preoccupation with the care and feeding of the rac—an animal much like a bull in size, strength, and temperament. In the Asu tribe, it is almost a social obligation to own at least one if not more racs. People not possessing at least one are held in low esteem by the community because they are too poor to maintain one of these beasts properly. Some members of the tribe, to display their wealth and social prestige, even own herds of racs.

3 Unfortunately the rac breed is not very healthy and usually does not live more than five to seven years. Each family invests large sums of money each year to keep its rac healthy and shod, for it has a tendency to throw its shoes often. There are rac specialists in each community, perhaps more than one if the community is particularly wealthy. These specialists, however, due to the long period of ritual training they must undergo and to the difficulty of obtaining the right selection of charms to treat the rac, demand costly offerings whenever a family must treat an ailing rac.

4 At the age of sixteen in many Asu communities, many youths undergo a puberty rite in which the rac figures prominently. Youths must petition a high priest in a grand temple. They are then initiated into the ceremonies that surround the care of the rac and are permitted to keep a rac.

5 Although the rac may be used as a beast of burden, it has many habits which would be considered by other cultures as detrimental to the life of the society. In the first place the rac breed is increasing at a very rapid rate and the Asu tribe has given no thought to curbing the rac population. As a consequence, the Asu must build more and more paths for the rac to travel on since its delicate health and its love of racing other racs at high speeds necessitate that special areas be set aside for its use. The cost of smoothing the earth is too costly for any one individual to undertake; so it has become a community project, and each member of the tribe must pay an annual tax to build new paths and maintain the old. There are so many paths needed that some people move their homes because the rac paths must be as straight as possible to keep the animal from injuring itself. Dr. Thapar also noted that unlike the cow, which many people in his country hold sacred, the excrement of the rac cannot be used as either fuel or fertilizer. On the contrary, its excrement is exceptionally foul and totally useless. Worst of all, the rac is prone to rampages in which it runs down anything in its path, much like stampeding cattle. Estimates are that the rac kills thousands of the Asu in a year.

6 Despite the high cost of its upkeep, the damage it does to the land, and its habit of destructive rampages, the Asu still regard it as being essential to the survival of their culture.

Comprehension

Answer the following questions. Your teacher may want you to answer orally, in writing, or by underlining appropriate portions of the text. True/False items are indicated by a T / F preceding the statement.

1. What society reveres the rac? _____

2. Where is the tribe located? _____

3. **T / F**   People who don't own racs are not respected in the Asu community.

4. Why does it cost so much to have a rac specialist treat an ailing rac?

    _____

5. **T / F**   An Asu must pass through a special ceremony before being permitted to keep a rac.

6. How is the rac helpful to the Asu?

    _____

7. What effects does the size of the rac population have on the life of the Asu?

    _____

8. **T / F**   Rac excrement can be used as fuel or as fertilizer.

9. According to the author, what is the worst characteristic of the rac?

    _____

10. **T / F**   The Asu feel that their culture cannot survive without the rac.

11. What is *rac* spelled backward? _____

Drawing Inferences

What is the author's attitude toward the rac? Why does she choose to present her opinion using this story about the Asu society?

Discussion/Composition

1. Is the rac essential to the survival of the Asu society? Of your society? What effects is the rac having on your society? Do people in your society revere the rac as much as the Asu do?

2. Describe some aspects of your culture from the point of view of an anthropologist.

3. In her essay "Who Can Tell My Story?" Jacqueline Woodson, an African American writer, speaks about people outside her home culture writing without true knowledge and insight.

> We want the chance to tell our own stories, to tell them honestly and openly. We don't want publishers to say, "Well, we already published a book about that," and then find that it was a book that did not speak the truth about us but rather told someone on the outside's idea of who we are.

Is it possible for "outsiders" to write with understanding about a culture? How do you feel when people on the outside write about your culture?

4. Can there be a scientific description of human behavior? The author of "The Sacred 'Rac'" constructed a culture she called the Asu. Many modern-day anthropologists believe that all cultural descriptions are really inventions—creations of the writer—and that the line between scientific and literary writing is not clear. Anthropological writing, they believe, is a place where art and science come together. Do you believe that studying human cultures is an art or a science or both?

Vocabulary from Context

Use the context provided and your knowledge of stems and affixes* to determine the meanings of the italicized words. Write a definition, synonym, or description in the space provided.

1. _____ Alex has had trouble studying for the final examination because he has been *preoccupied* (1) with happy thoughts of his summer vacation.

2. _____ Alice's dog is gentle and friendly; unfortunately, my dog doesn't have such a pleasant *temperament* (2).

3. _____ Peter wants to be a lawyer because he feels it is a very *prestigious* (3) occupation, and he has always wanted to hold a high position in society.

4. _____ Do you know a doctor who has experience *treating* (4) children?

5. _____ Instead of complaining to me that you're *ailing* (5), you should see a doctor to find out what's wrong with you.

6. _____ Many people believe that only primitive societies have a special ceremony to celebrate the time when a child becomes an adult; however, anthropologists say that advanced cultures also have *puberty rites* (6).

7. _____ The criminal was to be killed at dawn, but he *petitioned* (7) the president to save him and his request was granted.

8. _____ Doctors believe that smoking cigarettes is *detrimental* (8) to your health. They also *regard* (9) drinking alcohol as harmful.

9. _____

*For a list of all stems and affixes that appear in *Reader's Choice*, see Appendix B.

UNIT 9

Longer Reading
Psychology

This unit addresses issues of obedience to authority. Before you begin the longer reading in this unit, you will need to complete the Attitude Questionnaire and discuss The Question of Obedience. These selections will provide an introduction to the longer reading, "The Milgram Experiment."

Attitude Questionnaire

In the following questionnaire you are asked to predict your behavior in particular situations and to predict the behaviors of others. Specifically, you are asked to indicate three things.

1. What you, yourself, would do in the situations. Indicate your opinion on the scale marked *S* (for self).

2. What you think would be the reactions of people from your native culture. Indicate this opinion on the scale marked *C* (for native culture).

3. What you think would be the reactions of people in the United States. Indicate this opinion on the scale marked *U* (for US native).

Example

The following item was marked by a college student from Japan.

> You are a department head in a company that has very strict rules concerning punctuality. One of your most talented and productive employees is habitually late for work in the mornings. Company policy is to reduce latecomers' wages. Do you obey the company rule?
>
> Definitely Yes ◄————————► Definitely No
> S   ____ ____ ____ ✓ ____ ____ ____
> C   ✓ ____ ____ ____ ____ ____ ____
> U   ____ ____ ____ ____ ____ ____ ✓

Explanation

The checks on the scale indicate that the student believes that there is some difference between her and her fellow citizens and that there is substantial difference between her and US natives. She indicates that she would probably follow the company rule, while she thinks that most of the people from her native culture would definitely follow the rule and that most US natives would definitely not follow the rule.

In the questionnaire that follows you will be asked to respond to a number of items such as the preceding one. Remember, there are no right answers. What matters is your honest opinion.

After you have responded to all of the items, your teacher may want you to discuss your answers in small groups.

1. You travel on business a great deal with all expenses paid by your company. On one trip a waiter offers to leave the space blank on your receipt so that you can fill in whatever amount you wish. Do you accept the offer?

    Definitely Yes ◄――――► Definitely No

    S ____ ____ ____ ____ ____ ____
    C ____ ____ ____ ____ ____ ____
    U ____ ____ ____ ____ ____ ____

2. You have been attending a course regularly. An acquaintance, who rarely comes to class, asks for help with the take-home exam. Do you agree to help?

    Definitely Yes ◄――――► Definitely No

    S ____ ____ ____ ____ ____ ____
    C ____ ____ ____ ____ ____ ____
    U ____ ____ ____ ____ ____ ____

3. The police ask you for information about a friend who has strong political views. Do you give it to them?

    Definitely Yes ◄――――► Definitely No

    S ____ ____ ____ ____ ____ ____
    C ____ ____ ____ ____ ____ ____
    U ____ ____ ____ ____ ____ ____

4. You are in love with a person who is a devout follower of a different religion. What do you do?

Continue to see the person, hoping your differences in religion will not matter.	Change your religion.	Attempt to change the religion of your lover.	End the relationship.
S ____	____	____	____
C ____	____	____	____
U ____	____	____	____

5. You are the manager of a grocery store. You notice a woman stealing food. She is an acquaintance whom you know to be the unemployed single mother of three small children. What do you do?

Report her to the police.	Speak to her privately; allow her to replace the food.	Ignore the situation.	Secretly pay for the food she took.
S ____	____	____	____
C ____	____	____	____
U ____	____	____	____

6. In a high-level meeting with all of the bosses in your company, a superior takes credit for work of a colleague who is not present. Do you correct the information?

    Definitely Yes ◄――――► Definitely No

    S ____ ____ ____ ____ ____ ____
    C ____ ____ ____ ____ ____ ____
    U ____ ____ ____ ____ ____ ____

7. The police have captured a man who they say is a dangerous criminal and whom they hope to convict of a series of violent crimes. You have been brought in to see if he is the same person who robbed you recently in the park. He is not the man who robbed you, but the police are pressing you to testify against him. Do you identify him as the robber?

    Definitely Yes ◄――――► Definitely No

    S ____ ____ ____ ____ ____ ____
    C ____ ____ ____ ____ ____ ____
    U ____ ____ ____ ____ ____ ____

8. Your boss is about to fire a woman for a mistake that you know she did not make. You think the woman is not a very good employee. Do you correct your boss?

    Definitely Yes ◄――――► Definitely No

    S ____ ____ ____ ____ ____ ____
    C ____ ____ ____ ____ ____ ____
    U ____ ____ ____ ____ ____ ____

9. You discover that your brother is selling important information to a foreign power. What do you do?

Report him to the police.	Try to convince him to stop.	Ignore the situation.
S ____	____	____
C ____	____	____
U ____	____	____

10. Your company is about to sign an extremely important contract. Your boss asks you to not mention a production problem you have been trying to solve because knowledge of the problem might cause the client to go to a different company. In a meeting with the client you are asked if there are any production problems. Do you tell the truth?

    Definitely Yes ◄――――► Definitely No

    S ____ ____ ____ ____ ____ ____
    C ____ ____ ____ ____ ____ ____
    U ____ ____ ____ ____ ____ ____

11. Your boss is having marital difficulties with her husband. She decides to take a weekend vacation with another man. She instructs you to tell her husband that she is at a business meeting. Do you follow her instructions?

Definitely Yes ←——————→ Definitely No

S   ____ ____ ____ ____ ____ ____
C   ____ ____ ____ ____ ____ ____
U   ____ ____ ____ ____ ____ ____

12. You work for a large firm that owns many apartment buildings. You have been instructed to evict all tenants who are behind in their rent. Mr. and Mrs. Jones are hardworking people who have always paid on time. They have five children to support. They have both just lost their jobs and are unable to pay the rent. Do you evict them?

Definitely Yes ←——————→ Definitely No

S   ____ ____ ____ ____ ____ ____
C   ____ ____ ____ ____ ____ ____
U   ____ ____ ____ ____ ____ ____

13. You are taking a college psychology class. The professor asks you to participate in an experiment that requires you to lie to your friends. Do you do as you are told?

Definitely Yes ←——————→ Definitely No

S   ____ ____ ____ ____ ____ ____
C   ____ ____ ____ ____ ____ ____
U   ____ ____ ____ ____ ____ ____

Examine your answers to the questionnaire. Did you tend to see yourself as agreeing more with citizens of your native culture or with citizens of the US? Do you see yourself as a "member of the group" or as an "individualist?" Did your answers differ markedly from those of other members of your class? What kinds of evidence did people give to support their points of view?

The Question of Obedience

The preceding questionnaire and the longer reading in the next section raise the question of obedience to authority. There are times when we must follow the orders of people in authority and times when we must follow our own consciences. Use the items below to guide your discussion of this conflict between authority and conscience. True/False items are indicated by a T / F preceding a statement.

1. The following individuals are authority figures in most cultures. Indicate the extent to which they should be obeyed. Compare your responses to those of others in your class.

Most Obedience ←——————→ Least Obedience

a.	employer	____	____	____	____	____	____
b.	police officer	____	____	____	____	____	____
c.	friend	____	____	____	____	____	____
d.	grandmother	____	____	____	____	____	____
e.	mother	____	____	____	____	____	____
f.	teacher	____	____	____	____	____	____
g.	judge	____	____	____	____	____	____
h.	father	____	____	____	____	____	____
i.	military officer	____	____	____	____	____	____
j.	religious leader	____	____	____	____	____	____
k.	grandfather	____	____	____	____	____	____

2. **T / F** Authority figures should be obeyed even when they order you to do something you disagree with.

3. What do you mean when you use the word *obedience?*

    a. Are there situations when one should unquestioningly obey an authority? List occasions when this is true._____

    _____

    b. Can you obey someone without doing *exactly* what that person tells you to do? _____

    c. Are there times when children should not obey their elders?_____

The Milgram Experiment

Psychological experiments can have unexpected consequences. According to the *Atlantic* online:

> In the fall of 1958 Theodore Kaczynski, a brilliant but vulnerable boy of sixteen, entered Harvard College. There he encountered a prevailing intellectual atmosphere of antitechnological despair. There, also, he was deceived into subjecting himself to a series of purposely brutalizing psychological experiments that may have confirmed his still-forming belief in the evil of science.

Thirty years later he was arrested as "the Unabomber," an American antitechnology terrorist who over the course of seventeen years sent bombs to people involved in science and technology.

    The experiments that Kaczynski was exposed to were precursors of the famous psychological experiments conducted by Yale psychologist Stanley Milgram. During the 1960s, Milgram conducted a study to determine the extent to which ordinary people would obey clearly immoral orders…. The results were disturbing and led Milgram to conclude that "ordinary people, simply doing their jobs, and without any hostility on their part, can become agents in a terrible destructive process." In the Discussion/Composition section on pages 251–253 you will be asked to compare Milgram's analysis of his data with an alternative interpretation.

    The article that follows summarizes the experiment conducted by Milgram. Your teacher may want you to do Vocabulary from Context Exercise 1 before you begin reading. Read the first eight paragraphs to understand the design of the experiment and then answer the questions that follow. Your teacher may want you to discuss your answers before continuing with the reading.

The Milgram Experiment

1   After World War II the Nuremberg war trials were conducted in order to try Nazi war criminals for the atrocities they had committed. In many instances the defense offered by those on trial was that they had "only followed orders." During the Vietnam War American soldiers accused of committing atrocities in Vietnam gave basically the same explanation for their actions.

2   Most of us reject justifications based on "obedience to authority" as mere rationalizations, secure in our convictions that we, if placed in the same situation, would behave differently. However, the results of a series of ingenious and controversial investigations performed in the 1960s by psychologist Stanley Milgram suggest that perhaps we should not be so sure of ourselves.

3 Milgram wanted to determine the extent to which people would obey an experimenter's commands to administer painful electric shocks to another person. Pretend for a moment that you are a subject in one of his studies. Here is what would happen. On arriving at a university laboratory in response to a classified ad offering volunteers $4 for one hour's participation in an experiment on memory, you meet another subject, a pleasant, middle-aged man with whom you chat while awaiting the arrival of the experimenter. When the experimenter arrives, dressed in a laboratory coat, he pays you and then informs you and the other person that one of you will be the subject in the experiment and that the other will serve as his assistant. You are chosen by lot to be the assistant, but in reality you are the subject.

4 The experimenter explains that the study is concerned with the effects of punishment on learning. Accompanied by you, the "subject" is conducted into a room and strapped into a chair, and a large electrode is attached to his wrist. He is told that he is to learn a list of word pairs and that whenever he makes an error he will receive electric shocks of increasing intensity. On hearing this, the "subject" responds, "When I was at the West Haven V.A. Hospital a few years ago, they detected a slight heart condition. Nothing serious, but are these shocks dangerous?" The experimenter replies in an unconcerned manner that although the shocks may be painful, they will cause no permanent tissue damage.

5 You and the experimenter then proceed to an adjoining room connected by an intercom so that the "subject's" responses can be heard. You are seated in front of an apparatus with 30 toggle switches ranging from 15 volts to 450 volts (see Figure 1). Your task is to administer the learning task to the "subject." Whenever he gives an incorrect answer, you must give him an electric shock, starting at the lowest level (15 volts) and increasing the level by 15 volts each time. You are given a sample shock of 45 volts and find it moderately painful.

6 What you are unaware of at this point is that you are in a carefully contrived situation. The learner is actually an actor who receives no shock at all, and the responses you hear over the intercom are tape-recorded so that they will be exactly the same for each "assistant." The experimenter's actions are also carefully programmed.

7 As the experiment proceeds, the learner makes error after error. You increase the shock level steadily until he is clearly experiencing pain. The tape-recorded responses are programmed to correspond to the shock intensities as follows:

75 volts Ugh!

90 volts Ugh!

105 volts Ugh! *(louder)*

120 volts Ugh! Hey, *this* really hurts.

135 volts Ugh!!

150 volts Ugh!!! Experimenter! That's all. Get me out of here. I told you I had heart trouble. My heart's starting to bother me now. Get me out of here. I told you I had heart trouble. My heart's starting to bother me. I refuse to go on. Let me out.

165 volts Ugh! Let me out. *(shouting)*

180 volts Ugh! I can't stand the pain. Let me out of here! *(shouting)*

195 volts Ugh! Let me out of here. Let me out of here. My heart's bothering me. Let me out of here! You have no right to keep me here! Let me out! Let me out of here! My heart's bothering me. Let me out! Let me out!

210 volts Ugh!! Experimenter! *Get* me out of here. I've had enough. I won't be in the experiment any more.

225 volts Ugh!

240 volts Ugh!

255 volts Ugh! Get me out of here.

270 volts *(Agonized scream).* Let me out of here. Let me out of here. Let me out of here. Let me out. Do you hear? Let me out of here.

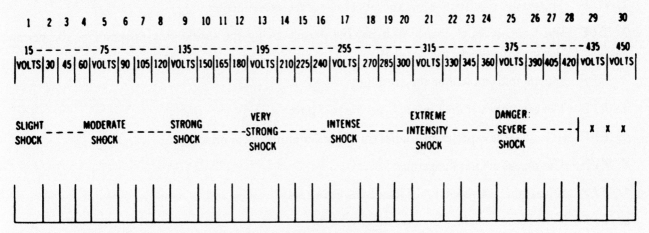

FIGURE 1 The control panel of the shocking apparatus used in the Milgram research. Copyright © 1974 by Stanley Milgram. Reprinted by permission of Harper & Row, Publishers, Inc.

285 volts *(Agonized scream).*

300 volts *(Agonized scream).* I absolutely refuse to answer any more. Get me out of here. You can't hold me here. Get me out. Get me out of here.

315 volts *(Intensely agonized scream).* I told you I refuse to answer. I'm no longer part of this experiment.

330 volts *(Intense and prolonged agonized scream).* Let me out of here. Let me out of here. My heart's bothering me. Let me out, I tell you. *(Hysterically)* Let me out of here. Let me out of here. You have no right to hold me here. Let me out! Let me out! Let me out of here! Let me out! Let me out!

345 volts *(At 345 volts and thereafter, there was only silence.)*

8   But supposing you express unwillingness at some point to continue shocking the learner? In that event the experimenter, sitting at a nearby desk, would respond in one of the following ways:

"Please continue" or "Please go on."

"The experiment requires that you continue."

"It is absolutely essential that you continue."

"You have no other choice. You must go on."

Comprehension

Exercise 1

Pretend you have volunteered to participate in Milgram's experiment as you answer the following questions. True/False items are indicated by a T / F preceding a statement.

1. **T / F** The person you first meet at the laboratory is the experimenter.

2 **T / F** You have an equal chance of being the person giving the shocks (the assistant) or the person receiving the shocks (the learner).

3. **T / F** You are told you will be the assistant.

4. **T / F** The experimenter does not tell you the true purpose of the experiment.

5. **T / F** In reality, the experiment studies the effects of punishment on learning.

6. **T / F** The shocks are not dangerous.

7. **T / F** When you pull a switch, the learner receives a shock.

8. **T / F** Some learners make more mistakes than others.

9. **T / F** If you say that you do not want to continue, the experimenter stops the experiment.

10. Why is *subject* in quotation marks in Paragraphs 4 and 5? _____

11. If you were a participant in this experiment, at what point would you *stop* administering "shocks?"

_____

12. What results would you predict for the experiment?

   a. Do you think most people would continue pulling the switches? How long do you think most people would continue?_____

   b. Do you think there would be different results depending on the subject's age, education, nationality, sex?_____

Now, read the rest of the article, and answer the questions that follow.

9   Having now experienced the Milgram situation at least in your imagination, how long do you think you would continue to administer shocks? Most of our students maintain that they would not go beyond 105 volts before refusing to continue the experiment. A panel of psychiatrists predicted before the experiment that perhaps only 1 percent of the subjects would proceed to the 450-volt level.

10 In fact, however, the "shock" produced by the results of this study was much more startling than the simulated shocks in the experiment. Forty men ranging in age from 20 to 50 and representing a cross section of the population, participated in the investigation. The maximum shock levels they administered are shown in Table 1. Nearly two-thirds of them administered the 450-volt maximum shock, and the average maximum shock they administered was 368 volts.

TABLE 1. Maximum shock levels administered by subjects in the Milgram experiment.

Shock level	Verbal designation and voltage level	Number of subjects giving each maximum shock level
1	Slight Shock 15	
2	30	
3	45	
4	60	
5	Moderate Shock 75	1
6	90	
7	105	
8	120	
9	Strong Shock 135	
10	150	6
11	165	
12	180	1
13	Very Strong Shock 195	
14	210	
15	225	
16	240	
17	Intense Shock 255	
18	270	2
19	285	
20	300	1
21	Extreme-Intensity Shock 315	1
22	330	1
23	345	
24	360	
25	Danger: Severe Shock 375	1
26	390	
27	405	
28	420 XXX	
29	435	
30	450	26
	Average maximum shock level	368 volts
	Percentage of obedient subjects	65.0%

11 Virtually all the people who administered high levels of shock exhibited extreme discomfort, anxiety, and distress. Most verbally refused to continue on one or more occasions. But continue they did when ordered to do so by the experimenter, who assured them that what happened in the experiment was his responsibility.

12 By contriving a situation with many real-life elements, Milgram succeeded in demonstrating that a high percentage of "normal" people will obey an authority figure even when the destructive effects of their obedience are obvious. The conclusions that he draws from his work are chilling indeed:

13 A commonly offered explanation is that those who shocked the victim at the most severe level were monsters, the sadistic fringe of society. But if one considers that almost two-thirds of the participants fall into the category of "obedient" subjects, and that they represented ordinary people drawn from working, managerial, and professional classes, the argument becomes very shaky. After witnessing hundreds of ordinary people submit to the authority in our own experiments, I must conclude that [Hannah] Arendt's conception of the *banality of evil* comes closer to the truth than one might dare imagine. The ordinary person who shocked the victim did so out of a sense of obligation—a conception of his duties as a subject—and not from any peculiarly aggressive tendencies.

14 This is, perhaps, the most fundamental lesson of our study: ordinary people, simply doing their jobs, and without any particular hostility on their part, can become agents in a terrible destructive process. Moreover, even when the destructive effects of their work become patently clear, and they are asked to carry out actions incompatible with fundamental standards of morality, relatively few people have the resources needed to resist authority. A variety of inhibitions against disobeying authority come into play and successfully keep the person in his place (Milgram, 1974, pp. 5–6).

15 Milgram's method of investigation also generated shock waves among psychologists. Many questioned whether it was ethical to expose subjects without warning to experiments that were likely to generate considerable stress and that might conceivably have lasting negative effects on them. But supporters of Milgram's work argue that adequate precautions were taken to protect participants. There was an extensive debriefing at the conclusion of the experiment, and participants were informed that they had not actually shocked anyone. They had a friendly meeting with the unharmed "subject." The purpose of the experiment was explained to them, and they were assured that their behavior in the situation was perfectly normal. Further, supporters argue, the great societal importance of the problem being investigated justified the methods the experimenters used. Finally, they cite follow-up questionnaire data collected by Milgram from his subjects after they received a complete report of the purposes and results. Eighty-four percent of the subjects stated that they were glad to have been in the experiment (and several spontaneously noted that their participation had made them more tolerant of others or otherwise changed them in desirable ways). Fifteen percent expressed neutral feelings, and only 1.3 percent stated that they were sorry to have participated.

16 The controversy over the ethics of Milgram's research has raged for decades. In combination with other controversial issues, it has prompted a deep and abiding concern for protecting the welfare of subjects in psychological research. Because of such concerns, it is most unlikely that Milgram's research could be conducted today.

Exercise 2

Answer the following questions. Your teacher may want you to do this exercise orally, in writing, or by underlining appropriate portions of the text. True/False items are indicated by a T / F preceding a statement. Some items may not have a single correct answer. Be prepared to defend your choices.

1. What was the purpose of Milgram's experiment?_____

2. **T / F** Most of the subjects continued to shock the learners when the shock level reached the danger level.

3. **T / F** The subjects appeared to enjoy the opportunity to hurt other people.

4. **T / F** The people who shocked the learners at the most severe level were mentally disturbed or in other ways antisocial.

5. **T / F** Today we are far more sophisticated than we were in the 1960s, and therefore we do not have to worry about people submitting to an immoral authority.

6. **T / F** Most professionals, schoolteachers for example, are incapable of inflicting pain on others while following a superior's orders.

7. The authors state that the subjects were visibly shaken by the experience and that many refused to continue. Why *did* they continue if it was so painful for the learner and so upsetting for them? Why didn't they just refuse to go on?_____

_____

8. Follow-up studies indicated that the subjects' opinions of the experiment were generally positive.

    a. **T / F** These positive evaluations could be attributed to the subjects' respect for the experimenter, and their obedience to his authority.

    b. **T / F** The results of the experiment should cause us to doubt the validity of the follow-up studies.

9. **T / F** If Stanley Milgram participated in such an experiment, he would probably agree to push the shocks above the comfort level.

Vocabulary from Context

Exercise 1

Both the ideas and the vocabulary in the exercise below are taken from "The Milgram Experiment." Use the context provided to determine the meanings of the italicized words. Write a definition, synonym, or description of each of the italicized vocabulary items in the space provided.

1. _____ Many people, when forced to justify poor behavior, come up with *rationalizations* (1) that seem convincing but are really just excuses.

2. _____ The experiment was cleverly organized to appear as if it were real, but in fact it was merely a *simulation* (2) in which all of the participants were actors.

3. _____ Extraordinary evil is very frightening, but when it appears as if evil has a common, everyday quality about it, its *banality* (3) is even more frightening.

4. _____ Scientists cannot agree on the value of the Milgram study. Heated debate and angry disagreement have surrounded the *controversial* (4) research ever since the first experiment was completed.

5. _____ We are all comforted by the thought that society is governed by a system of moral principles and human values. It is, in fact, our confidence in the *ethical* (5) nature of the common person that gives us peace of mind.

Exercise 2

This exercise gives you additional clues to determine the meaning of vocabulary in context. In the paragraph of "The Milgram Experiment" indicated by the number in parentheses, find the word that best fits the meaning given. Your teacher may want to read these aloud as you quickly scan* the paragraph to find the answer.

1. (1) Which word means *extremely wicked or cruel acts*? _____

2. (2) Which word means *very clever*? _____

3. (3) Which word means *give*? _____

4. (3) Which word means *person studied in an experiment*? _____

5. (6) Which word means *constructed; designed*? _____

6. (11) Which word means *almost*? _____

7. (13) Which word means *cruel; experiencing pleasure from others' suffering*? _____

8. (15) Which word means *a session provided to give information to an experimental subject after the experiment*?
_____

Figurative Language and Idioms

This exercise is designed to give you additional clues to understand the meanings of vocabulary in context, in this case figurative language and idioms. In the paragraph of "The Milgram Experiment" indicated by the number in parentheses, find the word or phrase that best fits the meaning given. Your teacher may want to read these aloud as you quickly scan* the paragraph to find the answer.

1. (3) What phrase means *by chance; at random*? _____

2. (10) What phrase means *a wide variety*? _____

3. (12) Which word means *frightening*? _____

---

*For an introduction to scanning, see Unit 1.

4. (13) What phrase means *the edge of normal society*? _____

5. (16) What phrase means *has occurred energetically and violently*? _____

Discussion/Composition: Revisiting the Experiment

1. Some scientists argue that experiments such as this violate basic human rights of the subjects because they deceive the participants. Others claim that the deception is justified because of the importance of the findings. What do you think?

   a. In what ways are the subjects deceived?

   b. What might be the negative effects upon the subjects of having participated in the study? Recall that "the Unabomber" took part in similarly disturbing experiments. Do you think the negative effects could be so severe that they could create someone like "the Unabomber?"

   c. What is the importance of this sort of study? What do you know now about society that you did not know before reading the article?

2. The following are adapted from guidelines written after the Milgram experiment in an effort to protect the rights of participants in psychological studies. As you read the principles take note of how they address aspects of the Milgram experiment.

Ethical Principles and Code of Conduct for Psychologists

Principle A: Beneficence and Nonmaleficence

Psychologists strive to benefit those with whom they work (beneficence) and also to take care to do no harm (nonmaleficence). Because psychologists' scientific and professional judgments and actions may affect the lives of others, they must avoid personal, financial, social, organizational, or political factors that might lead to abuse of their power.

Principle B: Integrity

Psychologists seek to promote accuracy, honesty, and truthfulness in the science, teaching, and practice of psychology. In these activities psychologists do not steal, cheat, or engage in intentional misrepresentation of fact.

Principle C: Respect for People's Rights and Dignity

Psychologists respect the dignity and worth of all people, and the rights of individuals to privacy, confidentiality, and self-determination.

   a. Beneficence is taking an action to do good. Nonmaleficence is avoiding doing something that will cause harm. Milgram would probably argue that his research constituted beneficence because it would help us understand obedience to authority—a benefit for humanity even if possibly a risk for individuals in the experiment. Do you agree?

b. T / F By explaining the experiment to the participants after the study and then following up with them later to discover how they were doing, Milgram was practicing nonmaleficence.

c. T / F Because the participants in the experiment did not actually receive electrical shocks, Milgram was practicing nonmaleficence.

d. In what ways did Milgram violate Principle B?

e. What do you believe to be the rights of all people with regard to authority? How did Milgram violate the dignity of the experiment participants?

f. Under what conditions would you agree to participate in a psychology study?

3. The Milgram experiment asks the question, "How can good people, ordinary people, do very bad things?" Milgram's explanation is that people "submit to authority." In paragraph 14, you read his description:

> Even when the destructive effects of their work become patently clear, and they are asked to carry out actions incompatible with fundamental standards of morality, relatively few people have the resources needed to resist authority. A variety of inhibitions against disobeying authority come into play, and successfully keep the person in his [or her] place.

This description does not address the question, What is the source of these inhibitions? Recently, sociologist Fred Emil Katz has offered an intriguing extension of the Milgram findings:

> It seems to me that we must interpret Milgram's experiments as more than centering on obedience to authority. Although, to be sure, obedience to authority was what Milgram meant to investigate—and did indeed investigate—he surely created a situation in the laboratory where a *specific morality prevailed*. It had its own ultimate values: the prime importance of science, its ultimate importance of yielding greater knowledge that can benefit humankind; and the ongoing behavior that must adhere to "scientific" conduct of inquiry, where personal feelings must be excluded in the pursuit of dispassionate, objective knowledge. Along the way the individual participant became part of a team, a social community (temporary, to be sure) that would labor to bring about the grand goal of increasing our scientific knowledge, even if it included having to do some awful things along the way. Science was given top priority, overcoming the participants' personal squeamishness about hurting innocent people. Here in the laboratory, a distinct morality prevailed, one I [call] a Local Moral Universe. That Local Moral Universe explicitly excluded values on which one was brought up (notably, that one does not hurt innocent people) while one acted within the confines of an immediate, locally defined moral community.

To summarize, Milgram explains good people doing bad things because they are obeying authority. Katz goes further, to ask why people obey authority. He argues that ordinary people do extraordinarily bad things as members of a community, in the context of a Local Moral Universe (LMU). You might think of this as similar to "peer pressure." Respond in writing or by discussing some or all of the following questions.

a. Do you believe people are "authority prone," that is, that in the right circumstances, almost everyone will follow orders? Give examples for your position. (If you have read "The Lottery" in Unit 6, is this a good example?)

b. Do you agree with Katz that good people do bad things because of the attitudes of people around them, their Local Moral Universe? Give examples for your position.

c. Near the end of his book *Confronting Evil*, Katz says that it is only the first step to understand LMUs. The next step is to find ways to change them, end their control, use them for good, instead of evil: "For this I invite your suggestions and your help." How can we end the influence of Local Moral Universes that encourage people to treat other people badly?

Word Study

Stems and Affixes

Below is a list of some commonly occurring stems and affixes.* Study their meanings, and then do the exercises that follow. Can you think of other words that derive from these stems and affixes?

Prefixes		
by-	aside or apart from the common, secondary	*bypass, by-product*
de-	down from, away	*descend, depart*
dia-	through, across	*diameter, diagonal*
epi-	upon, over, outer	*epidermis*
hyper-	above, beyond, excessive	*hypersensitive*
hypo-	under, beneath, down	*hypothesis, hypothermia*
Stems		
-capit-	head, chief	*captain, cap, decapitate*
-corp-	body	*corporation, incorporate*
-derm-	skin	*epidermis, dermatology*
-geo-	Earth	*geology, geography*
-hydr-, -hydro-	water	*hydrogen, hydrology*
-ortho-	straight, correct	*orthodox, orthography*
-pod-, -ped-	foot	*podiatrist, pedestrian*
-son-	sound	*sound, sonic*
-therm-, -thermo-	heat	*thermal, hypothermia*
-ver-	true	*verity, veritable*
Suffixes		
-ate, -fy	to make	*activate, liquify*
-ize	to make	*crystallize*

---

*For a list of all stems and affixes that appear in *Reader's Choice*, see Appendix B.

EXERCISE 1

Word analysis can help you to guess the meanings of unfamiliar words. For each item, using context clues and what you know about word parts, write a synonym, description, or definition of the italicized word or phrase.

1. _____ Adam is employed at a *hydroelectric* power plant.

2. _____ Before Cindy gets dressed in the morning, she looks at the *thermometer* hanging outside her kitchen window.

3. _____ Some doctors prescribe medication to calm *hyperactive* children.

4. _____ I'm not sure if that information is correct, but I'll look in our records to *verify* it.

5. _____ Susan wants to replace the *pedals* on her bicycle with a special kind that racers use.

6. _____ After spending so many days lost in the desert, he was suffering from severe *dehydration.*

7. _____ June's father's hobby is photography, so she bought him a top-quality *tripod* for his birthday.

8. _____ He will never learn how to improve his writing unless he stops being so *hypersensitive* to criticism.

9. _____ Dr. Robinson said that just the sight of a *hypodermic* needle is enough to frighten many of his patients.

10. _____ Although she finished her degree in dentistry in 2005, she wants to go back to school next year to specialize in *orthodontics.*

11. _____ The immigration authorities *deported* Bob Jensen because he did not have a legal passport.

12. _____ The average *per capita* annual income in this country for people between the ages of sixteen and sixty-five has risen dramatically in the last ten years.

13. _____ Sam Thompson made an appointment with a *dermatologist* because he noticed small red spots on his hands.

14. _____ Scientists have developed a sensitive instrument to measure *geothermal* variation.

15. _____ Anthropologists say that bipedalism played an important role in the cultural evolution of the human species. Because early humans were *bipedal,* their hands were free to make and use tools.

16. _____ They doubted the *veracity* of his story.

17. _____ The Concorde, which flew at *supersonic* speed, could cross the Atlantic in about three hours.

EXERCISE 2

Following is a list of words containing some of the stems and affixes* introduced in this appendix and the previous ones. Definitions of these words appear on the right. Put the letter of the appropriate definition next to each word.

1. _____ *hyperbole*	**a.**	the tissue immediately beneath the outer layer of the tissue of plants
2. _____ *hypodermis*	**b.**	a quotation printed at the beginning of a book or chapter to suggest its theme
3. _____ *epicentre*	**c.**	the outer layer of skin of some animals
4. _____ *epidermis*	**d.**	an exaggeration; a description that is far beyond the truth
5. _____ *epigraph*	**e.**	the part of the Earth's surface directly above the place of origin of an earthquake

6. _____ *orthography*	**a.**	fear of water
7. _____ *hydrate*	**b.**	agreeing with established beliefs
8. _____ *decapitate*	**c.**	fat; having a large body
9. _____ *orthodox*	**d.**	to cut off the head of
10. _____ *hydrophobia*	**e.**	correct spelling; writing words with the proper, accepted letters
11. _____ *corpulent*	**f.**	to cause to combine with water

12. _____ *bypass*	**a.**	of or related to walking; a person who walks
13. _____ *pedestrian*	**b.**	a dead body
14. _____ *by-product*	**c.**	a passage to one side; a route that goes around a town
15. _____ *corporeal*	**d.**	a secondary and sometimes unexpected result; something produced (as in manufacturing) in addition to the principal product
16. _____ *corpse*	**e.**	the care and treatment of the human foot in health and disease
17. _____ *podiatry*	**f.**	bodily; of the nature of the physical body; not spiritual

18. _____ *deflect*	**a.**	to turn aside from a fixed course
19. _____ *decentralize*	**b.**	of or relating to the form of the Earth or its surface features
20. _____ *diaphanous*	**c.**	to divide and distribute what has been concentrated or united
21 _____ *verisimilitude*	**d.**	the quality of appearing to be true
22. _____ *geomorphic*	**e.**	characterized by such fineness of texture that one can see through it

*For a list of all the stems and affixes that appear in *Reader's Choice*, see Appendix B.

APPENDIX B

Below is a list of the stems and affixes that appear in *Reader's Choice*. The number in parentheses indicates the unit in which an item appears. A indicates Appendix A.

Prefixes

(5) **a-, an-**   without, lacking, not
(3) **ante-**   before
(5) **bene-**   good
(5) **bi-**   two
(A) **by-**   aside or apart from the common, secondary
(3) **circum-**   around
(1) **com-, con-, col-, cor-, co-**   together, with
(3) **contra-, anti-**   against
(A) **de-**   down from, away
(A) **dia-**   through, across
(A) **epi-**   upon, over, outer
(A) **hyper-**   above, beyond, excessive
(A) **hypo-**   under, beneath, down
(1) **in-, im-, il-, ir-**   in, into, on
(1) **in-, im-, il-, ir-**   not
(3) **inter-**   between
(3) **intro-, intra-**   within
(1) **micro-**   small
(5) **mis-**   wrong
(5) **mono-**   one, alone
(7) **multi-**   many
(7) **peri-**   around
(5) **poly-**   many
(3) **post-**   after
(1) **pre-**   before
(1) **re-, retro-**   back, again
(7) **semi-**   half, partly
(3) **sub-, suc-, suf-, sug-, sup-, sus-**   under
(3) **super-**   above, greater, better
(5) **syn-, sym-, syl-**   with, together
(3) **trans-**   across
(7) **tri-**   three
(7) **ultra-**   beyond, excessive, extreme
(7) **uni-**   one

Stems

(5) **-anthro-, -anthropo-**   human
(5) **-arch-**   first, chief, leader
(7) **-aster-, -astro-, -stellar-**   star
(1) **-audi-, -audit-**   hear
(7) **-auto-**   self
(7) **-bio-**   life
(A) **-capit-**   head, chief
(3) **-ced-**   go, move, yield
(1) **-chron-**   time
(A) **-corp-**   body
(7) **-cycle-**   circle
(A) **-derm-**   skin
(1) **-dic-, -dict-**   say, speak
(3) **-duc-**   lead
(5) **-fact-, -fect-**   make, do
(3) **-flect-**   bend
(5) **-gam-**   marriage
(A) **-geo-**   earth
(1) **-graph-, -gram-**   write, writing
(5) **-hetero-**   different, other
(5) **-homo-**   same
(A) **-hydr-, -hydro-**   water
(1) **-log-, -ology-**   speech, word, study
(5) **-man-, -manu-**   hand
(7) **-mega-**   great, large
(3) **-mit-, -miss-**   send
(5) **-morph-**   form, structure
(7) **-mort-**   death
(5) **-onym-, -nomen-**   name
(A) **-ortho-**   straight, correct
(5) **-pathy-**   feeling, disease
(7) **-phil-**   love
(1) **-phon-**   sound
(A) **-pod-, -ped-**   foot

(3) **-pon-, -pos-** put, place

(7) **-polis-** city

(3) **-port-** carry

(7) **-psych-** mind

(1) **-scrib-, -script-** write

(3) **-sequ-, -secut-** follow

(A) **-son-** sound

(1) **-spect-** look at

(3) **-spir-** breathe

(7) **-soph-** wise

(3) **-tele-** far

(5) **-theo-, -the-** god

(A) **-therm-, -thermo-** heat

(3) **-ven-, -vene-** come

(A) **-ver-** true

(1) **-vid-, -vis-** see

(3) **-voc-, -vok-** call

Suffixes

(3) **-able, -ible, -ble** capable of, fit for

(A) **-ate** to make

(1) **-er, -or** one who

(A) **-fy** to make

(5) **-ic, -al** relating to, having the nature of

(5) **-ism** action or practice, theory or doctrine

(1) **-ist** one who

(7) **-ity** condition, quality, state of being

(A) **-ize** to make

(7) **-ness** condition, quality, state of being

(5) **-oid** like, resembling

(3) **-ous, -ious, -ose** full of, having the qualities of

(1) **-tion, -ation** condition, the act of

References

Grateful acknowledgment is made to the following authors, publishers, and journals for permission to reprint previously published materials. Every effort has been made to contact the copyright holders for permission to reprint borrowed material. We regret any oversights that may have occurred and will rectify them in future printings of this book.

"2021 International Tourist Arrivals." Available from: https://www.unwto.org/impact-assessment-of-the-covid-19-outbreak-on-international-tourism

"Carbon Dioxide Peaks at 420 Parts per Million at Mauna Loa Observatory." *NOAA News.* June 7, 2021.

"City Populations, World Cities." World Population Review. September 26, 2022. Available from: https://worldpopulationreview.com/world-cities

"Climate Change Science." *Future Atmosphere Changes in Greenhouse Gas and Aerosol Concentrations. U.S. Environmental Protection Agency.* Available from: http://www.atmo.arizona.edu/students/courselinks/fall06/nats101s6/ClimateMaterial/NOAA_futureac.html

"Ethical Principles of Psychologists and Code of Conduct." *American Psychological Association*, March 2017, https://www.apa.org/ethics/code.

"Fashion-conscious chimps ape habits of their friends" by Steve Connor August 22, 2005 http://news.independent.co.uk/world/science_technology/article307447.ece from The Independent captured 3/31/07

"Garbage Patches." Marine Debris Program, National Oceanic and Atmospheric Administration. Available from: https://marinedebris.noaa.gov/info/patch.html#1

"Global CO2 emissions by World Region, 1751 to 2015." Available from: https://ourworldindata.org/co2-and-other-greenhouse-gas-emissions

"Global Map of Biotech Crop Countries and Mega-Countries in 2018." *ISAAA.* 2018.

"Global Mean Estimates Based on Land and Ocean Data." *NASA.* 2020.

"GMO Crops." *ISAAA.* 2016.

"How Multi-tasking Affects Human Learning." *Weekend Edition, Saturday. NPR.* March 3, 2007. Available from: https://www.npr.org/2007/03/03/7700581/how-multitasking-affects-human-learning.

"International tourism expenditure." *UNWTO Tourism Highlights 2016 Edition.* Pg. 13. Available from: https://www.e-unwto.org/doi/pdf/10.18111/9789284418145

"Manhattan Subway Map." City Maps, Inc., Courtesy of *Metropolitan Transportation Authority.* 2006.

"Opinion: Unmasking Multitasking." *Los Angeles Times.* June 30, 2008. Available from: https://www.latimes.com/archives/blogs/opinion-la/story/2008-06-30/opinion-unmasking-multitasking.

"Percentage of correct answers to factual knowledge questions in physical and biological sciences, by region or country: Most recent year." *Science & Engineering Indicators.* 2018. Available from: https://www.nsf.gov/statistics/2018/nsb20181/report/sections/science-and-technology-public-attitudes-and-understanding/public-knowledge-about-s-t

"Street-Savvy: Meeting the biggest challenges starts with the city." Scientific American. Springer Nature America, September 1, 2011. https://www.scientificamerican.com/article/street-savvy/#:~:text=As%20Kavita%20N.,get%20education%20for%20her%20children.%E2%80%9D

"Regulations on GM Products by Country." *The Digital Literacy Project.* www.geneticliteracy.org

"The Globalization of Tourism." *The UNESCO Courier.* July/August 1999. Pgs. 26-27. Available from: https://unesdoc.unesco.org/ark:/48223/pf0000116585

"The Great Pacific Garbage Patch." *5W Infographics.* 2013. http://www.5wgraphics.com/

"Twilight of the Gods." *Time.* November 24, 1975. Pg. 107.

"Unearthing the Past." *Research News.* 23, no. 5 (November 1972). Pg. 6.

"UNTWO Tourism Towards 2030: Actual Trend and Forecast 1950-2030." *Markets, Performance, and Prospects.* October 2012, pg. 17. Available from: https://webunwto.s3.eu-west-1.amazonaws.com/imported_images/37729/item_4_c_tourism_towards_2030_e.pdf

"UNWTO tourism towards 2030 international tourism by region." October 2011. Pg. 36. Available from: https://www.globalwellnesssummit.com/wp-content/uploads/Industry-Research/Global/2011_UNWTO_Tourism_Towards_2030.pdf

"UNWTO tourism towards 2030 international tourism by region." October 2011. Pg. 38. Available from: https://www.globalwellnesssummit.com/wp-content/uploads/Industry-Research/Global/2011_UNWTO_Tourism_Towards_2030.pdf

"Why Does Ice Cream Cause Brain Freeze?" *Medical News Today.* March 2017. Available from: https://www.medicalnewstoday.com/articles/244458.

"Word Entries." Dictionary.com. Available from: https://www.dictionary.com/

Anonymous. "To the City We Go." *Scientific American.* September 201. Pgs. 40-41.

Aratani, Lori. "Teens Can Multitask, But What Are Costs? Ability to Analyze May Be Affected, Experts Worry." *Washington Post.* February 26, 2007.

Bahrani, Ramin. "Plastic Bag." Gigantic Studios. Available from: https://vimeo.com/144928861

Bingham, Hiram. *Lost City of the Incas, the Story of Machu Picchu and Its Builders.* New York: Duell, Sloan and Pearce, 1948.

Bonnard, Pierre. "Meditating on modernism: A French master reassessed." The Economist. The Economist Newspaper Limited, February 5, 2009. https://www.economist.com/books-and-arts/2009/02/05/meditating-on-modernism

Bower, B. 2001. "Math Fears Subtract from Memory, Learning." *Science News.* 159 (26): 405. doi:10.2307/3981545.

Bower, Bruce. "Math Fears Subtract From Memory, Learning." *Science News.* June 27, 2001. Available from: https://www.sciencenews.org/article/math-fears-subtract-memory-learning

Brody, Jane. "Are GMO Foods Safe." *The New York Times.* April 23, 2018. Available from: https://www.nytimes.com/2018/04/23/well/eat/are-gmo-foods-safe.html.

Dillinger, Jessica. "The Largest Cities in North America." *World Atlas.* July 25, 2019. Available from: https://www.worldatlas.com/articles/largest-cities-in-north-america.html

Elgendy, Karim and Natasha Abaza. "Urbanization in the MENA Region: A Benefit or a Curse?" Friedrich Ebert Stiftung. February 20, 2020. Available from: https://mena.fes.de/press/e/urbanization-in-the-mena-region-a-benefit-or-a-curse

Emil Katz, Fred. *Confronting Evil: Two Journeys.* State University of New York Press, 2004. Pg. 171.

Fagan, John, Michael Antoniou, and Claire Robinson. *GMO Myth and Truths, 2nd Edition.* 2014.

Fecht, Sarah. "How Exactly Does Carbon Dioxide Cause Global Warming?" *State of the Planet, Columbia Climate School: Climate, Earth, and Society.* February 25, 2021.

Fernandez, Bob "New Life for Used Clothes" The Philadelphia Enquirer, January 16, 2005. Available from: https://www.seattletimes.com/business/new-life-for-used-clothes/

Flatow, Ira, Host. "The Myth Of Multitasking." *Talk of the Nation, NPR.* May 10, 2013. Transcript available from: https://www.npr.org/2013/05/10/182861382/the-myth-of-multitasking.

Gardiner, Stephen M. and Laura Hartzell-Nichols. "Ethics and Global Climate Change." *Nature Education Knowledge*, 3 (10):5.

Goleman, Daniel. "Major Personality Study Finds that Traits Are Mostly Inherited." *The New York Times Archive.* December 2, 1986, Section C, Page 1. Available from: https://www.nytimes.com/1986/12/02/science/major-personality-study-finds-that-traits-are-mostly-inherited.html#:~:text=For%20most%20of%20the%20traits,and%20other%20experiences%20in%20life.

Gore, Al. *An Inconvenient Truth.* Viking Press, 2008.

Hamilton, Jon and Daniel Weissman. "Bad At Multitasking? Blame Your Brain." *NPR.* October 16, 2008. Available from: https://www.npr.org/templates/story/story.php?storyId=95784052.

Hamilton, Jon. "Multitasking Teens May Be Muddling Their Brains." *NPR.* October 9, 2008. Available from: https://www.npr.org/2008/10/09/95524385/multitasking-teens-may-be-muddling-their-brains.

Haney, James E. "Health and Motor Behavior: Measuring Energy Expenditures." *Research News.*

Hayutin, Adele M. "Graying of the World Population" Public Policy and Aging Report, Col. 17, No 4. (2007). Available from: https://drive.google.com/file/d/1Lj0KzO4bwMugV6YB-dfwW4_Y5xv-a8xd/view?usp=sharing

Hegarty, Stephanie. "The Myth of the Eight-Hours Sleep." *BBC News Magazine.* 22 February 2012. Available from: http://www.bbc.com/news/magazine-16964783

Hempel, Amy. "The Man in Bogota." *The Collected Stories of Amy Hempel.* New York: Scribner, 2007. Pages. 73-74.

Hoornweg, D., & Pope, K. "Population predictions for the world's largest cities in the 21st century." *Environment and Urbanization,* 29(1). 2017. Pgs. 195–216. https://doi-org.proxy.lib.umich.edu/10.1177/0956247816663557

Hughes, Patricia. "The Sacred 'Rac.'" Fersh Seymour, Editor. 1974. *Learning About Peoples and Cultures.* Evanston Ill: McDougal Littell, 1974.

Jackson, Shirley. "The Lottery." *The New Yorker.* June 18, 1948 Issue. Available from: https://www.newyorker.com/magazine/1948/06/26/the-lottery.

Jha, Alok. "Chimp culture reveals roots of human society." *The Guardian.* August 22, 2005. http://www.guardian.co.uk/uk_news/story/0,,1553671,00.html

Kaufman, Anna. "What is the World's Most Populous City? To Ten Most Populous Cities in the World, US Ranked." USA Today. September 26, 2022. Available from: https://www.usatoday.com/story/news/2022/09/26/most-populous-city-in-world/10427581002/

Klinenberg, Eric. *Going Solo: The Extraordinary Rise and Surprising Appeal of Living Alone.* NY: Penguin Books, 2013.

Kosinski, Jerzy. *Blind Date.* Grove Press: New York, 1977.

Kruger, Justin ; Wirtz, Derrick ; Miller, Dale T. "Counterfactual Thinking and the First Instinct Fallacy." Journal of Personality and Social Psychology. Washington, DC: American Psychological Association, n.d. doi:10.1037/0022-3514.88.5.725.

Langdon, John. *Wordplay: Ambigrams and Reflections on the Art of Ambigrams.* New York: Harcourt Brace, 1992.

Livermore, Roy. "Plate Tectonics by Jerks." *The Tectonic Plate Are Moving.* Oxford University Press, 2018.

Longman, Phillip J. "The World Turns Gray." *US News & World Report.* March 1, 1999. Available from: http://globalag.igc.org/pension/world/gray.htm

Ma, Michelle. "Access to Electricity is Linked to Reduced Sleep." Available from: https://www.washington.edu/news/2015/06/19/access-to-electricity-is-linked-to-reduced-sleep/

McCrum, Robert, William Cran, and Robert MacNeil. *The Story of English.* New York: Penguin, 1986.

McNeill, David. *The Acquisitions of Language: The Study of Developmental Psycholinguistics.* New York: Harper and Row, 1970.

Stanley Milgram. *Obedience to Authority: An Experimental View.* New York: Harper & Row, Publishers, 1974.

National Academies of Sciences, Engineering, and Medicine. 2016. *Genetically Engineered Crops: Experiences and Prospects.* Washington, DC: The National Academies Press. https://doi.org/10.17226/23395.

Nicholson-Lord, David. "The Politics of Travel." *The Nation.* October 6, 1997.

Nye, Naomi Shihab. "Gate 4-A." 2007. Poetry Selection Titled: "Gate A4." From *Honeybee* by Naomi Shihab Nye Read By: Naomi Shihab Nye. Text copyright (C) 2008.

Passer, Michael and Ronald Smith. "Myth or Reality? When Taking Tests, Stick with Your First Instinct." *Psychology: The Science of Mind and Behavior.* NY: McGraw-Hill, 2011. Pg. 8

Passer, Michael and Ronald Smith. "When Do People Help?" *Psychology: The Science of Mind and Behavior.* NY: McGraw-Hill, 2011. Pgs. 664-665.

Peterson, Ivar. "The Troubled State of Calculus: A Push to Revitalize College Calculus Teaching Has Begun." *Science News.* April 5, 1986, pgs. 201-21.

Preston, Richard. *First Light: The Search for the Edge of the Universe.* New York: Random House, 1996.

Randall, Megan. "'Dreamland:' Open Your Eyes To The Science Of Sleep." *NPR.* August 03, 2012. Available from http://www.npr.org/2012/08/07/158087512/dreamland-open-your-eyes-to-the-science-of-sleep

Ravilious, Kate. "Eat, Sing, and Be Merry." *The Guardian.* January, 2003.

Satterthwaite, David. "The World's 100 Largest Cities from 1800 to 2020, and Beyond." *International Institute for Environment and Development.* January 16, 2020. Available from: https://www.iied.org/worlds-100-largest-cities-1800-2020-beyond

Schrank, Jeffrey. *Deception Detection.* Boston: Beacon Press, 1975. Pg. 53.

Silver, Marc. "Memo To People Of Earth: 'Third World' Is An Offensive Term!" *NPR.* January 1, 2021. https://www.npr.org/sections/goatsandsoda/2021/01/08/954820328/memo-to-people-of-earth-third-world-is-an-offensive-term.

Slabbekoorn, Hans and Margriet Peet. "Ecology: Birds Sing at a Higher Pitch in Urban Noise." *Nature.* Vol. 424. July 17, 2003.

Smith, Ronald E. Irwin G. Sarason, and Barbara Sarason. "The Milgram Experiment." In *Psychology: The Frontiers of Behavior.* NY: Harper & Row, 1978.

Sohoulande, Clement & Singh, Vijay. (2015). "Impact of Climate Change on the Hydrologic Cycle and Implications for Society." *Environment and Social Psychology.* 1. 10.18063/ESP.2015.01.002.

Sullivan, Bob and Hugh Thompson. "Brain, Interrupted." *The New York Times.* May 3, 2013. Available from: https://www.nytimes.com/2013/05/05/opinion/sunday/a-focus-on-distraction.html.

Summit, Ginger and Jim Widess. *The Complete Book of Gourd Craft.* New York: Lark Books, 2000.

Tagliabue G. "The EU legislation on "GMOs" between nonsense and protectionism: An ongoing Schumpeterian chain of public choices." *GM Crops Food.* 2017 Jan 2;8(1):57-73. doi: 10.1080/21645698.2016.1270488. Epub 2016 Dec 21. PMID: 28001470; PMCID: PMC5592980.

Tan, Amy. "Mother Tongue." Copyright © 1990 by Amy Tan. First appeared in The Threepenny Review. Reprinted by permission of the author and the Sandra Dijkstra Literary Agency.

The American Heritage Dictionary of English Language. Houghton Mifflin, 2000

Thoryn, Mike. "Clement Collection Features Forgeries." *The Michigan Daily* 78, no. 18 (1967): 1.

Thrupp, Sylvia L., Editor. *Early Medieval Society.* New York: Appleton-Century Crofts, 1967.

U.S. Environmental Protection Agency. "Climate Change Indicators in the United States." Accessed [June 2022]. www.epa.gov/climate-indicators.

Underwood, Tim B. *The Story of the Cherokee People.* S.B. Newman Printing Co., 1961. Pg. 13.

United Nations, Department of Economic and Social Affairs, Population Division . "World Population Ageing 2017 - Highlights." 2017. Available from: World Population Ageing

United Nations, Department of Economic and Social Affairs, Population Division. "World Population Ageing 2017 - Highlights." Pg. 7. 2017. Available from: <u>World Population Ageing</u>

Vanderbilt, Tom. "Traffic as Culture." In *Traffic: Why We Drive the Way We Do (and What it Says About Us).* NY: Alfred A. Knopf, 2008.

Vinovskis, Maris. "Historical Perspectives on the Development of the Family and Parent-Child Interactions." In *Parenting Across the Life Span.* Edited by Jane B. Lancaster, Jeanne Altman, Alice S. Rossi, and Lonni R. Sherrod. Aldine de Gruyter, 1987.

Waters, Thomas, MD. "Did you Really Lose Most of Your Body's Heat Through Your Head?" *Family Medicine.* Cleveland Clinic, 2021.

Wernick, Robert. "Summits of Yore: Promises, Promises, and a Deal or Two." *Smithsonian.* 17, no. 6. September 1986. Pg. 58.

Whiten, Andrew, Victoria Horner and Frans B. M. de Waal. "Conformity to cultural norms of tool use in chimpanzees." *Nature.* 437, Pgs. 737-740. 29 September 2005; doi:10.1038/nature04047.

Williams, Ray. "Nightly 8-Hour Sleep Isn't a Rule, It's a Myth." *Psychology Today in Wired for Success.* March 3, 2014. Retrieved from <u>http://www.psychologytoday.com/blog/wired-success/201403/nightly-8-hour-sleep-isnt-rule-its-myth</u>

Wong, Kate. "Chimps found to conform to cultural norms." Scientific American. Aug. 22, 2005 <u>http://www.sciam.com/article.cfm?chanID=sa003&articleID=000CBEE6-2096-1306-A09683414B7F0000</u>

Wyss, Hal H. *Hummingbirds: A Portrait of the Animal World.* New Line Books, 1999.

YourDictionary.com. Available from: <u>https://www.yourdictionary.com/</u>